More Than Words Can Say

The Ink Spots and Their Music

Marv Goldberg

The Scarecrow Press, Inc.
Lanham, Md., & London
1998

SCARECROW PRESS, INC.

Published in the United States of America
by Scarecrow Press, Inc.
4720 Boston Way
Lanham, Maryland 20706

4 Pleydell Gardens
Kent CT20 2DN, England

British Library Cataloguing in Publication Information Available

Library of Congress Cataloging-in-Publication Data

Goldberg, Marv, 1944–
   More than words can say : the Ink Spots and their music / Marv Goldberg.
       p.   cm.
   Includes bibliographical references and index.
   ISBN 0-8108-3568-1 (cloth) : alk. paper)
   1. Ink Spots (musical group)   2. Singers—United States—Biography.
   I. Title.
ML421.I53G65   1998   98-35748
782.42164'092'2   CIP
[B]—dc21   MN

To Jerry Daniels, the last survivor.

To Jimmy McGowan, always an inspiration.

To the memory of my partner, Mike Redmond.

To Marcia, who put up with a lot.

To Danny.

If I didn't care
More than words can say . . .

Jack Lawrence

Contents

Foreword
by Peter A. Grendysa

What's in a name? Plenty, if the name is "Ink Spots." It's been more than fifty years since that foursome of dynamic and consummate performers first caught the public ear, and a very long time since that name appeared on a hit record. Yet, the mere mention of the name still evokes images of a silvery high tenor voice bending the notes of a romantic lyric. Over the intervening years, "Ink Spots" has very nearly become a generic term to the extent that impostors still find easy work in clubs, hotels, and resorts, playing to audiences who are blissfully unaware or uncaring that the last of the original hit group has long passed on to that grandstand in the sky.

This phenomenon of American music is almost unique in popular culture. It's the equivalent of having multiple formations of Mills Brothers, Rolling Stones, or Beach Boys roving the country and drawing good crowds everywhere they play. The lasting power of the Ink Spots, at least in name, is like the afterimage of a flashbulb—so brilliant, so intense was their popularity that they have transcended decades of change in music.

The foundations upon which the Ink Spots built their fame were an integral part of the black American experience. Singing in harmony was by no means an exclusively black innovation, but instead of singing in unison or harmonizing on the same note, the black quartets, sextets, and octets of the first two decades of the twentieth century developed a style distinct from their white counterparts. Bass voices accentuated the rhythm of the tunes, while floating tenor/baritone harmonies provided a backdrop to the lead vocalist.

In the 1920s, hot jazz bands enjoyed a sudden rise in popularity among both blacks and whites while vocal groups continued to concentrate on spirituals, hymns, and traditional folk melodies. Every black college had a number of singing groups formed as fund-raising vehicles, and these choirs and quartets toured the country and the world, playing to sophisticates and the moneyed classes. The astounding popular success of the Mills Brothers, who increased their income tenfold during 1932, was accomplished by the simple trick of taking pop, show, and jazz tunes and adapting them to syncopated vocal arrangements with voices taking the place of instruments. Their fame was spread via radio, the entertainment choice of the masses during the Depression, and record sales and concert bookings followed.

By the end of 1932, it was estimated that the Mills Brothers, all of them under twenty-one years old, would earn $125,000 a year. Suddenly the woods and city streets were full of black pop quartets. None of them could achieve the national breakthrough that had launched the Brothers. In an attempt to field a hit group to counter the Brothers on the CBS network, rival NBC gave a jive trio from Philadelphia, the Three Keys, a major promotional shove, but their supercharged combo versions of standards and current hits failed to excite the masses. The Ink Spots took a similar route with their raucous, jivey renditions of black jazz, and found even less acceptance.

The Ink Spots mugged like Fats Waller, cavorted on stage like Cab Calloway, and sang while they plucked out hot string band jazz. They gained only a toehold in big-time show business, and it took a radical change in style to bring them to the top ranks in American popular music. After ten years of struggle on the fringes, the deceptively simple Ink Spots "formula" was the key they needed. The times were right for dramatic love songs; the remarkable clear high tenor of their new lead singer had few traces of "blackness," and the spoken interludes by the bass voice injected gentle humor and pathos.

While the Mills Brothers were the group to follow in terms of financial and popular achievement, the Ink Spots set a whole new standard for black vocal group technique. Their singing transcended all that had come before and sparked hosts of imitators. No sooner had this revolution been set in motion, when the Ink Spots themselves began to change. Aside from the lead singer and "formula" spoken bass parts, the rest of the group was relegated to nondescript humming in the background. With the exception of the talking bass, the Ink Spots essentially became a solo act.

The years of the Second World War were those of major changes in American society and music, and that short period marked both the rise and fall of the Ink Spots. The development of rhythm and blues was a return to earthy roots that the Ink Spots had left behind in their quest for mass market acceptance. The group's recordings vanished from the R&B charts after 1948. The perception was that they sang "white." Likewise the start of the Korean Conflict in 1950 produced a new cynicism in war-weary America, and sentimental songs of hope and hearth declined in popularity. The last Ink Spots hit record came in 1951.

In their place in rhythm and blues came a multitude of vocal groups with strong leads, both tenor and bass, intricate harmony, and soulful delivery rooted in black gospel. The early instrumental imitations of the Mills Brothers lived on in the backing vocals, and reached their exaggerated culmination in doo-wop. The soaring, ethereal, high-tenor leads came from the Ink Spots, often augmented with floating, wordless vocal obbligatos from a second, even higher, tenor.

As an important vocal group, the Ink Spots had ceased to exist by the time their legacy was realized. Remnants and spin-offs of the group moved into the same venues that accepted the Mills Brothers—glitzy hotels and resorts—but without the benefit of familial continuity that the Brothers enjoyed. Still, it is the name "Ink Spots" that means black vocal group to many people, not the Mills Brothers. And it is the Ink Spots who are recognized as the progenitors of the rhythm and blues vocal groups, from the Ravens, Orioles, and Clovers, to the Moonglows, Flamingos, Miracles, Temptations, and Spinners.

Every legend has a basis in cold fact, and in the case of the Ink Spots, the truth of their beginning, rise to fame, and precipitous decline has been clouded with carefully contrived show business mummery and fluff. The truth, as always, is far more fascinating than the fiction, especially press agent pipe dreams.

The story of the Ink Spots is one of those rags-to-riches tales so beloved in American lore, and their success inspired countless hundreds to try for the gold at the end of the rainbow. More than that, they produced a musical style and sound that has proven timeless in its appeal to listeners. Whatever the reality behind the glitter and bright lights of show business, the only lasting effect is that found in the hearts and minds of the audience, and in this most important way, the Ink Spots are here to stay.

Acknowledgments

Thanks are due to many people who helped me in my research. The original work was an extensive article in the rhythm and blues magazine *Yesterday's Memories* (Number 9, March 1977), written in the main by Pete Grendysa, George Moonoogian, and Rick Whitesell, with information provided by my interviews (augmented by their own research). The section on the Brown Dots is a synopsis of an article that I wrote with my friend and partner in *Yesterday's Memories*, Mike Redmond.

Most of the photographs of the Ink Spots used herein are from the collection of Paul Scriven, unless otherwise credited. Paul provided me with a carton full of photos and clippings, many of which were indispensable. Michael Ochs, of the Michael Ochs Archives/Venice, California, sent me loads of photostats of various Ink Spots groups that I used to attempt to sort out personnel changes over the years.

For more recent help, I have to thank Ray Funk, Galen Gart, Bob Pruter, Bill Proctor, Mike Caldarulo, and Andy McKaie and Barbara Kaufman (of MCA Records). Also, thanks to George Moonoogian and Dave Hinckley, for taking the time to read and critique the manuscript.

Thanks are also due to the following periodicals, whose publishers graciously granted me permission to quote from their publications: BPI Communications (the *Billboard*), *Variety,* the *Chicago Defender*, the *Afro-American Co. of Baltimore City* (T/A the *AFRO-AMERICAN NEWSPAPERS*—the *Baltimore Afro-American*), the *New York Post*, the *Boston Herald*, the *New York Amsterdam News*, the *Cleveland Call And Post, Down Beat* magazine, and the *New York Times*. All direct quotes are copyrighted by these publications, on the dates given in the notes.

Quotes from Deek Watson's book *The Story Of The Ink Spots* were used by permission of Shirlita H. Watson (aka Lee Stephenson).

Finally, it's difficult to remember any project that I've worked on that didn't include thanks to Ferdie Gonzalez (or should have, if I left it out). His discographical work in rhythm and blues and rock and roll is beyond measure. Almost all the record listings appearing in this book were based on entries in the latest version of his book *Disco-File*.

Introduction

No matter what generation you're from, no matter what singers you've listened to, you've probably heard of the Ink Spots. Not the first crossover black group, but the most successful and most imitated. Most rhythm and blues groups of the '40s and '50s took their cue from the Ink Spots; the rock and roll groups of the '50s built on that (directly or indirectly); the soul groups of the '60s carried on a strong tradition; and even as I am writing this paragraph, there is, in all probability, an Ink Spots group somewhere that's within twelve hours, either way, of a performance.

Of course, like any formulaic sound, the Ink Spots' style became ritualized, which is why for decades, groups have both imitated and parodied them. But the formula worked: Herb Kenny has said of his brother Bill's lead singing: "Bill painted a picture with every phrase. Some of his high notes would take your breath away."[1]

Although it's been over fifty-five years since "If I Didn't Care" became a huge hit, their records *still* sell today (MCA has released their greatest hits on a compact disc). And though all of the original members have passed away (the last one in late 1995), there are still numerous "Ink Spots" groups appearing today—this, above all, shows the strength of their appeal.

Their first hit (although their thirteenth record), "If I Didn't Care," featured a soaring tenor paired with a bass "talking bridge," and the combination went over so well (too well?) with the public that ensuing recordings seemed to be little more than carbon copies of that initial success. The Ink Spots found their niche and carved it so deep that it ended up becoming a rut.

When the Ink Spots became famous, their origins became enshrouded in the mists of fiction—a fiction created by the press agents of their manager and their own recording company. The most common account, something out of a Hollywood "B" movie, is found on liner notes that Decca Records trotted out on more than one occasion (this particular variant was taken from the liner notes of a 45 sleeve):

> "We struggled along for five years doing jive arrangements," they confessed, "but nothing happened. We were on the verge of disbanding because we couldn't get work. As a matter of fact, we were working. It was at the New York Paramount Theatre, but we were not out in front as singers—we were backstage as porters and the only singing we did was between pushes with brooms and mops! It was a good thing we did keep practicing as a group, though, because an artist-representative happened to hear us one night. We were signed to contracts and next thing we knew we had recorded 'If I Didn't Care' for Decca."[2]

Many years later, Decca issued "The Best Of The Ink Spots" two-record set. The liner notes not only repeated that story, but finally acknowledged it to be a myth (without admitting, of course, that it was Decca itself that had originally reported and repeatedly perpetuated that myth).

Decca also wrote, as part of the mythos:

> Contrary to belief, the Ink Spots did not get their name because of their dusky complexions. The actual fact is both more casual and more surprising. The four young men and their manager were sitting in an office trying to think up a likely name for the quartette. They had rejected such trite characterizations as "Harmony Four," "Rhythm Quartet," "Jazz Melodeers," and a score of others, when their manager idly glanced at the blotter on which he was doodling with his pen. The pen had gone dry and he shook it impatiently. Four blots appeared. "The Ink Spots!" he shouted, and the Ink Spots they were and still are.[3]

Because press agents have had a free hand, and because literally dozens of singers have claimed (and still claim) to be "original" members, an exhaustive history of the Ink Spots is needed.

Just to get it out of the way here and now, there are only *five* singers who can claim to be original members of the Ink Spots: Jerry Daniels, Deek Watson, Charlie Fuqua, Orville "Hoppy" Jones, and Bill Kenny (who was not there from the beginning, but was the most famous member nevertheless)—and all are dead! Of course there were others who sang with the Victor/Decca group (the only legitimate Ink Spots group as far as this history is concerned): Bernie Mackey, Cliff Givens, Billy Bowen, Huey Long, Herb Kenny, Adriel McDonald, Teddy Williams, Ernie Brown, and Jimmy Kennedy. There were also the pianist/arrangers: Bob Benson, Ace Harris, Bill Doggett, Ray Tunia, and Harold Francis. This list comprises nineteen people; there just *weren't* any others!

Of those nineteen, I interviewed the following members for this history: Jerry Daniels, Herb Kenny, Bernie Mackey, Ray Tunia, Adriel McDonald, Billy Bowen, Bill Doggett, and Huey Long. I cannot overstate the thrill of having had the opportunity to speak with them, and to relive their memories of a Golden Era.

Others interviewed included Jimmie Nabbie (of the Brown Dots and lead of a later Ink Spots group), Leonard Puzey (of the Ravens, who was with a "spin-off" Ink Spots in the mid-1950s), and Richard Lanham (of the Tempo-Tones, who was with a 1960s Spots incarnation).

As well as exploring the origins and activities of the Ink Spots, we'll delve into the workings of the music business of their time. The Spots didn't exist in a vacuum; what went on around them affected their recordings and performances. We'll take a look at the ASCAP/BMI War, the Petrillo strikes (of the American Federation of Musicians), shellac shortages, gas rationing, the War of the Record Speeds, vinyl shortages, and lawsuits (most definitely lawsuits). Some of these may seem tangential to the story, but they'll all fit in.

A note on the reviews: most of the record reviews were taken from Billboard, which tended to give favored-singer status to the Ink Spots (although there are times when the sameness of the style seems to grate on them, too). It's important to keep in mind that these reviews weren't meant for the general public, but for jukebox operators. (An "operator" was the person who actually owned the boxes, sometimes hundreds, and placed them in juke joints, bars, drug stores, even railway stations. The operator was constantly on the road servicing his machines and trying to guess which records would make the public part with their nickels—the reviews were his guide.) These reviews were also meant for retail store buyers (especially chain stores). Fortunately, I've managed to find reviews for most of the Spots' tunes. The earliest charts in *Billboard* listed up-and-coming songs; but it was the song itself that got the review, not the artist/song combination. Other charts listed a song's popularity by how many times it was heard on the radio that week (which mostly reflected how well the song pluggers, not the artists, were doing their job). Only in the early '40s were positional charts started; prior to then, it's difficult to gauge what a Number 1 song was. There were reviewers who disliked the Ink Spots intensely; their reviews are included for balance.

Similarly, the theater reviews were not meant for the general public, but were there to help theater owners book acts that would appeal to their clientele. These reviews show that the Ink Spots kept their performance appeal long after their records stopped being hits.

One caveat must be mentioned. In several places I have used Deek Watson's autobiography, *The Story Of The Ink Spots*, as a source. Unfortunately, it's an uneven document. The chronology bounces forward and backward from one year to another in no particular order (nor is the reader always aware of where, in time, the story is). Also, Watson does not mention his departure from the Ink Spots in 1944, his formation of the Brown Dots, or the personality clashes between himself and Bill Kenny. The book is, however, fascinating for Watson's anecdotes (although I'm never sure if they're true). Part of the problem is that Deek and Bill Kenny didn't get along (except that they both loved to gamble), and some of what Deek writes may just be sour grapes.

I've had a great deal of fun working on this book; I hope it's as much fun for you to read.

Long Island, New York
January 1998

Prelude: The 1920s to 1931

World War I has just ended; the world begins to slide inexorably into the next conflict. U.S. Senate refuses to ratify League of Nations Covenant. Prohibition experiment begins. Women get the vote. Civil war rages in Ireland. Byrd and Amundsen fly over North Pole in separate flights; Byrd flies over South Pole. Kellogg-Briand Pact renounces aggressive war. Washington Disarmament Pact. Japan seizes Manchuria. Saudi Arabian, Iraqi and Transjordanian monarchies established. Chiang Kai-shek suppresses the Chinese warlords. Turkey becomes a republic. Art deco begins. "Teapot Dome" scandal. Scopes "monkey trial." Sacco and Vanzetti found guilty, later executed. Joseph Stalin assumes power on the death of Lenin. Congress declares Native Americans to be citizens. Lindbergh solos the Atlantic. Empire State Building opens. "Lost Generation" writers express the aimlessness of life. "Talkies" come to the movies. Stock market crashes and the world is in the grip of a depression. But all is not lost: in 1920, the first licensed radio broadcasts begin.

Where to begin with the story of the Ink Spots?

Let's go back to Indianapolis, Indiana, at the start of the Roaring Twenties. Let's begin with Orville "Hoppy" Jones and Mifflin "Miff" Campbell, meeting in an ice cream parlor where Campbell was a waiter and Jones made ice cream. Finding a mutual interest in dancing (the nickname "Hoppy" seems to have come from his dancing moves), they formed an act called "Jones and Campbell," playing in small-time vaudeville, carnivals, and clubs.[1]

By 1928, Leonard Reed had been added, and "Jones and Campbell" had become "The Peanut Boys." Reed can be seen in the group's photo holding a tipple. Jones danced and played the "bass fiddle." Actually, Hoppy would do *anything* to avoid the clumsiness of a stand-up bass; in the beginning, he used a guitar, held upright and supported by the shaft of a cane (this can be seen in some of the photos); later he switched to a cello, tuned to sound like a bass.

Jones and Campbell (ca. 1925): "Miff" Campbell (left) and "Hoppy" Jones.

At the same time, Ivory "Deacon" (usually shortened to "Deek") Watson was also making music. He began in Indianapolis in the mid-1920s with a "coffee-pot band" known as the "Percolating Puppies," and it was there that Deek learned to play the ukulele and the four-string tenor guitar. Basically, coffee-pot bands consisted of teenagers performing the music of their contemporary heroes, such as Duke Ellington, Cliff "Ukulele Ike" Edwards, Barney Rapp and the New Englanders, and the idolized McKinney's Cotton Pickers. In order to re-create band material, these groups had to be skillful at improvising a sound based on harmony vocals, often simulating wind, brass, and reed instruments with their voices, as well as "playing the strings," such as tipples, ukuleles, guitars, tenor guitars, banjos, and bass fiddles. A tipple, once a common instrument, was a little larger than a ukulele and had ten strings. A tenor guitar was a regular guitar with the low E and A strings removed; it was really an extension of a ukulele, capable of playing more octaves.

The coffee pot was used as an echo chamber for a kazoo; by blowing kazoos into the pots, you could simulate a whole reed section. Jerry Daniels said that "the larger the coffee pot, the more resonant the tone."[2] Therefore, the bands had various sizes of them. Many of the bands also had dancers—true self-contained entertainment units. And they weren't only trios, quartets, and quintets; some of these units could have as many as fifteen members (probably only the extremely good ones, otherwise it wouldn't have been financially feasible).

What was a coffee-pot band like? According to Deek Watson:

> I had a group called the "Percolating Puppies." We played a small tea pot, a medium sized coffee pot, and a very large coffee pot, plus guitars. The sounds we were able to make were fantastic. We played on the streets. At the end of each such performance we passed the largest of the pots among the audience. The toughest thing about this way of making money was the fact that all of us had to keep our eyes on the cat who passed the collection for the evening, or else some of the money found its way from the pot to his pocket before dividing time arrived.[3]

Around 1929 Leonard Reed left the Peanut Boys; he would have subsequent careers as a dancer, comedian, straight man (for Joe Louis' stage act), producer, and songwriter. As of the early 1990s, he was still active in show business. Deek Watson was then recruited to join Hoppy Jones and Miff Campbell as Reed's replacement. Another new member was Oliver "Slim" Green (whose name is sometimes spelled "Greene"). He was a musician, singer, and dancer, who had been part of a dancing act with Marion "Taps" Miller. Once again there was a name change, this time to the "Four Riff Brothers." The "Riffs" got the chance to do a fifteen-minute radio program on WLW in Cincinnati (about a hundred miles from Indianapolis), replacing the departing Mills Brothers. This group was together until 1931, when both Watson and Green left to do solo acts. (Green had at least four releases on Decca's Sepia series in 1935. Despite later stories about his death in the '30s, Slim lived on until around 1960, when he died of pneumonia in Detroit.)[4]

The Peanut Boys (1928): Miff Campbell, Leonard Reed, Hoppy Jones. (Courtesy of Jerry Daniels.)

Meanwhile, in 1928, guitarist Charlie Fuqua started out with an aggregation called the Patent Leather Kids, which included Sid Ballantine, Fred Wisdom, Slick Helm, and Paul George. In the following year, he left them and teamed up with Jerry Daniels (whom he knew from the neighborhood, although they lived on different sides of a canal that ran through town). The third member of this unnamed coffee-pot band was Bernie Mackey. Charlie ran a shoeshine stand across from the Stutz Bearcat automobile factory, and he and his pals got together to serenade the workers.[5] They all sang and played guitar, with Jerry doubling on the ukulele. Fuqua (sometimes known as "Satchelmouth") had an uncle, Chauncey Lee, who was a classical guitarist and Fuqua's inspiration. (Note that Harvey Fuqua of the famous '50s vocal group the Moonglows is a nephew of Charlie's—a musical family indeed! Interestingly, Charlie pronounced his name "Foo-kway," whereas Harvey pronounces it "Foo-qua.")

Around 1930, Charlie and Jerry decided to "turn pro" and left Bernie Mackey behind (we'll meet him again later, though). The duet was called, after a lot of thought perhaps, "Charlie and Jerry." With Jerry's tenor voice, ukulele, and tenor guitar, and Charlie's baritone/tenor voice, guitar, and tenor banjo, the two appeared in vaudeville and were also stars of a radio show on WKBF (Indianapolis).

Charlie and Jerry (ca. 1930): Charlie Fuqua (left) and Jerry Daniels. (Courtesy of Jerry Daniels.)

The Four Riff Brothers (ca. 1929): Miff Campbell (with tipple), Deek Watson (tenor guitar), Hoppy Jones (with a tenor guitar that he's playing as a bass—he's cut down a cane to make a support for it!), Slim Green (tipple). (Courtesy of Jerry Daniels.)

1932

Twelve million jobless in the United States. Severe famine in Russia. Lindbergh baby kidnapped, later found dead. World War I veterans stage Bonus March on Washington, D.C. Polaroid process invented by Edwin Land.

The year 1932 found Charlie and Jerry touring the Midwest with the Whitman Sisters vaudeville show, one of the most popular programs in TOBA (the Theatre Owners Booking Agency), the main booking agency for black theaters. By July, the show having disbanded for the summer, the pair found themselves on vacation in Cleveland. It was here that they ran into Deek Watson, performing as a single. These three alumni of the Indianapolis street corners decided to form a trio.[1]

First calling themselves the "Swingin' Gate Brothers," they became the "King, Jack, and Jester" about the time they landed a job on WHK (Cleveland); Deek was the "King," Charlie the "Jack," and Jerry the "Jester." Like many other acts of the day, they did a sustaining fifteen-minute show three times a week. A "sustaining" show was one with no sponsor; you were an employee of the station itself, which paid for the show. At this time, commercial radio was still in its infancy, and anything and everything was being broadcast to determine listeners' tastes (the same thing was to happen in the early days of television).

Later that year they moved to WLW (Cincinnati), where they did commercials for the Crosley Broadcasting Company; Red Barber, future sportscaster for the Brooklyn Dodgers and New York Yankees, was their announcer. Then, to add a final touch to the group, Watson recruited his former "Riff Brother," Orville "Hoppy" Jones, as a fourth member. Without giving the matter too much thought, they changed their name to the "King, Jack, and the Jesters."[2]

Hoppy was the grand old man of the group, turning twenty-seven in 1932. That year the others would have been: Jerry (seventeen), Deek (nineteen), and Charlie (twenty-one).

Throughout 1932-33, they built up a following among midwestern listeners. Although there were many black vocal groups around, few got much recognition. Two who did were the extremely popular Mills Brothers (who had a 1931 smash with "Tiger Rag"), and the Three Keys. Jerry Daniels pointed out that the sound of his group was quite unlike the more polished style of these contemporaries. The style of the King, Jack and the Jesters (and also of the early Ink Spots) was "swing," derived from the big-name jazz bands, vaudeville acts, and the coffee-pot street-corner bands of Indianapolis.[3]

The King, Jack, and Jester (ca. 1932) at WHK (Cleveland): Jerry Daniels, Deek Watson, Charlie Fuqua. (Courtesy of Jerry Daniels.)

1933

Hitler comes to power in Germany. Japan occupies Inner Mongolia. FDR takes office, then closes the banks. United States off the gold standard. Prohibition ends. Tennessee Valley Authority established. Walt Disney wins an Oscar for The Three Little Pigs.

In 1933 Grace Raines, pianist and vocal director at WLW, decided to relocate to New York and she asked the group to join her. This was too good of an offer to pass up; Indianapolis, Cleveland, and Cincinnati were good for exposure and fine-tuning, but New York was one of the entertainment capitals of the country.

However, don't think that WLW was small-time radio. Known as "The Nation's Station," WLW advertised (in September 1938) that it had a staff of fifty radio voices and fifty-three musicians. In 1934, WLW, located at 700 on the AM dial, had started using an experimental 500,000-watt transmitter (by comparison, big stations today use about one-tenth of that wattage). With that much power, they were probably heard in most parts of the country. But the Federal Communications Commission (FCC) deemed this wattage excessive and unsuccessfully took the station to court to try to force it back to 50,000 watts. The station continued to transmit at 500,000 watts until March 1939, when the FCC finally won the battle and made it settle down to a more respectable 50,000 watts (even though crediting the station with materially contributing to radio knowledge).

When the King, Jack, and the Jesters got to New York late in 1933, they faced stiff competition within the entertainment world, as well as a problem over their name. Orchestra leader Paul Whiteman already had a vocal group within his band called the "King's Jesters," and when a conflict arose, it was not difficult to figure out who would yield. The newcomers from the Midwest renamed themselves the "Riff Brothers" for a while, and then the "Four Ink Spots."

Many fanciful stories have been told about the origin of this name. The truth, however, is rather dull: their manager simply sat down and decided on it. It's a little harder to determine just *who* this manager was: Jerry Daniels said that the name came from Moe Gale; Deek Watson said it was a Mr. Heffman (their first manager when they got to New York; he also managed bandleader Ozzie Nelson and comedian Joe Penner). They had gone through a couple of managers before ending up with Gale, owner of Harlem's Savoy Ballroom, but it isn't clear exactly when he took them over.

Nor were they the first to use "Ink Spots." When they came to New York, that name was being used by a small-time dance group, which was going nowhere. Somehow their manager (whoever he may have been) got involved, and decided to let the Riff Brothers try the name, which was tailor-made for a black group.[1]

There was a "Christmas-card" ad in the January 2, 1934, *Variety* from the Gale agency that listed his acts: Don Hall Trio, Southern Singers, Phantom Strings, Morton Bowe, and Helen Gordon. The Ink Spots are conspicuous by their absence. Either Gale wasn't yet managing the Spots, or he didn't yet consider them to be of headline quality (since the ad stated that they all had shows on NBC).

The Spots were lucky to hook up with Moe Gale, who not only managed many of the black acts of the day, but also owned the Savoy Ballroom on Lenox Avenue and 140th Street (the most popular nightclub in Harlem in the '30s, with the largest dance floor, nicknamed "The Track").

Probably Gale's most important act was the orchestra of drummer William Henry "Chick" Webb, the Savoy's unofficial house band. Edgar Sampson, one of Webb's arrangers, wrote the tune "Stomping At The Savoy," later recorded by the Ink Spots, as well as by Webb, Benny Goodman, and Ozzie Nelson, among many others. In 1935 Webb hired neophyte singer Ella Fitzgerald. This was the first big break for "Miss Ella" (who had really wanted to be a dancer). Later in our story we'll meet her again.

The Ink Spots (1933): Jerry Daniels, Deek Watson, Hoppy Jones, Charlie Fuqua. (Jerry and Deek have four-string tenor guitars, and Hoppy has his trademark cello.) (Courtesy of Jerry Daniels.)

1934

U.S. troops pull out of Haiti (they'd been there since 1915). Battle of Toledo Ohio (police and National Guard attack workers who were attacking scab laborers). General strike in San Francisco. Teamsters strike in Minneapolis. John Dillinger killed by FBI agents.

The Ink Spots appeared in "white" theaters as well as on the so-called "Chittlin' Circuit" (a group of theaters, including the Apollo, Royal, Howard, Earle, and Regal, that was to black performers what the Catskills "Borscht Belt" was to Jewish performers). Thus, they played such divergent spots as the Waldorf-Astoria; the Apollo (newly moved in 1934 from the old Lafayette Theater); New York's Roxy and Washington's Howard Theaters; the Savoy Ballroom (owned by Moe Gale and managed by Charlie Buchanan) in Harlem; and the West End Theater in Philadelphia, where they gave that city's first Sunday performance.

Their stage show at the time had a "socko" ending—the Ink Spots' version of "Tiger Rag" and their own dance routine, which impressed reviewers.

However, their early appearances at the Apollo certainly weren't financial successes:

> ... in 1934, the already famous Mills Brothers were headlining at a then-fabulous $3,000 a week, while the yet relatively

unknown Ink Spots, later to become all-time greats, shared a weekly salary of $160.[1]

Contrast this with the way things turned out years later:

> Another star who believed in body banking [carrying large amounts of cash] was Bill Kenny, the tall, lean tenor who led the Ink Spots to fame and fortune with his rendition of "If I Didn't Care."
> Bumping into Bill by accident one day, Dad [Apollo Theatre owner Frank Schiffman] was alarmed at a bulge in Bill's side. "You're not carrying a gun, are you?" Dad asked worriedly.
> "Who, me, Pop?" was the good-natured reply. "I never carried a gun in my life."
> Bill reached into his jacket and pulled out a money belt stuffed with bills. It was at least four inches thick, and there wasn't a "single" visible in the bunch: there had to be at least ten thousand dollars in that roll.[2]

In the fall of 1934, the Ink Spots were hired by British bandleader Jack Hylton, who was putting together a group of acts for a tour of the British Isles. According to Moe Gale, "[Hylton] gave them [an] audition on a Friday afternoon at 4:00 pm. The next morning at 11 they were on the [ocean liner] *Ile de France*."[3] (Jerry Daniels said that this is essentially correct.)

It started with a headline proclaiming, "Hylton Here Hunting Acts":

> Jack Hylton will take in Chicago and other key cities during his American sojourn in a search for attractions he plans to take back to England.[4]

It's unclear what Hylton planned to accomplish on his American "sojourn," since he only took two acts back with him:

> Jack Hylton, English bandleader, sailed back Saturday (29) for London taking over with him two American acts, the 4 Ink Spots (colored) and the 3 Gay Lords, femme trio, whom he caught in hideaway joints around N.Y. a couple of days before sailing. This necessitated some high pressure passport

and passage booking but they got away okay with Hylton in time.

English maestro wanted the 6 Spirits Of Rhythm from the Onyx Club, but they're committed to some intensive Decca recordings this winter which, their own managers figure, will increase their potential value for foreign bookings. Hence Hylton's compromise on the Ink Spots.

Both acts almost missed sailing time, getting over the gangplank with less than 10 minutes to spare. Of the colored quartet two were on time, the other two arriving five minutes before the 11 am sailing time Saturday morning.[5]

Hylton's first choice, the Spirits Of Rhythm, had recorded for Brunswick in 1933. They later had releases on Decca, Columbia, and Black & White.

Moe Gale (right) and his brother, Tim.

The day they left, Jerry Daniels sent a telegram home that read: WE GOT THE BREAK SAIL FOR LONDON AT 11 OCLOCK. SON.

The troupe departed on September 29, 1934, along with Johnny Weissmuller, his wife Lupe Velez (whose movie nickname was "The Mexican Spitfire"), and comedian Joe Penner. Moe Gale also sent his brother, Tim, with them as a road manager. The trip across the Atlantic was a rough one and proved traumatic for Hoppy, who was scared of the sea, wearing a life jacket at all times, even when sleeping.[6] Deek says that they entertained the other passengers on the crossing: "Johnny Weissmuller's favorite song was one that I had written, and that we had recorded, called 'Your Feet's Too Big.'"[7]

This probably would have come as a shock to the actual writer of the song (whoever that might have been—Jerry Daniels said it wasn't Deek;[8] the Ink Spots' 1935 Victor recording of the tune credits "Jack Hancock;" their 1936 re-recording for Decca credits "Ink Spots-Ada Benson-Fred Fisher;" and the 1939 Fats Waller version credits only Benson and Fisher—see the next chapter for more on this mystery). Also note that, Deek's remark notwithstanding, they hadn't yet recorded *anything*.

In England, the Ink Spots toured with Hylton, playing Birmingham, Manchester, Liverpool, and London, as well as Edinburgh and Glasgow in Scotland. Other acts with them were pianist Alec Templeton, singer Tessie O'Tish (a Sophie Tucker type), and Dutch singer Leo Fould.

Here's another interesting "fact" thrown out by Deek:

> Then came a really big thrill. We played at the Coronation
> of the Prince of Wales, when he became King, and at the Ball
> that night![9]

Only one sentence, and yet three problems: (1) the Prince of Wales became king Edward VIII on January 20, 1936, more than a year after the Ink Spots returned to the United States; (2) a coronation is a solemn, formal, historic ceremony, at which there would have been no "playing" by the Ink Spots or anyone else; and (3) Edward never *had* a coronation (hence no Coronation Ball), abdicating that same year. When asked about this, Jerry Daniels said that they never had anything *at all* to do with the Prince of Wales.[10]

In terms of media exposure, the trip paid off well. Transatlantic broadcasts over the BBC airwaves in London increased the Ink Spots' popularity back home as well, and following their December 26, 1934, return to New York (this time on the *Queen Mary*), bookings and broadcasts kept them busy.

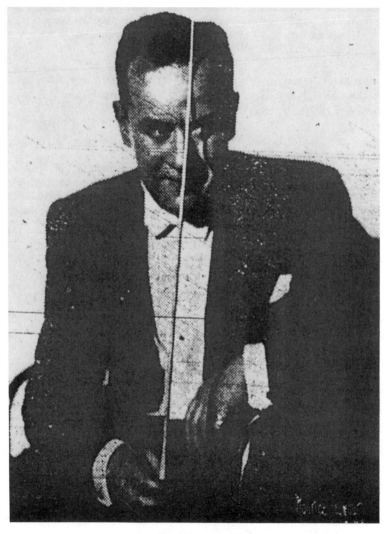

Bandleader Jack Hylton.

PERFORMANCE REVIEWS

Roxy (New York—part of the Fanchon and Marco vaudeville theater chain)

> More vocalizing (plus string tickling) is dished by the Four Inkspots [sic], colored lads, who get lowdown and plenty effective and end with a hotcha dance. (*Billboard*, 9/1/34)

The Ink Spots were reviewed the following week as a "New Act," based on that same show (a New Act was either the first appearance of an artist or a new routine by an established artist):

> *Reviewed at the Roxy, New York, Style—Singing, instrumental and dancing. Setting—In one. Time—Thirteen minutes.*
> Four colored lads who sing and play stringed instruments while grouped around the mike. Excellent arrangements and catchy hotcha style put them over easily. Went across heavy when caught. End the act with a dance which is hot and effective. Easy favorites with any audiences with a yen for Harlem jazz. (*Billboard*, 9/8/34)*

And this is what *Variety* had to say:

> Four Inkspots [sic] do a radio style act that got them back for a hand since they did not require much urging. (*Variety*, 8/28/34)

---

* Like any other profession, show business has its jargon, which can be unintelligible to outsiders. I'll try, whenever possible, to translate. For example, "Went across heavy when caught" means that on the day the reviewer saw the act, they went over extremely well with the audience.

At the Roxy Theater (8/28/34): Jerry Daniels, Deek Watson, Charlie Fuqua, Hoppy Jones. (Courtesy of Jerry Daniels.)

1935

Hitler openly begins rearmament, then annexes the Saar. Italy invades Ethiopia. Will Rogers killed in Alaska plane crash. Louisiana Governor Huey Long assassinated. George Gershwin's Porgy And Bess *opens. Social Security enacted. Wagner Act passed (allows collective bargaining rights). Joe Louis defeats Max Baer.*

The competition: Begin The Beguine, Blue Moon, Cheek To Cheek, Deep Purple, I'm Gonna Sit Right Down And Write Myself A Letter, I'm In The Mood For Love, I've Got Plenty Of Nothin', Just One Of Those Things, Lovely To Look At, Lullaby Of Broadway, The Music Goes Round And Round, Red Sails In The Sunset, Stardust.

Based on the success of their British tour, the Ink Spots got a recording contract. On January 4, 1935, they recorded four songs for Victor Records. One of these, "Your Feet's Too Big" featured successive choruses by Jerry, Deek, Charlie, and Hoppy. Anyone who only knows the later Fats Waller version of this song is missing something: the Ink Spots present more lyrics and deserve as much recognition as Waller.

Also recorded was "Swinging On The Strings," featuring frenetic vocals and finger-spraining lead guitar by Daniels, backed up by Watson and Fuqua on tenor guitars, and Jones on bass-tuned cello. (When I visited Jerry Daniels in the mid-1970s, he could *still* play guitar like that.) The weak link instrumentally was Hoppy Jones, who couldn't really keep up with Daniels' and Fuqua's frantic playing. Another wild tune was "Don't 'Low No Swingin' In Here," in which "mamma," before leaving for work, cautions her "children" against "swinging" while she's gone. Of course, once she's out the door, a wild swing session occurs, stopped only by her return.

It would be nice to give credit where credit is due on their recordings. According to the labels, all four Victor tunes were written by "Jack Hancock." Jerry Daniels was actually the author of "Swinging On The Strings" and "Swing, Gate, Swing." He didn't know who wrote "Don't 'Low No Swingin' In Here," but it was based on "Mama Don't 'Low No Easy Riders Here," credited to Charles Davenport in 1929. Who was "Jack Hancock"? The answer comes from ASCAP, which lists "John Hancock" as one of the pen names of Fred Fisher (others included "Tom Jones," "Washington Irving," "Dan Parker," "Joe Williams," "Reid Summey," and "The Roaming Ranger"). Fisher, along with Ada Benson, would eventually be credited with writing "Your Feet's Too Big." Why was his name placed on the other songs? After sixty years, it's probable the answer is buried so deep that we'll never know.

Almost buried as well was their recording career, seemingly cut short when they left Victor, after receiving an advance and nothing more.

But success was creeping up on the Ink Spots. They landed a three-times-a-week sustaining (nonsponsored) show on WJZ, the flagship station of the RCA/NBC Blue Network. Starting on February 25, the fifteen-minute show was heard on a coast-to-coast hookup Mondays, Wednesdays and Fridays, at 11:30 p.m.[1] They performed both vocals and instrumentals, indicating that they had a large reservoir of material to draw from.[2] With performances on network radio, an act could become more widely known in a few weeks than in years in vaudeville, or in any medium other than movies; thus began vaudeville's decline.

According to their manager, the show got great reviews:

> The marvelous reception received by the "Four Ink Spots" from their three times a week WJZ-NBC broadcast which began only two weeks ago has caused the quartet to be seriously considered for a full week schedule as a sustaining feature, according to announcement of Gale, Inc., RKO Bldg., managers of the successful young singers.[3]

They went over so big, in fact, that they got a *second* show. Heard over WENR (Chicago), this was a thirty-minute Monday evening (9:00 p.m.) spot, sponsored by Sinclair Oil.[4] Although it was only supposed to last for a month, the exposure made it worthwhile; their booking fee was raised to $1750 per week. The year 1935 also saw the beginning of their movie career: they appeared in a Smith and Dale movie short, "Oh, What A Business," filmed in Queens, NY, and shown in Broadway's Trans-Lux Theater in May.[5] The Spots were only one of the acts in this half-hour extravaganza, singing and dancing their way through "Don't 'Low No Swingin' In Here" and "Tiger Rag."

The first recording. Note the title is also in Spanish. I dare anyone to do a foxtrot to this! (Courtesy of the RCA Records Label, a unit of BMG Entertainment.)

SONGS RECORDED

01/04/35	BS-87269	Swinging On The Strings
	BS-87270	Your Feet's Too Big
	BS-87271	Don't 'Low No Swingin' In Here
	BS-87272	Swing, Gate, Swing

NOTE: Throughout the text, these listings give the recording date, the company's master number, and the title.

RECORDS RELEASED

VICTOR

24851	Your Feet's Too Big	01/04/35	BS-87270	01/35
	Swinging On The Strings	01/04/35	BS-87269	
24876	Swing, Gate, Swing	01/04/35	BS-87272	03/35
	Don't 'Low No Swingin' In Here	01/04/35	BS-87271	

NOTE: Throught the text, these listings give the company, its record number, the title, the recording date, the company's master number, and the record's release date.

RECORD REVIEWS

SWINGING ON THE STRINGS/YOUR FEET'S TOO BIG

Strictly for the jazzhounds, the campus wisies [probably means hip college kids] and Lindy's herring-tearers [sic, ?]. This very modern combo (two guitars, cello and a cymbal [?]) gives out two Harlemaniacal ditties by Jack Hancock captioned "Your Feet's Too Big" and "Swinging On The Strings" wherein the male quartet tells all about it to strict foxtrot tempo. They also simulate the jazzique [sic, ?]. Jack Hylton imported them to England on a recent trip. The guitars are very hotcha. (*Variety*, 2/5/35)

DON'T 'LOW NO SWINGIN' IN HERE/SWING, GATE, SWING

The Ink Spots on Victor 24876 are a colored quartet who make a lot of impression with Jack Hancock's two ditties, "Don't 'Low No Swingin' In Here" and "Swing, Gate, Swing," both brisk foxtrots. (*Variety*, 3/27/35)

PERFORMANCE REVIEWS

WJZ radio program (fifteen minutes, sustaining)

Four voices and string instruments who air late with their Harlem chamber music. Arrangements first are slow and exacting, while again they dip into typical za zu za stuff. Nothing new in the talent way, in fact it resembles all the other foursomes who do the same thing. But what they do is easy to listen to.

Came out of WLW, and have also had some dates in Europe. NBC using them thrice weekly at 11:30 pm EST. (*Variety*, 3/20/35)

1936

Hitler annexes the Rhineland. Stalin's "Great Purge" begins. Francisco Franco's rebellion in Spain, which leads to the Spanish Civil War. Gone With The Wind *is published. Jesse Owens wins four gold medals in the Berlin Olympics. FDR wins second term. Sit-down strikes at Goodyear Rubber and General Motors.*

The competition: All My Life, A Fine Romance, The Glory Of Love, Goody-Goody, I Can't Get Started With You, In The Chapel In The Moonlight, It's A Sin To Tell A Lie, I've Got You Under My Skin, Moon Over Miami, Pennies From Heaven, Summertime, There's A Small Hotel, These Foolish Things, Until The Real Thing Comes Along, The Way You Look Tonight, When Did You Leave Heaven.

In the early part of 1936, Jerry Daniels became the first to leave the Ink Spots. Deek claimed that Daniels was too physically ill to continue—Jerry himself said that the problem was more basic: the only thing he was "sick" of was making so little money. While trade papers proclaimed the Ink Spots were making as much as $5,000 weekly per member, Daniels saw earnings of only a couple of hundred dollars.[1]

Rumors of Daniels' discontent had filtered back to Moe Gale, who sensed that the group might fall apart if they were one member short. Now that they were beginning to make a name for themselves, Gale had a vested interest in keeping them together (in addition, they were usually billed as the Four Ink Spots). He therefore brought lanky 6-foot 2-inch tenor Bill Kenny to an Ink Spots' rehearsal, announcing that he was to be a new member. At that point, Daniels went back home to Indianapolis.

Actually, twenty-one-year-old Bill Kenny hadn't been the only choice. There was also Chuck Richards, a radio announcer and singer (with Lucky Millinder's Orchestra). But in the end, Bill won out.[2]

Bill Kenny was a tenor vocalist from Baltimore who had won an amateur contest at the Ritz-Carlton Gardens in Atlantic City. The prize was a week's bookings (which were handled by Jack Berle, Milton's brother). He then came to New York and won amateur contests at the Apollo (singing a musical rendition of Joyce Kilmer's "Trees") and at Gale's Savoy Ballroom. Kenny had a wonderfully smooth voice, which ranged from tenor to soprano; he was meant to sing ballads. His inspiration was Irish tenor Morton Downey, a popular singer of the '20s and '30s. Bill would rush home from school to listen to Downey's daily radio show. (Downey, whose theme song was "Carolina Moon," had a hit with "I'll Always Be In Love With You" in 1929.)

Although Bill Kenny was destined to become the best-known Ink Spot, he initially had great difficulty filling Jerry Daniels' "spot." Uncomfortable with "swing" arrangements, and unable to play an instrument (although he occasionally played a cymbal with a drummer's wire brush), Kenny and the other three members went through intensive rehearsals to create a homogenized sound. Watson wrote of audience reaction to the early results of those efforts:

> . . . public taste is a funny thing, and the people didn't like the change. We still got bookings, but we had to take a terrible cut in money. Where before we got eighteen hundred dollars a week, now we only got seven hundred and fifty dollars a week.[3]

Part of the reason for the negative reaction is that, until he hit his stride with the romantic ballads that he was born to sing, Bill sounded uncomfortable in the group. His voice didn't fit in with what the group was doing, and at times it seemed like he was just trying to find something to do in the background. For example, in "Pork Chops And Gravy" (1938), Bill proves that he really *can* hit soprano (but he sounds silly doing it here). On "Brown

Gal" Bill can be heard in the background searching for something to do with his voice. While Bill knew what he had, it must have been frustrating for him to be constrained in that manner. In fact, it's difficult to understand why Moe Gale hired him in the first place. There's no evidence on their early recordings that the Ink Spots were going to end up singing romantic ballads. Fortunately for music history, Gale *did* hire him and *did* stick with him and Kenny *did* bide his time. The record-buying public ultimately benefited from that decision.

Around April of 1936, the group signed with the fledgling Decca label (only about two years old), where the talent roster included Bing Crosby, the Mills Brothers, Guy Lombardo, Jimmie Lunceford, and the Boswell Sisters (all for only 35¢ apiece).

Decca had been started in 1934 by the efforts of Jack Kapp, whose father was a record salesman for Columbia (he sold them door-to-door). At fourteen, young Jack became a part-time Columbia salesman himself. In his middle twenties, he joined Brunswick, where he mostly handled "race" records (although he also signed Guy Lombardo to a contract and supervised Al Jolson sessions). Kapp journeyed to England, where he met E. R. Lewis, head of British Decca, selling him the rights to make Brunswick records in England. Jack Kapp had a dream: a budget American label, whose records, in the midst of the Great Depression, would retail for 35¢ (when everyone else's cost 75¢). When Brunswick wouldn't go along, he left to form American Decca (with British Decca's backing), taking many Brunswick artists with him. (Later, in 1941, Decca would buy out Brunswick.) Although Kapp realized his dream, he found that dealers didn't like the cheap records because their profits were correspondingly smaller.

Comparing the Ink Spots' early Decca recordings to those on Victor, you can hear the shift in sound without Jerry Daniels. The breathy youthful enthusiasm of their "hotcha" sound was all but gone and in its place was a more restrained "swing" sound. Daniels' hot guitar work was replaced by Charlie Fuqua's adequate, but less acrobatic breaks. Whereas all the members formerly took turns on lead vocals, during this period, Deek was the usual lead singer.

"Your Feet's Too Big" was re-recorded for Decca at their first session on May 12, 1936. Ensuing releases included the bluesy "When The Sun Goes Down" and "Keep Away From My Doorstep"; vocal adaptations of big-band tunes, such as "Stompin' At The Savoy" (a wonderful rendition, with Hoppy actually doing some singing) and "Christopher Columbus" (kind of a Mills Brothers arrangement); and even show tunes, such as George and Ira Gershwin's "Let's Call The Whole Thing Off."

Their style was certainly not what future fans of the Ink Spots would remember, or even be able to identify for the most part. They did unison singing, swing, jive, scat, barbershop, and anything else they could think of. The one unifying thread was that they seemed to be having fun. For example, in "Swing High, Swing Low," Deek throws in a couple of "ribba doo dee" scats, then, as if to pull it all together, says, "One more 'ribba doo dee' will get it!"

FORM 1OM 4475 4/36 U. P. & N. CO.

DECCA RECORDS, Inc.

Date 5/12/36

Series 10 "

Matrix No. 61104

Record No.

Selection Your Feets Too Big (novelty song)

Talking Picture or Show

Artist Ink Spots

Rate

Composer Ada Benson and Fred Fisher

Domicile

Citizenship

Author

Domicile

Citizenship

Published by Joe Davis Inc. Date

Place

Other publications by Date

Place

Copyright owner U. S. Number Date

Other copyright owners Joe Davis, Inc. Countries

The entry in the Decca files for the first Ink Spots recording: "Your Feet's Too Big" on May 12, 1936 (here credited only to Ada Benson and Fred Fisher). It's marked "vocal quartette, 2 guitars, string bass."

SONGS RECORDED

05/12/36	61104	Your Feets Too Big
	61105	Tain't Nobody's Biz-ness If I Do
06/18/36	61188	Stomping At The Savoy
	61189	Old Joe's Hitting The Jug
	61190	Keep Away From My Door Step
	61191	Christopher Columbus

RECORDS RELEASED

DECCA

817	Tain't Nobody's Biz-ness If I Do	05/12/36	61105	ca. 06/36
	Your Feets Too Big	05/12/36	61104	
883	Christopher Columbus	06/18/36	61191	ca. 08/36
	Old Joe's Hitting The Jug	06/18/36	61189	
1036	Stomping At The Savoy	06/18/36	61188	ca. 12/36
	Keep Away From My Door Step	06/18/36	61190	

BLUEBIRD

6530	Swinging On The Strings	01/04/35	BS-87269	09/36
	Your Feet's Too Big	01/04/35	BS-87270	

NOTE: Bluebird was a subsidiary of Victor; these were presumably released to cash in on Decca's re-recorded "Your Feet's Too Big" (which was released with the title spelled both with and without the apostrophe).

RECORD REVIEWS

OLD JOE'S HITTING THE JUG/CHRISTOPHER COLUMBUS
The Ink Spots swing-vocalize in foxtrot tempo with "Old Joe's Hittin' The Jug" and corking arrangement of the now classic "Christopher Columbus." (*Variety*, 9/9/36)

Intermezzo I:
Jerry Daniels

Once he returned to Indianapolis, Jerry Daniels sang in a succession of local groups. The first of these was the Deep Swingin' Brothers, who tried to recapture somewhat the sounds of a coffee-pot band. The other members were Andrew Harris (piano), William "Jock" Johnson (guitar), and Lucian Anderson (bass). The act also included a dancer, remembered only as "Snookie." They played at drive-in restaurants, where they did pretty well with tips, and got to do some appearances at political campaigns. (1936 was an election year, and they supported the local re-election bid of Senator Homer Capehart.)

Jerry's next group was originally called the Ace, King, and Jack of Spades, later shortened to the Three Spades. This was an all-guitar group, with brothers Bill Jennings on six-string and Al Jennings on tenor guitar. They first appeared on WKBF in Indianapolis, then went to WLW in Cincinnati (there was also a spot on WKBF's sister station WSAI). Around 1938 they came to New York, and were heard the following year on WHN. They finally broke up because of lack of work.

Returning to Indianapolis, Jerry formed his last group: Mr. Words, Mr. Music, and Mr. Strings. This was an attempt at a King Cole Trio sound, with Wendell McMillan, a fireman, on bass, and Donald Overby, a teacher, on piano. They played a continuing engagement at Indianapolis' Stratford Hotel, remaining together until the end of 1942.

Occasionally, during this period, when the Ink Spots played Indianapolis, Jerry would get together to sing with them—but never again before an audience.[1]

In late 1942, Jerry was drafted. Entering the army in January 1943, he trained at Fort Clark, Texas, and finally became a line chief with the Signal Corps, in the Second Cavalry Division. He hoped, of course, that his musical experience would get him into Special Services, but his ability to distinguish between different tones was more beneficial to the army in listening to Morse code. Shipped overseas to Europe, he was at the Battle of the Bulge in December 1944.

After the war, Jerry attended Indiana University and also taught piano technique and guitar at the MacArthur Conservatory of Music in Indianapolis. In the early '50s, he became a deputy clerk in the County Clerk's Office, and then switched over to the State Excise Tax Office (which had to do with alcohol, tobacco, and firearms control), from which he retired in 1986. In 1988 the governor of Indiana proclaimed Jerry Daniels a Sagamore of the Wabash (an honor extended to those rendering a distinguished service to the state of Indiana), and in 1992 he received the keys to the city of Indianapolis from the mayor. Additionally, he wrote a music column for the *Indiana Herald*.

Jerry Franklin Daniels passed away on November 7, 1995, at the age of 79. There at the beginning, he was the last of the original Ink Spots to die.

Jerry Daniels (1992). (Courtesy of Mike Caldarulo.)

1937

Japan invades China. Amelia Earheart disappears. Golden Gate Bridge dedicated. Nationwide student strike against war. Germans bomb Guernica in Spain (the subject of one of Picasso's most famous paintings). Neville Chamberlain becomes prime minister of Britain, ushering in the era of "appeasement."

The competition: Bob White, Boo Hoo, The Dipsy Doodle, A Foggy Day In London Town, Harbor Lights, In The Still Of The Night, It's De-Lovely, I've Got My Love To Keep Me Warm, Johnny One Note, The Lady Is A Tramp, Marie, The Moon Got In My Eyes, Once In A While, Rosalie, September In The Rain, Song Of India, So Rare, Sweet Leilani, Thanks For The Memory, That Old Feeling, They Can't Take That Away From Me, Too Marvelous For Words, Vieni Vieni, Where Or When.

A strange article appeared about the social clubs in Bill Kenny's hometown of Baltimore:

> Cops have had to warn operators of Negro niteries and saloons they'll have to stop practice of shooting and blackjacking patrons who grow disorderly in their establishments. . . . The colored spots, presided over by Negroes almost entirely in

39

> Balto, seem to have got out of habit of calling in police if customers get tough or frisky.... Generally bouncers use black-jacks, and the bartenders the shootin' irons.[1]

Let us now digress to take a look at James C. Petrillo, who, over the years, would have a tremendous impact on the recording industry. At this time, he was the head of the Chicago Federation of Musicians and, by his own calculation, the highest-paid union leader in the country. While Joseph N. Weber, head of the parent American Federation of Musicians (AFM), and Petrillo's superior, received a salary of $20,000 a year (plus $3,000 expenses), the much more outspoken Petrillo got the following in 1937:

salary	$26,000
expense fund	5,000
income taxes paid for him	16,000
house	25,000
home furnishings	12,000
gardening	1,700
armored car and bodyguards	25,000

This gave a grand total of $110,700.[2] He didn't just sit back and collect money, however; he was constantly waging war with someone or other, in order to get more work and pay for his union members. Our first glimpse of James C. Petrillo comes in January 1937, when he has just announced a ban on all recording by Chicago musicians, to begin February 1 (unless there was a prior contract). Petrillo was never happy with recordings, considering them the "enemy" of musicians. The ban was meant to keep records off sustaining programs. This meant that shows with no sponsors would have to keep a studio orchestra around; if they did (and that orchestra contained at least as many members as there were on any record being played), then they could play as many discs as they wanted. This led many stations to abandon records altogether; why pay a band to sit around and do nothing?

While this smacks of featherbedding, his reasoning was that every time a record was played, a band wasn't getting paid to perform. Somehow, Petrillo came up with a figure (given in a speech at the AFM's national convention): "an orchestra receiving $1,500 for a recording would mean eventually a loss of approximately $1,500,000 in wages by the time the recording was discarded."[3]

The recording industry had others worried too:

> John G. Paine, MPPA chairman [Music Publishers Protective
> Association], declared that it was the publishers' belief that
> the whole mechanical reproduction situation should be rectified
> so that an artist before making a record will definitely know
> in what field the stencilling [record] will be used, and thereby
> be in a position to make an intelligent contract for his services.
>
> As the pubs [publishers] see it, the basic reason for Petrillo's
> action is that the musicians aren't able to control the recordings'
> sources of use. They make a phonograph record for what is
> presumed to be strictly home use and they find it being played
> on most radio stations and in thousands of cafes, barrooms,
> barbecue stands and whatnot. Artist, unaware of this situation,
> has made contracts which do not adequately remunerate him
> for his services, while the recording companies have by their
> lack of opposition to these extraneous uses allowed unlimited
> competition with every orchestra in the country. While one
> station with a live studio orchestra is faced with a substantial
> payroll, another outlet in the same community is allowed to
> get away with the investment of a few dollars in phonograph
> records.[4]

Petrillo's ban lasted until March. One of the regulations that emerged
from it was that any recording made in the Chicago AFM's bailiwick

> . . . cannot be used in the jurisdiction of another local without
> the permission of the local in the jurisdiction wherein the
> recordings are to be used.[5]

The chaos inherent in this is unimaginable.

Later that year the AFM, in a move to control jukeboxes, also declared
that

> . . . records cannot be used in places where otherwise musicians
> may be employed or where it has a tendency to destroy em-
> ployment opportunities of musicians.[6]

This move would hurt Decca more than the other record companies, since Decca placed more discs in jukeboxes than any other company:

> Reason Decca heads the field is that its wholesale rate is cheapest, 21¢ per record (no returns), and also because in its catalog it includes a long list of swing orchs and singers, which supply the favorite form of music of the coin-machine sluggers [patrons].[7]

Not everyone liked jukeboxes, though. They proliferated after the repeal of Prohibition, and it was difficult to find a bar in the country that didn't have one of the estimated 150,000 boxes. But they tended to be played mostly by drunks, who would fixate on a single record, playing it over and over and over, to the total distraction of the other patrons. Sometimes this led to the owner's getting rid of the box rather than risk losing his customers.

In spite of the depression, there was opportunity for all. The following is part of a review of a radio sports show called "Today's Winners," on station WHO in Des Moines:

> This sportscast summarizing the day's happenings in the world of sports will be handled by "Dutch" Reagan, WHO's ace sports announcer until he leaves next month for Hollywood to make pictures for Warner Bros.[8]

Wonder whatever became of him?

The Ink Spots continued their fledgling recording career with three more records released in 1937. Always casting around for a different sound, they decided to use a banjo on "Alabama Barbecue"!

As they would many times in the future, the Ink Spots raided the movies for tunes: "With Plenty Of Money And You" came from *Gold Diggers Of 1937* (the subject of a Dick Powell Decca recording); "Swing High, Swing Low" was taken from the film of the same name (also recorded on Decca by Glen Gray's Casa Loma Orchestra); "Let's Call The Whole Thing Off" and "Slap That Bass" were both from the film *Shall We Dance* (and both had been recorded by Fred Astaire on Brunswick).

1937 probably saw hard times for the Spots; not one of their records was reviewed by either *Variety* or *Billboard*, nor were any of their appearances reviewed. *Variety* didn't seem to have a standard record review policy; they did it whenever they got around to it. Strangely, at the precise times that Ink Spots records were being released, the reviewer went on hiatus for months at a time. (This isn't as bad as it sounds, however, their "reviews" were mostly an announcement that a record existed, rather than a critique of the disc.) This news blackout would continue through 1938.

The Spots were having more success on radio in 1937. Listings show them on NBC's Red Network on Wednesdays and Saturdays (11:15 p.m.) in March, and on NBC's Blue Network on Wednesdays (3:15 p.m.) in April.

The Ink Spots (ca. 1937): Bill Kenny, Deek Watson, Hoppy Jones, Charlie Fuqua.

SONGS RECORDED

02/05/37	61581	Alabama Barbecue
	61582	Don't Let Old Age Creep Upon You
	61583	With Plenty Of Money And You
	61584	Yes-suh!
04/09/37	62120	Whoa Babe
	62121	Let's Call The Whole Thing Off
	62122	Swing High, Swing Low
	62123	Slap That Bass

RECORDS RELEASED

DECCA

1154	Alabama Barbecue	02/05/37	61581	ca. 03/37
	With Plenty Of Money And You	02/05/37	61583	
1236	Swing High, Swing Low	04/09/37	62122	ca. 04/37
	Whoa Babe	04/09/37	62120	
1251	Let's Call The Whole Thing Off	04/09/37	62121	ca. 05/37
	Slap That Bass	04/09/37	62123	

1938

Munich Pact gives Czechoslovakia to Hitler. National Minimum Wage Act passed. "Wrong-Way Corrigan" flies to Dublin. Orson Welles' "War Of The Worlds" Halloween broadcast causes panic.

The competition: A-Tisket A-Tasket, Bei Mir Bist Du Schoen, Change Partners, Donkey Serenade, The Flat Foot Floogie (With The Floy Floy), I Let A Song Go Out Of My Heart, I Married An Angel, I've Got A Pocketful Of Dreams, Heart And Soul, Love Walked In, Mexicali Rose, Music Maestro Please, My Reverie, Nice Work If You Can Get It, September Song, Two Sleepy People, You Go To My Head, You Must Have Been A Beautiful Baby.

The Ink Spots spent 1938 included in package shows with other Moe Gale artists, such as Tiny Bradshaw, Chick Webb's Band (with Ella Fitzgerald), Willie Bryant, Teddy Hill, and Moms Mabley. They also appeared weekly on Chick Webb's "Good Time Society" NBC radio show.

Their "official" Decca career began in 1938, when "Oh! Red" and "That Cat Is High" became the first Ink Spots songs listed in the artists' section of Decca's interim catalog, sent out to dealers. While their song titles had been listed previously, this marked the first time that they were also listed in the artists' section. This probably means that Decca felt ready to promote them a bit (but only a bit, since the trade papers stubbornly refused to review their records).

The only mention of the Ink Spots that I could find between September 1936 and October 1938 was this abbreviated notice in the May 4, 1938, *Variety*:

> Four Ink Spots exited Levaggi's, Boston, April 29 to come to New York.

This shows that they certainly were "out there," but definitely not doing much to attract the attention of reviewers. Notice that it doesn't even say *where* in New York they were going to be appearing.

Years later, after Bill Kenny had gone out on his own, he returned to Levaggi's. At that time, they reminisced that the Ink Spots had first played at their Flamingo Room in 1938, as "extras" along with Chick Webb and Ella Fitzgerald.

One of the Spots' 1938 recordings was "Brown Gal." While it wasn't a hit for them, it would see many reincarnations down through the years. The tune was a Lil (Mrs. Louis) Armstrong composition, which she had recorded with "Her Swing Ork" for Decca in late 1936. In the late '40s, saxophonist Al Sears recorded it (as "Brown Boy") with a group called the Sparrows, whose lead singer was Clarence Palmer. The tune itself would reach its pinnacle in 1957, when Clarence tried his hand at it once again, this time with a group called the Jive Bombers and a re-title of "Bad Boy"; this outing reached Number 7 on the Rhythm and Blues charts. Even Deek would do a solo version of "Brown Gal," on Jubilee, in the early '50s.

By 1938 record sales had started to climb out of the depths of the Depression. Around 120 million records had been sold in 1929 (which industry analysts considered low; they blamed radio), with sales plunging to 12 million in 1932, and creeping back up to 35 million in 1938 (which put them at the 1912 level).

But few of those records were by the Ink Spots. As the year ended, hits were nonexistent, money was short, and spirits were low. They all lived together in an apartment (provided by Moe Gale) on Manhattan's Amsterdam Avenue.

Although it's true that there weren't any hits by the group, the *New York Amsterdam News* had this to say in January 1939, five days *before* "If I Didn't Care" was recorded:

Negro quartets have been definitely a part of New York's broadcasting world, with a more than generous representation. That group, naturally, would be headed by the Four Ink Spots, who've done right well for themselves via NBC for quite some time.[1]

This seems to indicate that the Ink Spots had a following, and could have continued for some time in the same vein.

Gale Agency ad for Christmas, 1938.

SONGS RECORDED

03/25/38	63494	Oh! Red
	63495	That Cat Is High
05/19/38	63813	I Wish You The Best Of Everything
	63814	When The Sun Goes Down
08/31/38	64485	Pork Chops And Gravy
	64486	Brown Gal

RECORDS RELEASED

DECCA

1731	Don't Let Old Age Creep Upon You	02/05/37	61582	ca. 03/38
	Yes-suh!	02/05/37	61584	
1789	Oh! Red	03/25/38	63494	ca. 04/38
	That Cat Is High	03/25/38	63495	
1870	I Wish You The Best Of Everything	05/19/38	63813	ca. 05/38
	When The Sun Goes Down	05/19/38	63814	
2044	Brown Gal	08/31/38	64486	ca. 10/38
	Pork Chops And Gravy	08/31/38	64485	

PERFORMANCE REVIEWS

Sans Souci Grill (Hotel Bennett, Binghamton, New York)

Spot is featuring the Four Ink Spots, colored musicians and entertainers, for a three-week period which commenced October 9. Ink Spots appeared here a year ago.

Their music consists of low Southern comedy, Harlem lingo, popular music and the hottest swing. Costumes are flashy and boys are neatly groomed in all respects. Broadcasting every day over WNBF. (Billboard, 10/29/38)

1939

Italy annexes Albania. Germany invades Poland for the official start of World War II. Russo-Finnish War. Albert Einstein advises President Roosevelt of an atomic bomb's capability. FDR opens New York World's Fair—the ceremony is carried on television, but only on an experimental channel. San Francisco has its own World's Fair on Treasure Island. Ten million still unemployed. Sit-down strikes declared unconstitutional by the Supreme Court. Charles Lindbergh and Henry Ford receive medals from Adolph Hitler. The Grapes Of Wrath *written;* Gone With The Wind *filmed.*

The competition: All The Things You Are, And The Angels Sing, Beer Barrel Polka, Deep Purple, Do I Love You, Heaven Can Wait, I Cried For You, Jeepers Creepers, Little Brown Jug, My Heart Belongs To Daddy, Our Love, Over The Rainbow, Penny Serenade, Scatter Brain, South Of The Border, Sunrise Serenade, Three Little Fishies, The Umbrella Man.

And then, as they say, fate stepped in. They went to Decca's recording studio in New York on January 12, 1939, with the express intention of cutting a typical jive selection entitled "Knock Kneed Sal." Aspiring songwriter Jack Lawrence showed up with a ballad he had just penned, and suggested that the Ink Spots record it. Needing something to put on the back of "Knock Kneed Sal," they decided to give it a try, using a completely different style.

The title, of course, was "If I Didn't Care," and the recording represented a radical departure from previous Ink Spots' disks: for the first time, the soaring tenor of Bill Kenny was paired with Hoppy Jones' booming bass talking part, addressed to his "honey chile." That combination was to become *very* familiar in years ahead.

While the prior story was widely circulated, it has holes in it, which require examination. To begin with, "If I Didn't Care" has a *lower* master number than "Knock Kneed Sal," meaning that it was recorded *first*, not as an afterthought. Ironically, the Spots didn't particularly *like* the song and only ran through the single copy of the lyrics a couple of times before recording it. Since none of them was totally familiar with the words, Deek ended up whispering them to Hoppy during the bridge. This created a certain hesitancy in the delivery that actually enhanced the popularity of the song.

This is as good a time as any to examine the elements of a "classic" Ink Spots tune. First of all, it's a romantic ballad. It has a simple guitar introduction, it's sung by a high tenor, and the second bridge isn't sung, but spoken by the bass (ofttimes to his "honey chile"). All this is present in "If I Didn't Care." But did it just happen? Actually, the separate elements had all been done by the Spots before; this was simply the first time they had all come together on record.

Both the guitar introduction and Bill Kenny's romantic ballad tenor lead had first been done in the May 1938 "I Wish You The Best Of Everything." Unfortunately, the Spots didn't really know what to do on the bridge of that one. The first time Hoppy had done a talking bass was way back in 1935, before Bill Kenny had even joined! Their arrangement of "The Old Spinning Wheel" featured Jerry Daniels and Hoppy Jones, in a style that was suggestive of things to come (although, it's true, the arrangement was still somewhat jive-oriented in spite of its being a ballad).[1] Even Charlie Fuqua had done a talking bridge way back in 1936 (in "Keep Away From My Doorstep," he addresses his "chocolate drop"). The combination of Bill's high-tenor lead and Hoppy's bass recitation had been heard during an NBC broadcast in August 1938, with the Spots' radio arrangement of the ballad "So Little Time (And So Much To Do)."

Thus, like most great inventions, "If I Didn't Care" was less a bolt out of the blue than a synthesis of bits and pieces, which evolved into the final product. Also note that while the guitar intro is what's remembered, the piano (played by accompanist Bob Benson) is just as prominent as Charlie's guitar.

It's also true that many of these elements were present in *other* groups' songs before "If I Didn't Care." The best known, if not the first, high-tenor lead of the '30s was the Charioteers' Billy Williams. They were primarily a gospel group at the time, but on their secular ballads (e.g., "Along Tobacco Road," recorded for Decca back in 1935), Williams was doing a dramatic tenor lead that was almost as high and smooth as Kenny's. On the Mills Brothers' 1932 hit "Rockin' Chair," there's both an almost-familiar guitar introduction and a talking bass ("old rockin' chair's got me, son"). Even the Norfolk Jazz Quartet had a talking bass on a 1921 record. Certainly the Ink Spots were familiar with the Charioteers and the Mills Brothers. Were the Spots consciously emulating them? It's a moot point. All these groups were singing a certain style of music and things were bound to rub off; as far as we know, the Ink Spots were the first to bring all these pieces together.

The other song done at that January session was "Just For A Thrill" also a ballad, but with no talking bridge, and with *Deek* doing the lead.

The Ink Spots had used recurring themes throughout their career. The introduction to their earlier songs wasn't a guitar but, more often than not, Deek saying "yass, yass." Other repeated catchphrases in their early works were "ah, you dog," "home cookin'," "it's in the bag," and "cushfoot." The word *cushfoot* means one who's shuffling along, going through life comfortably, without a care in the world (probably akin to having a "cushy" job).

When "If I Didn't Care" was released about a month later, it promptly drew a rave review from extremely influential columnist Walter Winchell, who awarded it "orchids" (with "scallions" in advance to any other act that recorded it). The Ink Spots suddenly found themselves thrust into the spotlight as a hot vocal group. "Care" made it all the way to Number 1 on the "Songs with Most Radio Plugs" chart in *Billboard* (on June 10, 1939). This was a kind of predecessor to the weekly charts that *Billboard* would begin in the '40s. In a survey done in 1940, "If I Didn't Care" placed Number 30 (out of 38) in the "Top Radio Tunes during the Past Year." While this may not sound like the top of the heap, remember that of *all* the songs released during the year, *only* 38 even made the list.

In fact, the Ink Spots were the hottest black group of the era, following with a string of smash hits in the same vein: "Address Unknown" (1939), "My Prayer" (1939), "When The Swallows Come Back To Capistrano" (1940), "Maybe" (1940), "We Three" (1940), "Do I Worry?" (1941), "I Don't Want To Set The World On Fire" (1941), "Don't Get Around Much Any More" (1943), "I'm Making Believe" (1944), "Into Each Life Some

Rain Must Fall" (1944), "The Gypsy" (1946), and "To Each His Own" (1946). There were also countless other ballads that are scarcely distinguishable from one another. There were a few deviations that harkened back to their roots: Deek did the lead on "Java Jive" and "Shout, Brother, Shout," but for the most part, Bill Kenny-led ballads had replaced the contagiously high-spirited "jive" numbers led by Deek Watson. The public didn't seem to mind a bit, although it must have been a bitter pill for Deek to swallow.

Speaking of those heady days following "If I Didn't Care," Bill Kenny said: "We knew our forte then, so we immediately countered with another ballad, 'It's Funny To Everyone But Me.' Combined with the total sales on our previous record, established a new high at Decca Studios."[2] We'll chalk this up to enthusiasm and ignore the strange grammar, but though *Billboard* reviewed its flip, "Just For A Thrill," "It's Funny" (another Jack Lawrence tune) wasn't mentioned at all and doesn't actually seem to have been a hit for the group. Note that far from making his living off the Ink Spots, Jack Lawrence also wrote "What Will I Tell My Heart," "Sunrise Serenade," "Sleepy Lagoon," "With The Wind And The Rain In Your Hair," "Johnson Rag," "All Or Nothing At All," and "Tenderly." (Incidentally, another Jack Lawrence song was "Linda," written in 1947 for his lawyer's young daughter. Linda grew up and married Paul McCartney, of the Beatles, who bought the rights to all of Lawrence's songs, including "If I Didn't Care.")

The success of "Care" didn't immediately change the basic way the Spots did business. On July 12, they did a show for NBC affiliate WFIL (Philadelphia), wherein four of the five songs they sang were still in the jive vein. Announced as "the home cookin' boys from up Harlem way," they sang "No Wonder," "Stairway To The Stars," "Pork Chops And Gravy," "It's Funny To Everyone But Me," and "Tiger Rag." "Funny" was the only Kenny-led tune, and "Stairway" featured Deek doing lead to Hoppy's talking bridge.

By this date, there were technically five Ink Spots, not four; pianist/arranger Bob Benson had been added, and was specifically mentioned by the announcer of that WFIL show. Benson, originally from Bluefield, West Virginia, had known the group from their Indianapolis days, playing in local bands in the '30s. He came to New York around the same time they had, but didn't actually hook up with them until 1938.

Their next release, "Address Unknown," made it to the "Songs with Most Radio Plugs" chart on August 12, 1939 (and was subsequently reviewed as a *new* pressing on October 7).

Since the Ink Spots were radio stars long before charting with their records, it's nice to note that by the end of 1939 they were still being advertised as "NBC broadcasting stars."

In December 1939, Decca announced the start of its 18000 series, to retail at 50¢, rather than 35¢. Reserved for artists performing old standards that the record-buying public would snap up, the Ink Spots would not appear on this series until 1942.

Instant classic.

SONGS RECORDED

01/12/39	64891	If I Didn't Care
	64892	Just For A Thrill
	64893	Knock Kneed Sal
05/17/39	65584	It's Funny To Everyone But Me
08/17/39	66118	You Bring Me Down
	66119	I Don't Want Sympathy, I Want Love
	66120	Address Unknown
	66121	Coquette
09/19/39	66608	My Prayer
	66609	Give Her My Love
10/03/39	66463	Memories Of You
10/06/39	66737	Thoughtless
	66738	I'm Through
	66739	What Can I Do
10/11/39	66752	I'm Getting Sentimental Over You
	66753	Bless You (For Being An Angel)

RECORDS RELEASED

DECCA

2286	If I Didn't Care	01/12/39	64891	02/39
	Knock Kneed Sal	01/12/39	64893	
2507	It's Funny To Everyone But Me	05/17/39	65584	ca. 06/39
	Just For A Thrill	01/12/39	64892	
2707	Address Unknown	08/17/39	66120	ca. 10/39
	You Bring Me Down	08/17/39	66118	
2790	My Prayer	09/19/39	66608	ca. 11/39
	Give Her My Love	09/19/39	66609	
2841	Bless You (For Being An Angel)	10/11/39	66753	ca. 12/39
	I Don't Want Sympathy, I Want Love	08/17/39	66119	

RECORD REVIEWS

IF I DIDN'T CARE

The Ink Spots, a real sob ballad and an excellent phono bet, as more and more ops are finding out to their pleasure. Guaranteed to add a few tears to one's beer. (*Billboard*, 4/29/39)

The Four Ink Spots are still wringing pleasurable tears out of beer-sippers and nickel-droppers with as sentimental a disc as has been waxed in some time. Bob Crosby adds a dance arrangement, but thus far operators [owners of jukeboxes] for some reason have been slightly apathetic toward his disc. It may catch on, however. (*Billboard*, 5/6/39)

This sob ballad was listed under Operators' Specials for several weeks during the early spring, and it was thought that the Ink Spots' disc of it would live and die in that category. Belatedly, however, the tune seems to be catching on with the general public and with band leaders. It's been getting air plugs and selling copies (No. 7 on this week's best selling list isn't bad), so a revival in the boxes [jukeboxes] would seem to be in order. The Ink Spots did well with it once and should again, and for dancing there's Bob Crosby's version. (*Billboard*, 6/17/39)

Seems as if this Ink Spots special won't leave its slot. The already famous quartet has made many sides since this one, and while many of them are getting a play, it's the first love that's still strong and still keeping the needle grinding away. (Billboard, 8/5/39)

JUST FOR A THRILL

If the nickel dispensers [jukebox customers] are getting a bit weary of the Ink Spots' *If I Didn't Care*, it might be a smart idea to replace it with another of this quartet's waxings. This particular one is not only the best for that purpose, but it has already started to prove its worth in the Cincinnati area, where operators report it as among the strongest current records. (*Billboard*, 8/12/39)

A great follow-up to the Ink Spots' recording of *If I Didn't Care* is this ballad, as operators are beginning to realize in increasing number. The record offers all that the first big hit did, and ought to be pretty successful on its own merit. (*Billboard*, 8/19/39)

ADDRESS UNKNOWN

Another week ought to see this hitting the high spots of phono popularity. Some reports nominate it as a prime favorite in their particular locality right now, but there isn't enough unanimity of opinion to shoot it up to the head of the class this week anyway. But it's a pretty powerful item right now as is, and it gives every indication of becoming better. The Ink Spots, of course. (*Billboard*, 10/28/39)

It should be no surprise to anyone to see this Ink Spots' follow-up to *If I Didn't Care* shoot up into the higher brackets this week. It's been heading for the top for a number of weeks now and it would have been much more surprising to see it miss. Unlike last week's entrant into this sanctified department, *South Of The Border*, it's not the song itself that matters so much here. Actually copies [other artists' versions] of it are not selling too well and its radio plug listing is nothing sensational. This is a clear case of a particular disk copping all the glory. [Translation of all this: it's the Ink Spots' singing, not the song itself, that's got people throwing nickels into jukeboxes.] The Ink Spots have done all right by operators with this and *Didn't Care*. (*Billboard*, 11/4/39)

MY PRAYER

The Ink Spots have another record here that the machines are beginning to take in a big way, but this time the foursome is challenged for phono supremacy by Glenn Miller's and Horace Heidt's dance versions. (*Billboard*, 11/11/39)

PERFORMANCE REVIEWS

Loew's State (New York)

The Ink Spots, vocalizing with the [Erskine] Hawkins band, drew the best reception of the evening. An NBC radio act, they are not only swell singers, swingers and harmonizers, but present a mess of personality. Two of the boys, the shortest and tallest, clown around, get the audience in their hand and really sell the act. They should have done at least one more number. (*Billboard*, 4/8/39)

Apollo Theater (New York)

Four Ink Spots, aided by a pianist [Bob Benson] in this spot, have a captivating routine with "Jeepers Creepers" and "Pork Chops," latter their composition. "If I Didn't Care," tabbed as quartet's latest recording, is tops in the lengthly repertoire, although "Who" supplies the best clowning selection. Their harmony combos went so well that two encores were needed. (*Variety*, 5/10/39)

Hippodrome (Baltimore)

Lads proceed to mop up with four-way harmony renditions of "What Are You Going To Do," "It's Funny To Everyone But Me," "Your Feet's Too Big" and the inevitable "If I Didn't Care" [already, in August 1939, it's referred to as "inevitable"]. Vociferous demand for encore brings "Who" with interpolated Harlem hoofery [dancing] and jive stuff. (*Variety*, 8/30/39)

Paramount Theater New York)

The lack of a big name band is made up somewhat by the presence of the Ink Spots as added attraction and by Bert Wheeler. . . .

The Ink Spots, colored quartet shot into the name class thru music machine records, closed the bill and smashed over their trick harmonizing, accompanied by their own guitar and cello. The cellist's basso and the tall fellow's high tenor highlight the quartet's vocal effects which, along with their swell voice blending and swingy tempos, combine to arrest attention. Did *Undecided, Your Feet's Too Big, My Prayer, Honeysuckle Rose* and *If I Didn't Care.* Went over very big. (*Billboard*, 1/27/40—reviewing a show that had been running since late December)

1940

Germany annexes the Baltic States, conquers Denmark, Norway, France, and the Netherlands. British soldiers evacuated from Dunkirk. Battle of Britain takes place in the skies over England. Japanese occupy Indochina. Draft begins in peacetime. First electron microscope is demonstrated. Nylon stockings go on sale; an immediate hit. FDR wins unprecedented third term. "Grandma" Moses, at age 80, holds her first art show.

The competition: Blueberry Hill, The Breeze And I, Ferryboat Serenade, Fools Rush In, Frenesi, God Bless America, I Hear A Rhapsody, I'll Never Smile Again, Imagination, In The Mood, The Nearness Of You, Only Forever, Pennsylvania 6-5000, Sierra Sue, Tuxedo Junction, When You Wish Upon A Star, The Woodpecker Song.

The Spots were now so popular that in the early part of 1940, the first of the bogus Ink Spots groups appeared:

> When the Moe Gale office learned that four Negro singers were going around the South (a few days ahead of Gale's Inkspots' tour) under the name of the "Inkspots" it got busy trying to track the impostors down.

> In New Orleans they were found, billing themselves as the
> "Famous Inkspots, singing such songs as *If I Didn't Care*, and
> *My Prayer*." Gale office obtained an injunction from the U.S.
> court there to restrain use of the name and now the real Inkspots
> are carrying on with their tour.[1]

At the Paramount, attendance records were shattered as the Ink Spots
appeared with comedian Red Skelton and the Glenn Miller Orchestra, also
swinging on the crest of popularity. Eventually Moe Gale organized a tour
of his artists, and the foursome headlined a show featuring other black stars
such as Lucky Millinder and his band, Ella Fitzgerald, and popular comedy
acts. Actually, Gale's stable of talent had become so popular that

> Moe Gale announced this week that his organization, Gale,
> Inc., is broadening its scope to include booking activities on
> all attractions now being handled by the office. . . .
> Office's first task is the setting up of a tour of 60 one-nighters
> for the Ink Spots, one of Gale's top attractions due to the
> success of a series of recordings in automatic phonographs
> [jukeboxes]. Quartet is currently at the Famous Door here [New
> York]. Previously booked by General Amusement Corp., Ink
> Spots' GAC contract runs out in February, with the proposed
> tour under Gale booking due to start March 6. Boys will play
> ballroom dates, accompanied by the Sunset Royal Ork., most
> recent addition to Gale's properties.[2]

According to the *Chicago Defender*, the Ink Spots were voted the
"outstanding instrumental and vocal quartet of 1939."[3] You could see them
and "their" fourteen-piece orchestra (the Sunset Royal Ork., fronted by "Doc"
Wheeler Moran) at Chicago's Savoy Ballroom on April 21, 1940, for 60¢
(if you got there before 8:30 p.m.). The week before, they were at the East
Market Gardens (Akron, Ohio), where you had to shell out 95¢ in advance
($1.10 at the door).

In a tabulation of popular 1939 recording artists, based on the number
of mentions made in *Billboard*'s "Record Buying Guide" (directed at jukebox
operators), the Ink Spots didn't really make a respectable showing compared
with leaders Glenn Miller, Guy Lombardo, and Bing Crosby. However, they
were singled out as follows:

... the past year developed as standout recording successes the four Ink Spots, whose enormously popular disk of "If I Didn't Care" established them firmly as stellar lights in the entertainment picture. . . [4]

Of course, the public relations flacks were out there doing their job. This appeared in January:

Termed number-one men of the black and tan music world, the Four Ink Spots are namely Messrs. Ivory Watson, Billy Kenny, Orville Jones, and Chas. Fuqua. Their show is a genuine razzle-dazzle, zip-band, shouting, war whooping, frenzied fiesta that leads you to believe that the whole town has gone "whoopee" and that there's nothing left but to have jollification. [5]

and had been thoroughly reworked by October:

Number one men in the black and tan music world, the Four Ink Spots (Messrs. Ivory Watson, Billy Kenny, Orville Jones and Charles Fuqua) show a genuine razzle-dazzle, zip-band, shouting, war-whooping frenzied fiesta that leads you to believe, for the time at least, that the whole town has gone "whoopee." Yes sir, the Four Ink Spots are noisy in their vocal methods with little restraint at any time. [6]

Swamped by bookings, the Ink Spots still found time to sing on the "Kraft Music Hall" radio show (hosted by Bing Crosby—in those days, programs usually carried the name of the sponsor, not the name of the star). Somewhere along the way, unheralded in the press, they'd given up their own radio spot.

Radio was responsible for the world-famous diction that the Ink Spots always brought to their songs (at least after "If I Didn't Care"). Certainly for a good deal of their early career, radio microphones were of poor quality, and if you didn't enunciate clearly, you took the chance of not being understood.

Although the end result of touring was to present a show that would please the patrons, the traveling itself was monotonous, grueling, and sometimes even dangerous:

The bus in which the four Ink Spots and their accompanying 14-piece band were riding caught fire on their recent tour through here [Cumberland, Maryland], causing considerable damage to the bus but luckily no personal injuries, nor were any instruments damaged. The bus was coming down a mountain road four miles out of Cumberland when flames started to shoot out from under the hood. The fire was finally put out with the help of the bus' fire extinguisher.[7]

And this is what it took to play two simultaneous engagements in the same city:

Back in the Forties, the Ink Spots were engaged to play the Apollo for a week following a date at the Paramount Theatre on Broadway. Business at the downtown theater was so good, the Paramount decided to exercise its option to keep the four singers on an extra week. To solve the problem of how to meet two simultaneous contracts, the Ink Spots hired an ambulance to whisk them uptown and downtown for both engagements.[8]

That same story was also reported in *Variety*, under a review of their Apollo performance:

Inkspots [sic] were doubling from the Paramount for the first five days of the engagement here, traversing the distance from Times Square to 125th street in an ambulance four times daily. Holdover at the Par for a third week after the Apollo deal had already been set, caused the unusual arrangement.[9]

Around June 1940, *Billboard* began printing its first real record surveys. By August 3, the Spots' "When The Swallows Come Back To Capistrano" reached Number 7. By September 9, it was still Number 7, but "Maybe" had also charted, at Number 8. On October 5, they had an amazing *three* songs in the top ten: "Maybe" (#2), "When The Swallows Come Back To Capistrano" (#7—still!), and "Whispering Grass" (#10). They pulled the same stunt again on October 10, with "Maybe" (#4), "We Three" (#8), and "Swallows" (#9). "Maybe" could only rise as high as Number 2, however, being kept out of the top spot by Bing Crosby's "Only Forever."

Moe Gale claimed that he had an unusual but unbeatable way of ensuring that only top quality recordings were done by his acts:

> Every Gale, Inc. attraction carries a portable recording machine on tour and they make acetates of the tunes scheduled for the next recording session. These acetates are sent to the office and we listen to them, making special note of what pleases the ear and what doesn't. The tunes are played until everybody is satisfied and then finally okehed for final cutting. In short, we put in 10 times more work in preparing our records than in the actual studio work.[10]

Under the heading "Negro Employment Down [in the music industry]," a *Billboard* article stated that due to problems with mixed attendance at shows, only the highest-caliber black entertainers were able to secure work. It claimed that black bandleaders, during one-nighters, did their best to discourage black patrons from attending, in order to get whites in. There were, at that time, only four theaters left that had an all-black act policy: the Apollo (New York), the West End (New York), the Royal (Baltimore), and the Howard (Washington, D.C.). The article also went on to say:

> The Ink Spots are the colored act sensation of the year. Their prominence is due to their success on records, most of them played on the thousands of music machines [jukeboxes] throughout the country.[11]

Most of the Ink Spots' Decca recordings were also released in England, on the Brunswick label. Strangely, two of the sides they recorded in 1940 for Decca were never released in the United States at all, but *were* released on Brunswick: "I Wish I Could Say The Same," Brunswick 03673; and "Don't Ever Break A Promise," Brunswick 04183. Note that "I Wish I Could Say The Same" is a Deek-led ballad.

The Joy Boy Presents

THE 4 INK SPOTS

With The

SUNSET ROYAL ORCHESTRA

—Featuring—

Little Genevieve and Froshine Stewart

Wednesday Nite, April 24, 9:30 P. M. Until

EAST MARKET GARDENS

AKRON, OHIO

ADVANCE 95c ⋅ ⋅ ⋅ **AT DOOR $1.10**

If you were in Akron, with 95¢ to burn, you could see the Ink Spots.

SONGS RECORDED

05/13/40	67718	When The Swallows Come Back To Capistrano
06/11/40	67862	Whispering Grass
	67863	Maybe
06/18/40	67876	You're Breaking My Heart All Over Again (U)
06/24/40	67898	Stop Pretending
	67899	I'm Only Human
	67900	You're Breaking My Heart All Over Again
07/16/40	67928	We Three (My Echo, My Shadow, And Me)
	67929	So Sorry (U)
	67930	Puttin' And Takin'
	67931	Java Jive
08/08/40	67968	I'll Never Smile Again
	67969	I Could Make You Care
	67970	Do I Worry?
08/20/40	67990	My Greatest Mistake
	67991	Don't Ever Break A Promise (U—BR)
	67992	Ring, Telephone, Ring (U)
08/21/40	67999	In The Doorway (U)
12/23/40	68532	So Sorry
	68533	Ring, Telephone, Ring
	68534	You're Looking For Romance
	68535	I Can't Stand Losing You
	68536	That's When Your Heartaches Begin
	68537	I'm Still Without A Sweetheart
	68538	Why Didn't You Tell Me?
	68539	I Wish I Could Say The Same (U—BR)
12/30/40	68540	I'd Climb The Highest Mountain
	68541	What Good Would It Do?

NOTE: (U) indicates an unreleased song. (U—BR) indicates that the song was unissued in the United States, but was released on Brunswick in England (see text).

RECORDS RELEASED

DECCA

2966	I'm Through	10/06/39	66738	01/40
	Memories Of You	10/03/39	66463	
3077	I'm Getting Sentimental Over You	10/11/39	66752	04/40
	Coquette	08/17/39	66121	
3195	When The Swallows Come Back			
	To Capistrano	05/13/40	67718	06/40
	What Can I Do	10/06/39	66739	
3258	Whispering Grass	06/11/40	67862	07/40
	Maybe	06/11/40	67863	
3288	Stop Pretending	06/24/40	67898	08/40
	You're Breaking My Heart All			
	Over Again	06/24/40	67900	
3346	I'll Never Smile Again	08/08/40	67968	09/40
	I Could Make You Care	08/08/40	67969	
3379	We Three (My Echo, My Shadow,			
	And Me)	07/16/40	67928	10/40
	My Greatest Mistake	08/20/40	67990	
3432	Do I Worry?	08/08/40	67970	11/40
	Java Jive	07/16/40	67931	
3468	I'm Only Human	06/24/40	67899	11/40
	Puttin' And Takin'	07/16/40	67930	

RECORD REVIEWS

WHEN THE SWALLOWS COME BACK TO CAPISTRANO/ WHAT CAN I DO

The combination of this popular vocal group and a tune (*Capistrano*) that is attracting some attention around the country in music machines may result in a click record of *If I Didn't Care* proportions. Both sides are done differently than previous pressings of the Ink Spots, a well played piano chorus occupying the middle of the arrangements instead of the repetitive style of yore. The change is a decided improvement for the better. Excellent commercial prospects in this couplet. (*Billboard*, 6/29/40)

STOP PRETENDING/ YOU'RE BREAKING MY HEART ALL OVER AGAIN

After getting away from the pattern of *If I Didn't Care* and what seemed to be millions of similar disks after that click, the four Ink Spots return to it on the heels of a couple of recent releases that had the benefit of being a bit different. *Heart* brings them back to the familiar style and therefore it's got the same chance as hitting [sic], particularly in the automatic phonos, that *Care* had. *Pretending* is uneventful and not awfully good. (*Billboard*, 8/10/40)

WHISPERING GRASS

Another one that is setting no worlds on fire is the INK SPOTS' recording of this poetically titled opus. This is one of those numbers that find a great deal of favor in certain locations but don't seem able to make their popularity extend from Coast to Coast in a general, universal way. That can still happen, altho it isn't too likely. (*Billboard*, 9/14/40)

MAYBE

Really hitting the high spots now is this ballad from the Prohibition era that has found new life in its 1940 reincarnation. It's steady, speedy drive the past couple of weeks, in the INK SPOTS version, has carried it to the point of being one of the top coin phono numbers of the moment. The sepia quartet has the only recording to mean anything in a widespread, general way. (*Billboard*, 10/12/40)

I'LL NEVER SMILE AGAIN/I COULD MAKE YOU CARE

After a momentary departure on several recent sides from the style that made them famous with *If I Didn't Care*, the Ink Spots are once more back in the old groove of the half tenor-half talked-baritone vocal mugging. The tenor carries it a little too far here, and the style is wearing a little thin by this time. (*Billboard*, 9/28/40)

YOU'RE BREAKING MY HEART ALL OVER AGAIN

Many ops are meeting with great success via INK SPOTS recordings lately, and here is another one by the foursome, already starting to be noticed, that contains the same apparently magic formula for making them drop the nickels. (*Billboard*, 10/26/40)

MY GREATEST MISTAKE/WE THREE

The freak tenor, the talked baritone [sic] interlude, and the freak tenor again—in short, *If I Didn't Care* (and all the follow-ups) all over again. But this colored foursome has something that certainly pulls the nickels in the coin phonos, and there's every reason to believe a jackpot is just waiting to be hit here, too. (*Billboard*, 10/26/40)

DO I WORRY?/JAVA JIVE

Worry is the same old Ink Spots format all over again, and while it's wearing more than a bit thin artistically, its commercial qualities can't be denied, witness to that being the several currently popular Spots disks in the coin phonos. *Java Jive* happily breaks the routine, and offers the foursome in a slow tempoed lyric number, with harmony voicing, nice rhythm and humorous wordage. (*Billboard*, 11/30/40)

PUTTIN' AND TAKIN'/I'M ONLY HUMAN

The four Ink Spots vary their stock execution, if not the formula itself, on the A side here. The tenor first chorus is temporarily replaced by another voice, and there's a nice touch of humor in the talked-baritone middle half chorus. The companion piece, however, returns the boys to the old routine that has been so successful in the music machines so many times. (*Billboard*, 12/28/40)

PERFORMANCE REVIEWS

Apollo Theater (New York)

Harmonizing chromo quartet, at home on its old stompin' grounds, is considerably freer in action and sidetalk than in the awe-inspiring bigness of the Paramount [which they were also playing at the time]. Numbers are pretty much the same as at the midtown house, including "Undecided," "My Prayer" and "If I Didn't Care" for the encore. "Feet's Too Big," which they did at the Par, is better than "Just For A Thrill," being subbed here. Appearance emphasizes that the dusky four have still not acquired an arrangement to counterpart "If I Didn't Care," which catapulted them into a Harlem approximation of the U.S. Mint. "My Prayer," with beautiful pipework by the extra-tall lad, is the only thing that closely approaches "Care," although there is no gainsaying the quality of their general performance. (*Variety*, 2/7/40)

The Paramount Theater (New York)

. . . Nothing of sock caliber is around until the closing, when the Ink Spots show-stop.

The Ink Spots are a great quartet and as commercial as the Mills Brothers during their heyday. They sing, mug, dance, all in unorthodox but entertaining fashion. There is good contrast in the act which keeps it supplied with freshness and versatility. One has a high, freak voice, another low-pitched pipes, and a third gives out in comedy vein. Blend unusually well. Their tunes include *Java Jive, We Three,* and *Maybe,* all leaders on music machines. (*Billboard*, 12/14/40)

[Note that the Mills Brothers have already been written off as has-beens in 1940.]

In good company (ca. 1940): Bill, Deek, Count Basie, Hoppy, Charlie.

Prelude to War:
ASCAP vs BMI

In the late '30s, there was a certain amount of unpleasantness going on in Europe. But it was nothing compared to what was going on in radio broadcasting. And it all had to do with ASCAP.

ASCAP (the American Society of Composers, Authors, and Publishers) is an umbrella association that sees to it that its members get their rightful royalties for song performances. It had been formed in 1914 (just prior to that *other* unpleasantness) by the top composers of the day, led by Victor Herbert. The copyright laws then in effect gave royalties to composers only when their works were performed "for profit." At the time, many restaurants had singing waiters and other forms of entertainment, for which they did not pay royalties. Their reasoning was that they didn't charge admission, and, therefore, they were giving a nonprofit service and didn't have to pay. ASCAP challenged, and the case went all the way to the Supreme Court, where Justice Oliver Wendell Holmes voiced the unanimous decision, "PAY!" (in slightly more elegant terms).

The Hotel and Restaurant Association immediately gave battle to ASCAP, threatening to cut the size of the orchestras (thereby throwing musicians out of work). This caused the Musicians' Federation to boycott ASCAP tunes, which in turn led many composers to flee ASCAP, fearing that their songs would never get played. When the situation was finally settled in 1921, ASCAP took on its next opponent.

The owners of movie theaters had always provided music for their patrons. Silent films were only silent in that there was no dialogue associated with the movie; the theater itself was filled with music throughout the film. Originally, larger theaters had a full orchestra playing along with the screen action and smaller ones had at least a piano player (organists came later). Once again the argument was that the music was incidental to the main reason that people came to the theater; once again the courts sided with ASCAP. (The theater owners countered by forming their own association, the Music Publishers Protective Association, which was successfully challenged by ASCAP as a monopolistic restraint of trade—and the theater owners ended up paying.)

ASCAP was riding high. So high that it started having delusions of how powerful it actually was. Only *it* knew what "good" music was, so "hillbilly" and "race" composers were mostly excluded. Royalties received were pooled and distributed to members by a complicated formula which took into account the importance of a composer, rather than the importance of what had been written. Thus, if you were a lucky new composer who had had three consecutive hits, you probably wouldn't receive as much as an old-timer who hadn't had a hit for years (but who was a "big name").

And now a new medium was the target—radio. The radio stations tried to wriggle out of paying (shouldn't the composers be honored to have their songs showcased on radio?), but fared no better than the rest: ASCAP licenses were granted to radio stations. At this point in our story, all these licenses were due to expire on December 31, 1940.

ASCAP wasn't waiting for the last minute to work on the license renewals. In mid-1938, preparation started. Every once in a while something would leak out: the rates would double or the rates would include extra payments to help finance ASCAP's court cases. And radio started to fight back. "We won't stand for any extortionary raises," went the cry. But ASCAP didn't listen (why should they? this was all the same old tune to them). Radio actually *should* have worried more than it did, since almost *every* song played over the airwaves was ASCAP-licensed (two exceptions were pre-1900 songs and those registered with another organization, SESAC (Society of European Songwriters and Composers), which was nowhere near as far-reaching as ASCAP).

On September 1, 1939, the war in Europe formally began. In that same month, war was declared against ASCAP at a meeting of the National Association of Broadcasters (NAB). The most enduring legacy of that meeting was the mandate to set up an organization to compete with ASCAP, fixing royalties to no more than 50% of ASCAP's 1937 rates. The result, unveiled the following month, was Broadcast Music, Inc. (BMI). Interestingly, at the same time it was set up, provisions were put in place for it to be dismantled if ASCAP came to its senses.

The NAB thought it would be difficult at the start to get composers to affiliate with BMI. Many of them came from the ranks of "hillbilly" and "race" composers; many others were just . . . well, just people. (Up till now, "people" didn't write "popular" songs, ASCAP composers did.) There were two incentives to join BMI: it would actually take you in, no matter what kind of music you wrote, and BMI had a fair royalty distribution schedule—songs with the most play would make their composers the most money, period.

One of BMI's biggest coups was to secure the defection of Ed Marks, one of the old-time ASCAP composers, and a fixture of Tin Pan Alley. The battle lines were drawn, but there was another fly in the ointment.

Hollywood, since the earliest days of the "talkies," had had a love affair with music. This reached such proportions that the studios had started buying up publishing houses. There came a time when Hollywood found itself holding the copyrights to a phenomenal number of songs. In fact, Warner Bros. alone controlled a majority vote on ASCAP's governing board. Thus, the ASCAP/BMI war was, in reality, a movie/radio war.

All through 1940, BMI songs were introduced to the radio-listening public—about half the songs heard that year were from BMI; one of them was a smash Ink Spots tune: "Do I Worry?". In this way, the nation was being prepared for the possibility that ASCAP songs would disappear from radio.

Finally the terms were given: in August 1940, ASCAP announced that the rates, beginning January 1, 1941, would double. The NAB was just as firm in saying "no." Thus, the new year began with no ASCAP tunes heard over the airwaves. ASCAP was in its glory. They knew that only *they* could turn out "good" music and that no one wanted to hear anything else. The public would rise up and demand that the NAB settle and get the right kind of music played again. Well, they would, wouldn't they? Wouldn't they? Say, where *is* that rising public?

It turned out that the public didn't care *at all*. The BMI tunes were *just as good* as the ASCAP ones (at least to the public's collective ear), and the NAB hung tough. When it was all over, after ten months, it was ASCAP that caved in; the rates on the new licenses were *lower* than they had been in 1939.

However, one of the truly heartbreaking casualties of the feud was a seal, a radio performer that had been trained to honk out a song on bicycle horns. Since the only tune the seal knew was registered with ASCAP, the act was out of business on the first day of the ban.

Over the next twenty years, ASCAP would try many times to destroy BMI, failing at every turn. ASCAP went to war over BMI's supposed closeness to radio station owners and also over Rock and Roll (whose music was mostly written by those upstarts at BMI; the only song they didn't condemn was "Rock Around The Clock," written by two ASCAP composers). While beyond the scope of this book, the war culminated with the famed disk jockey "payola" hearings of 1960.

1941

Germany invades Russia. Lend Lease Act gives Britain much-needed supplies. Roosevelt and Churchill meet at the Atlantic Conference. Roosevelt proclaims the "Four Freedoms." Rubber tires become the first rationed item. Joe DiMaggio hits safely in fifty-six straight games. Japanese attack U.S. naval base at Pearl Harbor. The United States is at war.

The competition: Amapola, The Band Played On, Chattanooga Choo Choo (the first certified "million seller"), Daddy, Deep In The Heart Of Texas, Elmer's Tune, Green Eyes, Hut-Sut Song, I Guess I'll Have To Dream The Rest, I Hear A Rhapsody, It All Comes Back To Me Now, The Last Time I Saw Paris, Maria Elena, Perfidia, Racing With The Moon, There I Go, Yours.

And then the silver screen beckoned. In early 1941, the Spots were called to Hollywood to appear in the 20th Century Fox production *The Great American Broadcast* (starring Alice Faye, John Payne, Cesar Romero, Mischa Auer, Jack Oakie, and the Nicholas Brothers). Dressed as Pullman porters, they entertained the other "porters" with "If I Didn't Care" (only a portion of which appears in the movie) and "Alabamy Bound" (which concludes with the Nicholas Brothers doing one of their show-stopping dance numbers). Later in the film they sang "I've Got A Bone To Pick With You," and backed up Alice Faye and John Payne on "Where You Are" (although they don't appear in the scene where Alice and John are singing).

Note that only "If I Didn't Care" was ever commercially released, although both "Bone" and "Where You Are" wound up on 20th Century Fox dub discs. There seems to be only a single copy of each, so it's reasonable to suspect that these were recorded in advance and used on the sound track while the group lip-synched its way through the numbers.

The Spots reportedly received $25,000 a week for their performance,[1] and the publicity from the film was priceless:

> In person—direct from Hollywood—come the Four Ink Spots to appear in person on the stage of the Regal Theatre, South Parkway and Forty-seventh Street, the week starting on Friday, May 9. Fresh from their triumphs in the just-completed million dollar musical of Twentieth-Century Fox, "The Great American Broadcast," in which they are starred with Alice Faye, Jack Oakie and the Nicholas Brothers.[2]

That piece wasn't all hype. An interview with Moe Gale (whose press agent refers to him as "The Great White Father of Harlem") disclosed:

> Those Four Ink Spots of mine are spending like crazy since they clicked in Hollywood. They are coining $3,000 bucks a week playing one-nighters, and they will buy any-thing—anything that's marked Genuine!
>
> I am forcing them to save money, but with Hoppy Jones that is not so easy. He has bought a Deusenberg and also a station wagon. On one side of the station wagon he has had somebody paint the words, "Jones Acres." So far, Jones Acres is still an apartment somewhere up around my Savoy Ballroom.[3]

The same article went on to say that they were the second biggest record sellers in the country, right behind Bing Crosby.

As well as singing, Deek Watson actually got to speak a few lines in the film. It was some banter with Jack Oakie, who's trying to fix a radio. He's talking about getting the bugs out and "porter" Deek takes him literally

Off to Hollywood: (top) Bill Kenny, Bob Benson, Hoppy Jones; (bottom) Deek Watson, Charlie Fuqua.

about there being bugs in the radio. The scene was inane enough that neither of them was nominated for an Academy Award for the repartee.

The Ink Spots were always impeccably dressed for their performances (even being allowed to wear their own tuxedos in the film when the studio's didn't fit too well). They were so careful about their appearance, that by late 1940 their entourage included a valet for each of them, and a fifth valet to see to the costumes (they would joke that he was the valet to the other four valets).[4] However, by late 1941, they were down to a single valet, Russell Morrison.[5]

As early as 1941, the Ink Spots had made such a splash on the scene that biographers were inventing their history. This excerpt is from an unknown magazine, dated February 1941:

> The Four Ink Spots organized in 1926, and except for one member of the group, Slim Greene [sic], who died in 1937 [before he did some of his best recording work no doubt], the personnel has remained the same.

This was a powerful story, judging from the way it lingered on for over thirty years (we'll run into it again later). The same article stated:

> As a vocal quartet, the Four Ink Spots launched their professional career at the Indiana Roof Ballroom in 1926. They earned $5 per week per man at first, but since three of them were only youngsters still going to school, they didn't mind. They remained at the Roof for two years, and then got their first taste of big-time at radio station WLW Cincinnati, where they did sustaining and commercial programs from 1928 to 1931 inclusive.

This mélange probably came directly from Deek; in his book he mentions being at the Indiana Roof Ballroom. Possibly this is a capsule history of Deek's career both before and after joining the Ink Spots.

The Ink Spots were clearly on top. *Billboard* announced that Philadelphia's Earle Theater had grossed $34,000 for the week of November 21, 1941, when it offered the Ink Spots and the Erskine Hawkins Orchestra along with its movie.[6] That put them in a tie with Glenn Miller's Orchestra, which had also taken in the same amount in September.

There were many other black vocal groups around in the '40s, but nothing to match the Ink Spots. However, while Bill Kenny was the idol of aspiring black singers, few of the groups of the '40s cared to sing in the Ink Spots style (i.e., to appeal to white audiences as well as black).

Unlike other black vocal groups such as the Red Caps, Cats and the Fiddle, Four Blues, or Three Sharps and a Flat, the Ink Spots had crossed the racial barriers of the music industry and attracted a huge white following. The Deep River Boys and the Delta Rhythm Boys each had a single pop chart hit in the '40s; the Billy Williams Quartet and the Charioteers had seven (only one of them reaching the top ten). The Ink Spots, on the other hand, had more than forty pop-charted hits (although surveys are not very reliable before 1940).

Sometime in 1941, arranger/accompanist Bob Benson left, to be replaced by Ace Harris. Harris had been a member of the Sunset Royal Orchestra, which had toured with the Spots in the prior year. In fact, Ace had been the leader of the Royal Sunset Orchestra in 1938, when it backed several acts at the Apollo; he'd also danced and sung as part of the act.

In The Great American Broadcast *(1941): Deek, Bill, Hoppy, Charlie.*

SONGS RECORDED

01/23/41	TNY-911	Please Take A Letter, Miss Brown
02/04/41	68655	Driftwood
	68656	We'll Meet Again
07/25/41	69565	Keep Cool, Fool
	69566	Until The Real Thing Comes Along
	69567	Hey, Doc
08/12/41	69633	It Isn't A Dream Anymore
	69634	Nothin'
08/21/41	69660	I Don't Want To Set The World On Fire
	61-70	(masters not by the Ink Spots)
	69671	Don't Leave Now
10/06/41	69786	Foo-gee
	69787	Mine All Mine, My My
	69788	I'm Not The Same Old Me
10/13/41	69807	Someone's Rocking My Dream Boat
	69808	Shout, Brother, Shout
11/17/41	69949	It's A Sin To Tell A Lie
	69950	Is It A Sin?

RECORDS RELEASED

DECCA

3626	Ring, Telephone, Ring	12/23/40	68533	02/41
	Please Take A Letter, Miss Brown	01/23/41	TNY-911	
3656	We'll Meet Again	02/04/41	68656	03/41
	You're Looking For Romance	12/23/40	68534	
3720	That's When Your Heartaches Begin	12/23/40	68536	05/41
	What Good Would It Do?	12/30/40	68541	
3806	I'm Still Without A Sweetheart	12/23/40	68537	05/41
	So Sorry	12/23/40	68532	
3872	Driftwood	02/04/41	68655	07/41
	Why Didn't You Tell Me?	12/23/40	68538	
3958	Keep Cool, Fool	07/25/41	69565	08/41
	Until The Real Thing Comes Along	07/25/41	69566	

3987	I Don't Want To Set The World			
	On Fire	08/21/41	69660	09/41
	Hey, Doc	07/25/41	69567	
4045	Someone's Rocking My Dream Boat	10/13/41	69807	11/41
	Nothin'	08/12/41	69634	

20th Century Fox

56	Where You Are (the Ink Spots		TCF-56	—/41
	backing up Alice Faye and John Payne)			
57	I've Got A Bone To Pick With You		TCF-57	—/41

One-sided records only. Dubs of recordings used in the 20th Century Fox movie, *The Great American Broadcast*. These disks were probably used on the sound track, while the performers lip-synched.

RECORD REVIEWS

PLEASE TAKE A LETTER MISS BROWN/RING, TELEPHONE, RING

If the Ink Spots haven't a big coin phonograph number in the A side here, then something's wrong somewhere. Combining their usual style with a very amusing last chorus, the sepia foursome have hit upon something that certainly deserves to be rewarded in the commercial sense. The high tenor voice sobs thru a conventional first chorus, but the fun starts with the "talking" baritone that customarily follows on the second chorus on Spots' disks. But here the interpolations of "Miss Brown" to whom the "letter" is "dictated" are extremely comic. The obvious contrast between straight and funny, and the genuine and unforced humor ought to give this foursome one of its biggest disk clicks. Plattermate is straight, with a piano interlude replacing the middle baritone voice. But it's side A that will count here. (*Billboard*, 3/15/41)

WE'LL MEET AGAIN/YOU'RE LOOKING FOR ROMANCE

Two possible hits, these boys are potent with *We'll Meet Again* and *You're Looking For Romance*, back to back on Decca. In their famous *If I Didn't Care* style—should be terrific nickel-nabbers. (*Down Beat*, 4/15/41)

I'M STILL WITHOUT A SWEETHEART

One of the latest Ink Spots' arrangements on wax, and one that has begun to attract some attention in scattered locations. The Spots have done very well by music machine operators in the past, and at the moment this seems to indicate another phono success from these colored artists. (*Billboard*, 6/28/41)

I DON'T WANT TO SET THE WORLD ON FIRE/HEY, DOC

The four stellar sepia Spots are again making disks after a spell on the screen and stage. With this toothsome twosome, they again run away with all honors. The spark has already been applied to the ballad beaut on the A side [i.e., others have already released versions of it]. The Inkers, giving it their characteristic *If I Didn't Care* twist, top the torch tune with an interpretation that is bound to start a real blaze. The song is suitable to their singing and style, and the foursome gives all they've got. Equally effective is the Edgar Sampson-Kim Gannon jive ditty backing. The four voices give the opening lyrics a light and plenty lifto touch, with Deke [sic] digging the middle chorus with effective jiverie. The platter is expertly patterned for the youngsters, and it won't be long before the kids will be clamoring for the riff-enveloped *Doc* ditty. (*Billboard*, 9/27/41)

UNTIL THE REAL THING COMES ALONG

Billy Kenny's sickening, phony and pseudo-dramatic tenor soloing (voice, not a sax) continues on *Until the Real Thing Comes Along . . .* , but the Spots are their usual confident selves when Kenny isn't belching in a falsetto. Still the most popular vocal quartet in the business, either one of these is tailor-made for the jukes. But not for musicians. (*Down Beat* 10/1/41)

SOMEONE'S ROCKING MY DREAM BOAT/NOTHIN'

The jive experts do not pan out as expert for this doubling. The *Nothin'* dish of jive from the *Jump For Joy* show falls short by far in creating the spirit that the show conveys. Foursome add none of their individuality to the song and Deke's [sic] solo jive fails to jell. Tune is a natural for their talents, but the ink well is dry here, nor can the guitar chorus salvage the side. Ballad making for the B side is little better. Kenny solos the song, but doesn't sell it any too strongly. And the tune's triteness doesn't help the harmonizers any. (*Billboard*, 11/29/41)

This is the latest Ink Spots' rage in this territory [Mobile, Alabama]. Operators here report that there is always a title-strip reserved for these artists [identifying a song in a jukebox], and *Dream Boat* is the current favorite. Boys give this ditty their usual perfect treatment, and there's no reason why machines in other areas can't draw nickels with it, too. (*Billboard*, 12/6/41)

PERFORMANCE REVIEWS

Earle (Philadelphia)

Holding down the finale are the Four Inkspots [sic]. The quartet mixes up its offering neatly with sweet and jump stuff in equal doses. Opener is "Java Jive," a hodge-podge of double talk in the Inkspot manner. Other numbers are standbyes [sic]—"We Three," "Who" and "If I Didn't Care." The boys had trouble bowing off. Trio [?] is overmugging and thus spoiling the effect of their fine voice-blending. (*Variety*, 1/25/41)

Earle (Philadelphia) (same show, the two magazines are in agreement for once)

. . . It is their customary professional eclat for the harmonizing but the impression is not as thunderous as it might have been because of their over-mugging the songs to such a degree that it almost invites nausea. Moreover with the footwork of Tip, Tap, and Toe still fresh in the minds of the pew holders [audience], Ink Spots would do well to stick to their singing and forget their feeble attempt to create comedy with dancing. (*Billboard*, 2/1/41)

Steel Pier (Atlantic City)

Outstanding are the Ink Spots, who took over house with their harmonies. In white tuxedos and white ties, boys sing "Do I Worry" followed by "Brown Girl," [sic] which brought them tremendous applause. They came back with their perennial "If I Didn't Care," done with a smooth rhythm accompanied by guitar and cello. They had to beg off despite audience calls for favorite selections. (*Variety*, 7/6/41)

Club Bali (Philadelphia)

Four Ink Spots are the first to usher in the new season. They first created a furor introducing their *If I Didn't Care* at the next-door Little Rathskeller, operated by the same management. Following a three-week stretch, they will carry on at the adjoining Rathskeller.

. . . Alternated between the jive and ballad ditties for seven selections, all record rages, and there was still no giving the crowd enough. Opening with *Java Jive*, foursome flashed with *Do I Worry?; I'm Still Without A Sweetheart; Keep Cool, Fool; I Don't Want To Set The World On Fire; Who*; and their luckiest lullaby, *If I Didn't Care*. (*Billboard*, 10/4/41)

Singing "Until The Real Thing Comes Along" (1941): Bill, Deek, Hoppy, Charlie.

Being in a movie is great for publicity.

Hear the Famous

'FOUR 'INK SPOTS'

Trainon Ballroom
Oklahoma City, Oklahoma. .

Friday Night, April 18th.

Come and be thrilled by that famous
quartette making famous

'If I Didn't Care'

Purchase Your Advance Sale
Tickets At The Cut Rate Drug
Store

301 East Second Street

Advance sale price...............................86c
Box office $1.00

It paid to buy your tickets in advance!

1942

Allied invasion of North Africa. Japanese conquer Burma. Battles of Midway and Guadalcanal. U.S. citizens of Japanese descent moved to internment camps. Ocean liner Normandie *burns and capsizes at its pier. Bataan Death March. Doolittle bombs Tokyo. Gasoline rationed (three gallons a week is deemed enough for most people's use). Camus and Sartre create existentialist literature.*

The competition: Blues In The Night, Don't Sit Under The Apple Tree, I Don't Want To Walk Without You, Jingle Jangle Jingle, (I've Got A Gal In) Kalamazoo, Moonlight Cocktail, Praise The Lord And Pass The Ammunition, Skylark, Sleepy Lagoon, String Of Pearls, Strip Polka, Tangerine, This Is The Army Mr. Jones, When The Lights Go On Again All Over The World, White Christmas, White Cliffs Of Dover.

The year 1942 found the Spots in Hollywood again, this time for Universal's Abbott and Costello flick, *Pardon My Sarong*, at a reported fee of $20,000 for their entire contribution. "Money was the highest ever quoted to a musical group of this size, and even more fabulous is the fact that the colored quartet will only put in nine days on the lot."[1] (So much for the $25,000 figure quoted for *The Great American Broadcast*.) They happened

From Pardon My Sarong *(1942): Tip, Tap, and Toe, Bill, Hoppy, Charlie, Deek.*

to be in the right place at the right time for this one: they had been playing an engagement at the Golden Gate (San Francisco), when they got the call.

In *Sarong*, they appeared as "waiters" singing "Shout, Brother, Shout" (but were easily upstaged by the incredible dance routine done by Tip, Tap, and Toe in the middle of the song). Deek does the lead on this one (with a prop trumpet); look for Bill playing a cymbal with a wire brush. They also sang "Do I Worry?" and both tunes exist on Universal sound track disks (one-of-a-kind items, like the 20th Century cuts). Two other songs, cut from the final film, were "Java Jive" and "Someone's Rocking My Dream Boat"; these also appear on sound track platters. The film was released in August, and was the second most successful movie of 1942 (only Oscar-winning *Mrs. Miniver* made more money).

One of the problems with having a successful song is having to sing it—over and over and over. Sometimes a singer will do anything to break the monotony. On a test pressing of "Do I Worry?" (undated), instead of the usual line "Do I worry?/You know dog-gone well I do," Hoppy came out with "Do I worry?/You know God-damned well I do."[2]

In early 1942, accompanist Ace Harris left. He went on to be pianist and vocalist for the Erskine Hawkins Band, before recording on his own for Coral Records in the early '50s.

Harris was replaced by Bill Doggett, who had been a bandleader in Philadelphia until 1938, when his whole band was taken over by Lucky Millinder (at the time a bandleader without a band—they had all walked out on him and he had engagements to fulfill). In 1939 they came to New York, where the musicians' union forced them to break up (they all belonged to the Philadelphia local, and the New York local wouldn't let them perform until they got the proper union cards). When that was straightened out, Bill worked with tenor saxist Jimmy Mundy for a few months and then rejoined Millinder. Later, when the Ink Spots needed a new pianist/arranger, Millinder, who was another of Moe Gale's acts, recommended Doggett.

At the sessions, Bill Doggett played piano and Charlie Fuqua did the guitar work. However, by this time, Hoppy didn't play at all; they used a studio musician for the bass work. According to Doggett, the pianist/arranger only did the instrumental arrangements; the vocal arrangements for the Spots were done by Morty Howard.[3]

Another interesting piece of information from Doggett was that although the Ink Spots were known for their on-stage wardrobe, he was never dressed to match. While they bought him good (and expensive) suits, he was never made to feel like an actual *member* of the group, only a hired outsider. This is borne out by the fact that although their pianist was always on stage with them, there doesn't seem to be a single formal photo of the Ink Spots with *any* of the five men who held that position.

With World War II raging, record companies rushed their acts into the studios to record patriotic songs, morale boosters, and sometimes even sentimental heart-wrenchers. The Ink Spots were no exception, recording "This Is Worth Fighting For" (from the film *When Johnny Comes Marching Home*) and "Don't Get Around Much Anymore" (which was actually written prior to the war and makes more wartime sense when sung by a female but, as a weeper, was still apropos).

While most singers who have writing aspirations would write songs, not so with Bill Kenny. In 1942 he published a book of poems and sayings, entitled *The Smallest Container Of Treasure In The World*. He had been working on it ever since he'd been in high school in Baltimore.

During the summer of 1942, the famous "Petrillo Ban" began. James C. Petrillo, having worked his way up from the Chicago local, was now president of the American Federation of Musicians. He claimed that competition, on records, from amateur musicians was causing his members to be deprived of their livelihood. Consequently, union musicians were prohibited from playing on recordings (remember, he had never liked recordings to begin with). The strike was announced in June 1942, to begin August 1; therefore, record companies worked overtime to lay in stocks of prestrike masters (from dozens to hundreds). They sometimes kept the studios going around the clock, right up to the start of the strike, in order to have enough tunes to see them through what promised to be a minor inconvenience (the strike was expected to last about four months). It took a little longer than expected: in Decca's case, more than thirteen months.

Since Decca held no sessions from August 1, 1942, until settling with the union on September 18, 1943, all Ink Spots sides released during that period were from masters stockpiled before the strike began. In July the Ink Spots did a session which produced six masters; prior to this they had usually cut only two or three at a time.

As if the recording ban wasn't enough of a problem to recording companies, there was also a shortage of shellac, used in manufacturing records. This will be dealt with in the next chapter.

Meanwhile, the Ink Spots had found another home of a sort. In 1941 they had appeared at the seventh annual Harvest Moon Ball at Madison Square

Garden. This was the most prestigious popular dance contest in the United States, and it was an honor for them to be called back to entertain in 1942, as they were again in 1943.

We've seen how the Ink Spots traveled by ship and bus and ambulance. However, a serious problem for traveling acts during the war years was gas rationing, which forced the Ink Spots to make most of their trips by train during this period.[4] Even with that restriction, they closed out the year by playing not one, not two, but *three* engagements in Detroit on New Year's Eve: the Michigan, the Palm State, and the Broadway-Capitol (all Paramount theaters).[5]

SONGS RECORDED

05/19/42	70762	Don't Tell A Lie About Me, Dear
	70763	Who Wouldn't Love You?
06/23/42	70917	Ev'ry Night About This Time
	70918	Knock Me A Kiss (U)
07/28/42	71233	Street Of Dreams
	71234	I'll Never Make The Same Mistake Again
	71235	Just As Though You Were Here
	71236	If I Cared A Little Bit Less
	71237	Don't Get Around Much Anymore
	71238	This Is Worth Fighting For

NOTE: (U) indicates an unreleased song.

RECORDS RELEASED

DECCA

4112	Is It A Sin?	11/17/41	69950	01/42
	It's A Sin To Tell A Lie	11/17/41	69949	
4194	It Isn't A Dream Anymore	08/12/41	69633	03/42
	Shout, Brother, Shout	10/13/41	69808	
4303	Don't Leave Now	08/21/41	69671	04/42
	Foo-gee	10/06/41	69786	
18383	Don't Tell A Lie About Me, Dear	05/19/42	70762	06/42
	Who Wouldn't Love You?	05/19/42	70763	
18461	Ev'ry Night About This Time	06/23/42	70917	08/42
	I'm Not The Same Old Me	10/06/41	69788	
18466	This Is Worth Fighting For	07/28/42	71238	08/42
	Just As Though You Were Here	07/28/42	71235	
18503	Don't Get Around Much Anymore	07/28/42	71237	10/42
	Street Of Dreams	07/28/42	71233	
18528	If I Cared A Little Bit Less	07/28/42	71236	11/42
	Mine All Mine, My My	10/06/41	69787	

UNIVERSAL PICTURES

354	Do I Worry?	UPC-354	—/42
357	Java Jive	UPC-357	
355	Dream Boat	UPC-355	—/42
356	Shout, Brother, Shout	UPC-356	

The Universal Pictures disks (recorded for *Pardon My Sarong*) are also dubs to be lip-synched to during the filming of the movie. However, "Java Jive" and "Dream Boat" weren't used in the picture.

RECORD REVIEWS

IT'S A SIN TO TELL A LIE/IS IT A SIN?

The Ink Spots go sinful, in their characteristic song style, for both sides. For Billy Mayhew's oldie on the A side, taken at a moderately paced waltz tempo, it's the *If I Didn't Care* pattern. Almost as good, save for a high falsetto note coming on like a factory whistle and losing the touching character it hoped to create. The companion *Sin* is a slow ballad, establishing an identical song mood. Only it's dished up in jive style for the middle chorus. (*Billboard*, 1/24/42)

The Spots are fast becoming the ace schmaltz-dispensers of their race. The latest coupling drips with Billy Kenny falsettos and belchetoes. (*Down Beat*, 2/1/42)

SHOUT, BROTHER, SHOUT/IT ISN'T A DREAM ANYMORE

The Spots couple a jive spiritual on the A side with a dreamy torch ballad on the B side. Steeped in the tradition of *Yes, Indeed*, the A side is taken in a jump tempo, replete with plenty of shouting, singing and hand-clapping. However, the Spots are more effective for the slow ballad, treated in their characteristic sentimental style, with the top male voice carrying it all the way. (*Billboard*, 3/21/42)

DON'T LEAVE NOW/FOO-GEE

The inimitable spotters, with their customary singing eclat, come thru with two sock sides in this coupling. The slow ballad is on the A side, and for their *If I Didn't Care* pattern they have reached out to hillbilly lore. *Don't Leave Now* is one of those ever-tuneful torchers with a heavy outdoor flavor, written by Slim West and Jimmie Davis, and it's a natural for their sentimental style of singing. Erskine Butterfield's *Foo-Gee* is the typical jive tune that the Ink Spotters handle so well. It falls short of being another *Java Jive* only because the foursome takes it at a slow tempo instead of the bouncy beats, with the result that the side drags. (*Billboard*, 4/25/42)

WHO WOULDN'T LOVE YOU?/DON'T TELL A LIE ABOUT ME, DEAR

For sentimental song singing, the Ink Spots are without peers among the harmonizing troupes. And in *Don't Tell A Lie*, the foursome have a song that is tailor-made to their talents. The familiar pattern of their *If I Didn't Care* takes this ballad in good stride, and it's a natural for the Ink Spotters. *Who Wouldn't Love You?* is the rhythm ditty popularized on wax by Kay Kyser. The Ink Spots have been listening too attentively to the Kyser recordings. Side spans four choruses in medium tempo, each a solo-singing session, embellished by four drum-beats and whistling obbligatos a la Kay Kyser. Not only does the tune treatment lack originality, but the listless singing makes the side fall short. (*Billboard*, 6/27/42)

EV'RY NIGHT ABOUT THIS TIME/I'M NOT THE SAME OLD ME

A good song with a catchy title, this ballad should have no trouble taking itself up the line. Two disks out on it offer the operators two tempos to choose from. J[immy] Dorsey gives it a nifty dance beat, while the Ink Spots give it their typical slow treatment. Reverse side of the Ink Spots' disk, *I'm Not The Same Old Me*, is something that shouldn't be overlooked either. (*Billboard*, 8/15/42)

STREET OF DREAMS/DON'T GET AROUND MUCH ANYMORE

Already cutting a fancy figure in waxed circles as a result of Tommy Dorsey's recent recording, there is every indication that Sam L. Lewis's and Victor Young's *Street Of Dreams* will build even bigger today than it did when offered up on the song mart some years ago. Rich in melodic and lyrical qualities, these ballad requirements are tailor-made for the talents of the Ink Spots. Taking it at a slow tempo, the foursome follow their familiar *If I Didn't Care* pattern, and with excellent results. Flipover also finds the Ink Spots on the strong side. The slow blues tune was a Duke Ellington instrumental of earlier issue, and now it comes forth again with a new set of torch lyrics set by Bob Russell. Deke [sic] Watson carries this side, singing it in a low-down groove at a moderately slow tempo that is kept thoroly [sic] rhythmic. Piano cuts in for a half chorus to give the singers a breathing spell. No jive or scat to sell this side. Tune itself is based on a blues riff that fairly bounces, and the Ink Spots stick close to the melodic lines. (*Billboard*, 10/24/42)

MINE ALL MINE, MY MY/IF I CARED A LITTLE BIT LESS

This whimsical ditty finds the Ink Spots whipping up a bright disk to stimulate the meter clicks of the music phonos. Packing a melodic kick in their harmonizing about the joys of enjoying a honey who is "mine all mine," the foursome adds a novel twist in the song treatment by ringing in a jovial sermon admonishing the two-timing conduct of the playboys. Plattermate should also figure prominently in phono play, offering a sentimental ballad in *If I Cared A Little Bit Less* that follows their click *If I Didn't Care* song pattern. (*Billboard*, 11/28/42)

Mine is by far the least irritating of the Spots records in the past two years. Humorous and rocks for a change, and there ain't any of that FINE high falsetto tenor. (*Down Beat*, 12/1/42)

PERFORMANCE REVIEWS

Chicago Theater (Chicago)

...the only way they get off the stage is by staying on it while the curtains are drawn together.... Together they blend harmoniously and, what is more important, to the extreme pleasure of the paying customers. (*Billboard*, 1/3/42)

Orpheum (Minneapolis)

Four Ink Spots were a fitting climax to a good show. They opened with *Keep Cool, Fool*, followed by *Until The Real Thing Comes Along* and *Still Without A Sweetheart*. The audience wouldn't let them go and they anchored with *Hey Doc* and *If I Didn't Care*. Not since the Andrews Sisters were here last year has any group of singers received the ovation the Ink Spots got. (*Billboard*, 1/24/42)

Among the usual promotions were a Wurlitzer phono in the theater lobby, thru courtesy of Mayflower Novelty Company, with Ink Spots and [Erskine] Hawkins disks featured. (*The Billboard*, 1/24/42)

[At that show they grossed $17,000 for the week, in spite of two days of sub-zero weather.]

Paradise (Detroit)

Disappointment of the week was the Four Ink Spots at the Paradise who grossed just under $12,000. Figure is higher than the preceding two weeks, but about one-third of what the same act did at the Michigan about three months ago. (*Billboard*, 3/7/42)

[Blame was laid on mounting automotive industry unemployment and the fact that it was income tax time (in those days there was no withholding —the tax was due all at once; also the due date was March 15, not today's April 15).]

Hippodrome (Baltimore)

Four Ink Spots have lost none of their punch or popularity. Opened with *Have A Heart, Josephine*, following with *We'll Meet Again* and *Don't Sit Under The Apple Tree*, all well received. Ink Spots are masters of their particular style, and their gyrations and mannerisms are in themselves a show. (*Billboard*, 6/13/42)

Paramount (New York)

Ink Spots are almost a fixture at this house and got a big welcome. Sing out on *Shout, Brother, Shout; Don't Tell A Lie About Me; Your Feet Are Too Big* [sic] and close with a dramatic rendering of *This Is Worth Fighting For*. Boys still do their usual good job and pull down the house. (*Billboard*, 8/15/42)

Colonial (Dayton, Ohio)

It's a whopper of a show thruout, and when the Ink Spots appear it looks tough for them to top what has gone before, but they manage to do it and leave the audience begging for more. Opening with *Shout, Brother, Shout*, they swing into *Every Night About This Time* which, with *This Is Worth Fighting For*, constitute about the only calm spots on the program. Noteworthy in the two numbers is the solo work of Billy Kenny, baritone [sic!!!]. They close, of course, with the song that skyrocketed them to fame, *If I Didn't Care*. (*Billboard*, 10/24/42)

Shellac:
More Than You Ever Wanted to Know!

Shellac, a binding material in the manufacture of 78 rpm records, comes from an insect that inhabits Southeast Asia. Most of it was processed by India, and, due to the war, supply channels were not what they had been. The government was never quite sure if shellac was a strategic war material, but it ended up being rationed to record manufacturers. Actually, the companies had tons of the stuff in their warehouses, but rationing meant that the government would only let them use it a measured amount at a time.

As early as January 1942, Victor Records announced plans to buy up old phonograph records from distributors for recycling. Schoolchildren were offered a free record player (a Victrola, of course!) for turning in a set number of records. Charity organizations were asked to collect records and sell them back to Victor.[1] In certain cities, Victor posted a bounty of 2¢ for every old record brought in to be recycled, regardless of condition. At one point, record stores had a policy of selling a customer a new record only when an old one was brought in to be recycled. Think of all the great music (of all kinds) melted down! Records made from recycled materials didn't have the same fidelity or durability as regular production disks, but someone *did* once say that war was hell!

The shortage (especially when combined with the American Federation of Musicians' recording ban) hurt everyone, not always in obvious ways. It turned out that the shellac shortage hurt small publishers because record companies didn't want to take chances recording songs that might not sell.

The songs that were stockpiled by the record companies, although done on an assembly-line basis (remember, because of the AFM ban, record companies recorded around the clock, right up to the final minute), were carefully scrutinized by those with an ear for such things. Only those songs which they *knew* were going to be hits were recorded; this was no time for experimenting.

The small publishers also couldn't use payola, which, in those days wasn't money paid by record companies to disk jockeys to play records, but money paid by "song pluggers" (who worked for the publishers) to bandleaders to include arrangements of the songs in their repertoire. Bandleaders weren't about to take untried arrangements that they couldn't even record, especially when they had tons of arrangements that they'd recorded but couldn't play. This was because the records hadn't been released yet, which meant that the songs hadn't been published (the publishers and the record companies had made a deal that allowed publication of songs to be spread over a six-month period—the length of time they thought the strike would last). Since the bands had recorded what they thought was the publishers' best material, the rest of the tunes would have to wait. One way to eliminate song pluggers' payola attempts was announced by *Billboard*: they would continue to list the songs most played on the radio, but would do it alphabetically and without any indication as to how many times the song had been played. This would, it was hoped, keep pluggers from aiming their songs at the top spot on the chart.

Another complaint of the publishers was that sheet music sales were way down (helped, of course, by the ban, but in truth, that was the direction sheet music was headed anyway).

Back to shellac. The actual rationing went into effect in April 1942. By September there was real fear that shellac distribution would be cut off altogether:

> After more than four months of shellac rationing, during which there has been one alteration in the government's method of doling out the stuff and at least 5,000 false rumors about other changes, there continues to be no basis in fact for fears that War Production Board plans to cut off diskers' [record manufacturers] supply.
>
> The most recent WPB shellac order stating that diskers will henceforth be required to make formal application for each

allotment, caused a lot of the boys to assume that all was over, and that scrap would be the only source of the material from here on.[2]

Old Records for New

The fate of records in wartime. This cartoon appeared in the San Francisco Examiner *on July 3, 1943. (Reprinted with permission.)*

The major record manufacturers (Victor, Columbia, and Decca) were rationed 15% of their prior year's usage for the period from August 15 to September 30, 1942. That they could still turn out a respectable quota of records indicated that scrap salvage was working well.

As if the companies didn't have enough trouble, even if the ban were lifted and they were buried in shellac, their skilled pressing-plant employees were "gone with the draft," as were the repairmen who kept the machines working.

And if you think all this was bad, copper was a *real* strategic war material:

> Nellie Taylor Ross, Director of the Mint, said that experiments
> to make pennies out of glass had virtually been dropped.
> Experiments with plastics for the penny coin will continue.[3]

In November, the companies received 5% of their prior year's tonnage of shellac. Then the worst happened:

> Record industry's fears were realized Monday [11/2/42] when
> War Production Board sent word that, under present conditions,
> there would be no further amounts of shellac available for
> record manufacturers after this month.[4]

This declaration was followed by a hint from Washington that shellac might be cut off completely for the duration. Dealers' scrap quotas (as set by the record manufacturers) would have to be met or no new records would be shipped to them. Jobbers for Victor and Decca kept track of dealers' scrap returns; Columbia wasn't as tough. The current rule was to return one old disk in order to get three new ones.

A Decca executive tried to reassure the public:

> E.F. Stevens, Decca exec, asked what Decca will do,
> answered simply, "We are not going out of business and have
> every expectation of successfully overcoming the difficulty.
> Even if the difficulty works great hardship upon us, we are
> going to continue to do our utmost to keep going on an even
> keel. The value of records to civilian and service morale has
> been too well proven to admit the possibility of even a tempo-
> rary end to the industry."

> All the major record companies are in possession of substitute formulas for the usual shellac mixture which can be used in the absence of the real thing. Scrap shellac has been coming to the firms in such satisfactory quantity, however, as to put the substitute formulas in the background.[5]

The substitute formulas sounded great in theory, but they tended not to give the same fidelity and service life as shellac.

To make matters worse for the entertainment industry, the Office of Price Administration (in January 1943) imposed a ban on "pleasure driving," in order to conserve gas. This hit nightclubs and theaters wherever there wasn't adequate mass transit.

But things lightened up early in 1943, when the WPB declared itself ready to grant requests for new shellac—at 15% of the 1941 levels. This caused production of records to be stepped up, using shellac substitutes and scrap. Decca reported "satisfactory progress" in developing a shellac substitute, and claimed that it was maintaining production that was 55% of normal output.

> Despite severe materials restrictions, sales of Decca Records, Inc., for the first quarter [of 1943] were almost on a par with sales for the same 1942 quarter, company officials said following the annual meeting.
>
> Developments for substitutes [sic], as indicated in the annual report, is helping the company to maintain its sales. The company has not disclosed the nature of these substitutes altho it is known that one of the most important is used in the place of shellac, ordinarily the No. 1 material used by the company in making records. . .[6] [This seems to imply that there were other record ingredients in short supply too.]

And then, by mid-year, the sun came out:

> An inkling of good news for the juke box and record industries was released recently by government officials, who said that more shellac is coming in from India, or at least there are good prospects that there will be shipments soon. Officials estimate that some 2,000,000 tons of shipping will be added to the flow

of traffic from India as soon as the Suez Canal and the Mediterranean are opened. This is one of the good results of the victory in North Africa.[7]

And:

Loud cries of jubilation and heavy sighs of relief were heard in the offices of platter-making companies this week when the chemical division of the War Production Board released an order permitting the use of more shellac by disk moguls [executives of record companies].

The WPB order stated that for the first quarter of 1944 record makers could use 100 per cent of the quota they consumed in 1941. For the other three quarters of 1944 no ruling has been released. . . . [The second quarter also permitted 100%.]

Even tho the record industry will be using more shellac in 1944, it does not mean that there will be more platters produced. For one thing, New York execs say, man-power shortage will not allow it.

In some quarters the order did not bring jubilation. It brought groans. Some record makers have been stalling off artists anxious to make platters [with the end of the AFM ban] with the excuse that they couldn't do it because of shellac shortages. . . .[8]

This may sound a bit cryptic, so an explanation is in order. There was a ban on using union musicians, and therefore, most records released were either stockpiled from before the AFM ban or were "oldies." Then there was the shellac rationing, so new disks were being made from increasing quantities of scrap records. These platters weren't as good quality, having more surface noise and not holding up as well. If this wasn't enough, there was also wear and tear on the pressing-plant equipment (no new machines were available and most of the good mechanics were in the service). To top it off, there was gas rationing, and the Department of Defense Transportation had ruled that jukebox operators couldn't make as many trips to their boxes to replace needles and service the records. Therefore the disks in the jukes were deteriorating rapidly. The solution, as far as the manufacturers saw it, was to use the increased supply of shellac to upgrade the product to prewar standards; most new releases would have to wait.

September 1944 saw the end (almost):

> Shellac, bottleneck of the record situation, is now becoming available in goodly quantities, War Production Board officials informed *The Billboard* today. Consequently, record supply should be up in months ahead.
>
> Shellac, long marked critical by WPB, is now available from Defense Supply Corporation without red tape. Record companies, still short of the material, should advise WPB or go direct to Defense Supply for details of available supplies, it was stated. Other record-making materials have long been available, so that record-making industry should soon be back to normal, particularly as man-power situation eases.[9]

In October 1944, inventor John M. DeVell of Longmeadow, Massachusetts, patented a thermoplastic substitute for shellac, made from stump pine.[10] It was postulated that it could be used to replace 50% of natural shellac. Useful, but a bit late for all the headaches.

After the war shellac prices soared:

> Reason is that a group of speculators is said to have gotten control of the shellac output in India and is maneuvering to squeeze sky-high prices out of all trades using the stuff. Shellac has always been a product subject to speculator manipulation.[11]

While some of this may seem a bit far removed from our topic, the shellac shortage had one major effect that lasted for forty years: record companies started experimenting with other substances and hit on vinyl. Once records were made of vinyl, their fidelity was greatly enhanced and microgroove records were possible, leading to long-playing albums. This probably would not have been possible with shellac.

And now, back to our regularly scheduled program.

1943

Allies invade Italy. Income tax withholding begins. Race riots in Detroit and Harlem. Roosevelt and Churchill meet at Casablanca. Meat rationed (along with fats and cheese). California "Zoot Suit" riots. Mussolini deposed in favor of the former King of Italy, Victor Emmanuel III; Italy declares war on Germany.

The competition: All Or Nothing At All, As Time Goes By, Besame Mucho, Brazil, Comin' In On A Wing And A Prayer, For Me And My Gal, I Had The Craziest Dream, Let's Get Lost, Mister Five By Five, Moonlight Becomes You, Paper Doll, People Will Say We're In Love, Pistol Packin' Mama, Speak Low, That Old Black Magic, Warsaw Concerto, You'd Be So Nice To Come Home To, You'll Never Know.

While white audiences listened to the Spots' music and bought their records, there were still occasional problems. Deek Watson wrote of one experience in Savannah Beach, during the war, that shows what black artists had to contend with on tour.

Kenny and I went into the men's room to wash our hands.
I had finished and was waiting for Kenny to get through, when
two soldiers came into the wash room. They asked Kenny what

he was doing in there washing his hands. He told them he was one of the Ink Spots and that there was no other place to wash up before the show.

They said if we didn't get out of there, we would be the "dead spots."

I rushed out and got the road manager [at the time, Sam Flashnic]. He got the proprietor of the place, for whom we were doing the show. He went into the wash room, and instead of telling the soldiers to cut it out, he apologized to them. He told them we were from up North and just didn't know any better; and that it wouldn't happen again. Man it looked like all those people thought we started the war.

The same two soldiers that raised all this hell about us washing our hands in the men's room came to the show and had front-row seats.

I had just finished singing "Java Jive" when I happened to look down and spot them. They were applauding longer and louder than anybody! When they saw me looking right at them, they froze. Guess they didn't want to let me know they were enjoying the show after what had happened![1]

Sometimes the performances weren't *that* easy. In August of 1943, Deek and Charlie appeared at the Copacabana (New York) with foot injuries. Deek had had his big toe broken when a car door slammed on it, and Charlie fractured his leg when a bowling ball struck him.[2] Once again, stories vary wildly: *Billboard* reported that both had been in a car accident,[3] while Deek's book claims that Charlie had broken his *thumb* (AND, at the same time, Hoppy had fallen down the stairs, breaking his leg, AND Bill had had an automobile accident and had broken his arm)![4] The true story might be in there somewhere!

Soldiers may have been bigoted, but the draft board was color-blind. While Hoppy was too old by 1943 (thirty-eight), and Deek and Bill were both 4-F, Charlie was 1-A. He was drafted, and entered the service in September 1943. Before Charlie got his notice, they had all made an agreement that any member who was drafted would still receive his share from the remaining performers.[5] By February 1944, Charlie was playing with an army band in Camp Shanks, New York[6] (he would remain in the States throughout the war). The draft even took a toll on their name:

At a bond rally (ca. 1943).

Deek dances: Deek, Bill, Hoppy, Charlie.

> Ink Spots, playing Stanley [Theatre in Pittsburgh] last week, asked theatre management to drop the numeral 4 from their billing and advertise them merely as the Ink Spots. Quartet has passed along same word to other spots they're playing. When questioned about this, it was learned that one of their members expects to go into the Army shortly and indications were that remaining three would carry on without a replacement.[7]

But replacement there was. For the first time since 1936, a personnel change took place. Charlie picked Bernie Mackey, his old pal from Indianapolis, to be his replacement. Mackey joined the Ink Spots during an engagement at the Howard Theater in Washington, D.C., in the closing stages of the AFM strike.

At the time Mackey joined, the group was depending primarily on live gigs for income. Because of the AFM ban, they weren't being paid to record and Decca wasn't manufacturing as many records because of the shellac shortage, resulting in lower sales and royalties. Five Ink Spots records had been released by Decca during the strike period (and only one in all of 1943), all of which had been recorded prior to the ban.

One effect of the AFM ban was that disk jockeys started playing old records on the air in order to supplement the decreased number of titles received from manufacturers. They approached this with great trepidation: the public had always wanted the newest of the new; how would they react to the oldest of the old? Surprisingly, the public loved it.

In July 1943, Petrillo seemed to loosen up a bit. He said the union would allow recordings to be made, provided that their only purpose was for Service Canteen jukeboxes. This wasn't as altruistic as it sounds. There were about 7.5 million servicemen at this time, and bandleaders must have been pressuring Petrillo to allow them to reach this concentrated captive audience. The war would be over someday, and these were the listeners whose tastes would shape postwar music.

The Ink Spots were doing okay on the charts again: in July "Don't Get Around Much Anymore" hit Number 7 (it had been released the prior October), and "I Can't Stand Losing You" was Number 1 on the Harlem Hit Parade chart (the Mills Brothers' "Paper Doll" was a bit behind, at Number 5).

Finally, on September 18, Decca settled with the union, the first major company to do so. Petrillo, as a bonus, let talks with Victor and Columbia drag on, so that Decca (having seen the light) would get a recording advantage. (However, with all the shortages, Victor and Columbia were content to sit back and ride out the strike anyway.)

When the dust had settled, the strike had cost somewhere between $3.5 and $7 million (naturally estimates varied wildly). The biggest problem that the AFM had faced was the war. Record production was down about 50% anyway—due to shellac shortages and aging equipment, being maintained by a dwindling staff of repairmen. But the public snapped up whatever was released. Also, the union might have been too quick to announce the strike, giving manufacturers over a month to record everything and everyone in sight. The biggest potential hits were released first (from August to October, by which time, it was hoped, the strike would be over). Then, when it dragged on, releases were slower in coming, as the companies realized that what they had stockpiled would have to last. And still the public bought. Oldies were dug out and reissued; hillbilly songs (with nonunion musicians) started becoming hits; *a cappella* (voice-only) recordings were still being made; and bootleg records flourished (in this case "bootlegging" referred to union musicians recording under different names, or with no credit at all, for smaller companies). While the Supreme Court upheld the strike, it was conceded, even by Petrillo, that the best the union could hope for was a draw.

It took Decca a while to dust off the studios—there was no recording done the first week. Every act wanted to get back into the studio and record, but it didn't happen that way. Only the biggest names would be recorded immediately. (Bing Crosby and the Andrews Sisters, teaming on "Pistol Packin' Mama," had the honor of being the first Decca waxers.)

When Decca finally remembered the Ink Spots—Kenny, Watson, Mackey, and Jones—it teamed them up with Ella Fitzgerald to cut "Cow-Cow Boogie" on November 3, 1943. (Strangely, although Decca got them back into the studio within two months after the strike had ended, it certainly wasn't in much of a hurry to release anything—"Cow-Cow Boogie" didn't debut until February 1944. This may simply have been due to the shellac shortages.) The songstress and the quartet were paired to get maximum reception from the public: why not two acts instead of one? Besides, Bing and the Sisters' version of "Pistol Packin' Mama" had gone to Number 2 on the charts; maybe the Spots and Miss Ella could duplicate that feat.

Decca is repeating the pattern of teaming recording artists
on tunes that have been around for a long time, as it did with

Bing Crosby and the Andrews Sisters on *Pistol Packin' Mama*, mating Ella Fitzgerald and the Ink Spots to wax *Cow Cow Boogie* Wednesday (10) [actually it had been recorded a week earlier, on November 3].

While *Cow Cow* has not been the phenomenal hit *Pistol Packin'* has, it has sold 150,000 copies on the strength of one recording (Freddie Slack and Ella Mae Morse), with very few air plugs to boost it.[8]

As spiffy as they come: Deek, Bill, Hoppy, Charlie.

And in mufti: Bill, Deek, Hoppy, Charlie.

SONGS RECORDED

11/03/43	71482	Cow-Cow Boogie (EF)
11/17/43	71514	Don't Believe Everything You Dream
12/22/43	71609	A Lovely Way To Spend An Evening
	71610	I'll Get By

NOTE: (EF) indicates Ella Fitzgerald and the Ink Spots.

RECORDS RELEASED

DECCA

18542	I Can't Stand Losing You	12/23/40	68535	03/43
	I'll Never Make The Same Mistake			
	Again	07/28/42	71234	

RECORD REVIEWS

I'LL NEVER MAKE THE SAME MISTAKE AGAIN/
I CAN'T STAND LOSING YOU

The Ink Spots come up again with two of their standardly slow and sentimental torch tunes. Most impressive is *I Can't Stand Losing You*, in which Billy Kenny gave Joe Myrow and Kim Gannon a writing hand. In pattern and in appeal, it is virtually a sequel to their *If I Didn't Care*. Taken at a moderately slow tempo that keeps moving along, Kenny carries the opening refrain. Second stanza starts with Happy [sic] Jones's unique bass sermonizing, with Kenny carrying it up again at the bridge to sing out the side. Charlie Tobias's *I'll Never Make The Same Mistake Again*, also strongly on the sentimental side, offers much of the same standard treatment. Kenny starts off the side alone, taking liberty with the tempo in singing the short verse, and then right into the vocal refrain at the same moderately slow and easy tempo. Happy [sic] Jones again lights the torch with his characteristic word picture, and Kenny picks up the last half of the chorus to carry it out. (*Billboard*, 4/10/43)

Every new release by the Ink Spots seems to hit a new low in musical taste. All one can say of this coupling is that we don't believe the statement made in the first title. (*Metronome*, 4/43)

PERFORMANCE REVIEWS

Copacabana (New York)

However, the highlight of the occasion is the Gotham nitery bow of the Ink Spots, who prove to be as terrific in a cafe as they are in vaude. (*Billboard*, 8/7/43)

The Earle (Philadelphia)

Always heavy faves in this village, it's no exception this time for the return of the Four Ink Spots. Their characteristic brand of singing and jiving gets better as they go along, and even their inevitable *If I Didn't Care* is received by the mobbed house as tho they had just heard it for the first time. Sartorially correct in snow-white suits, the sepia foursome scores solidly from scratch with *Put Your Arms Around Me Honey*, and continues to build even bigger with Bill Kenny's soloing for *You'll Never Know*. Make the house jump with the jive for *Your Feet's Too Big* and crashing thru on the recall with Kenny's *I Can't Stand Losing You* and their *Care* classic. (*Billboard*, 9/18/43)

Paramount (New York)

Ink Spots appear to be losing their effectiveness just a mite, probably due to overly familiar routines. . . . It was only when the last title was announced [*If I Didn't Care*] that the audience showed it really cared. The jiving rhythm singer [Deek] has improved with time, but the tall balladeer's voice has lost a bit of its power even tho his presentation has become more intensely dramatic. (*Billboard*, 10/23/43)

1944:
We Were Winning the War,
but Losing the Ink Spots

Allied invasion at Normandy. Battle of Leyte Gulf. Paperback books re-introduced, due to wartime shortages. V1 flying bombs launched against England. GI Bill of Rights signed. Famed author Marv Goldberg born. FDR elected to fourth term. Plot to assassinate Hitler fails. Paris liberated. Battle of the Bulge. Cardinals beat Browns in the St. Louis-based World Series.

The competition: Amor, Bell Bottom Trousers, Besame Mucho, Dance With A Dolly, Don't Fence Me In, G.I. Jive, I Couldn't Sleep A Wink Last Night, I'll Be Seeing You, I'll Get By, I'll Walk Alone, It Had To Be You, Mairzy Doats, Oh What A Beautiful Morning, Poinciana, Rum And Coca Cola, Shoo-Shoo Baby, Swinging On A Star, There Goes That Song Again, Tico Tico, The Trolley Song, What A Difference A Day Made, You Always Hurt The One You Love.

In addition to personal appearances, radio still provided the Spots plenty of exposure. In 1944, Radio Daily conducted a poll to determine its readers' "Favorite Popular Singing Unit." Of 1,051 votes cast, the Ink Spots placed second, with 92, just behind the Fred Waring Glee Club, with 96. Other

117

Ella Fitzgerald.

Cootie Williams.

placers (far behind) were the Hour of Charm Choir, the Andrews Sisters, and the King's Men (a Paul Whiteman group).

By March, "Cow-Cow Boogie" brought the Ink Spots back to the charts. It was Number 1 on the Harlem Hit Parade chart at the end of the month, but never made a better showing than Number 10 on the National chart. One reason was that the song had already run its course in the prior year, having been a biggie for Freddie Slack (with vocalist Ella Mae Morse). Another reason was that the current competition was the similarly titled "Shoo-Shoo Baby" (Ella Mae's version of that tune made it to Number 4 and the Andrews Sisters' version went all the way to Number 1). In May the Spots were back on the charts, with "I'll Get By," which reached Number 7.

The Ink Spots toured constantly, usually with packaged shows. In 1944 the show also included Ella Fitzgerald, the Cootie Williams orchestra, Moke and Poke (comedy, dancing, and singing), and dancer Ralph Brown. (Strangely, in at least half the reviews from 1945, "Moke and Poke" is given as "Coke and Poke." This shows something, but I'm not sure what. Did the reviewers not go to the shows, relying on public relations material with misprints? If they went, surely the act was listed on the marquee, had photos in the lobby, and was announced by the emcee. Were there actually two acts with almost-identical names? Just another of life's mysteries.)

A typical Ink Spots' stage performance had them doing five tunes in eighteen minutes. For example, they might open with "Coquette," then follow it with "Java Jive," the inevitable "If I Didn't Care," another ballad for Bill Kenny, and another jump tune for Deek Watson.[1]

In March the Ink Spots appeared on the cover of *Billboard*. The accompanying "origins" text dragged out the porters bit again, but augmented it with a little piece about their having had their income "supplemented with singing for peanuts in a choir and little Brooklyn niteries. . . ."[2]

The Spots' fame brought them other opportunities: they got to endorse products. In a 1944 ad for Royal Crown Cola, the Ink Spots said "This cola tastes best!"[3] The ad featured Deek taking the "famous" cola taste test one "lucky" day.

A poll of high school students found the Ink Spots out in front in the "Singing Groups Most Preferred" category. Behind their 103 votes were the Andrews Sisters, with 64, and the Mills Brothers, with 48.[4]

In 1944 the Ink Spots got to do some non-Decca recording: both Armed Forces Radio Service (AFRS) disks and V-Disks were produced for the entertainment of servicemen. The Ink Spots would appear on some half-dozen AFRS disks (the last one being released in 1948). The first two (#78 and #100) were on the Jubilee series; the rest were on the Basic Music Library series. AFRS was an outgrowth of a 1942 homemade transmitter that some soldiers in the Aleutian Islands (Alaska) set up to pass the time. To have something to broadcast, they wrote to Hollywood stars requesting recorded messages. The response was so good that soon servicemen all over the world were receiving "official" AFRS disks.

V-Disks (that's "V" for Victory, folks) were also popular with service personnel, and most recording artists did them. In fact, they were also popular with bandleaders since they were immune from the Petrillo recording ban. The Ink Spots appeared on two in 1944 (both featuring "We'll Meet Again") and one in 1945.

During the summer of '44, the Gale Agency was booking "growl trumpet king" Charles "Cootie" Williams (and his orchestra), Ella Fitzgerald, and the Ink Spots as the "Big Three," an obvious reference to that other "big three": Roosevelt, Churchill, and Stalin (*they* didn't sing). In June this bill grossed $35,000 for a week-long stint at Pittsburgh's Stanley Theater and broke the house record at the Orpheum in Los Angeles.

The Ink Spots' recording of "I'll Get By" reached Number 13 on the national charts in June. Harry James' recording of the song (vocal by Dick Haymes) was Number 1 on the Most Played Juke Box Records chart at the same time.

While 1944 started so well for the Spots, it was not to end that way. In June, during an engagement in Chicago, Hoppy became ill and the group had to finish without him, Deek filling in on the mandatory talking parts.[5] Jones returned in August, but in the meantime, damage had been done. With Hoppy ill, the conciliatory father figure who was nicknamed "The grand old man" of the "Dukes of the Jukes," was missing—infighting between Bill and Deek, which had formerly just smoldered, now flared up unchecked. It was to get worse.

A *Billboard* article in July proclaimed, "Decca Stops Cutting for 30-Day Period," and went on to say:

> Decca isn't recording this month, making first time in plant's history that disking department has shut down of its own accord.

There was an over-a-year period when nothing was waxed
because of the Petrillo ban, but this time no-waxing period
is to catch up on back masters that Decca has been cutting
by the score since signing with the AFM last November.[6]

Another July article claimed that Moe Gale was poised to sue "three Negro
newspapers" in Los Angeles, which had criticized Deek

> . . . for using "an Uncle Tom" routine during recent engage-
> ment at the Orpheum theater which Negroes regarded as
> degrading to their race.
>   Phil Carter, in the *Los Angeles Tribune*, characterized The
> Inkspots [sic] as "four singing chimpanzees." Carter, following
> Gale's tirade against the papers and his threats to "close them
> up," came back with reprints of publicity sent out on the
> Inkspots by Ted Yates of New York which, Carter contends,
> emphasized objectionable and false Negro characteristics.[7]

This charge was to be leveled against Deek for the remainder of his performing
days. We'll run into it again.

And the troubles went on. After an engagement at the State Theater in
Hartford (probably in September), Deek quit. Bernie Mackey's assertion
was that Moe Gale had given Bill Kenny a raise at this time, but not Deek
or Hoppy.[8] After being edged out of the singing leadership of the hottest
black group in the country, this was more than Deek could take. Almost
immediately he began putting together his own competing Ink Spots group
(see Intermezzo III).

The Spots did their next two appearances (at Newark's Adams Theater
and Baltimore's Royal) with only three singers. Then, in early October, when
they reached the Howard Theatre in Washington, D.C., Moe Gale sent down
a new fourth member: Billy "Butterball" Bowen.[9]

Bowen had known the group from the early '30s, when he had met Charlie
Fuqua and Jerry Daniels. At that time Bowen had just replaced Benny Carter
as the leader of McKinney's Cotton Pickers, the legendary jazz outfit that
recorded for Victor. During the '40s, Bowen found himself on tour with
the Ink Spots, as a saxophonist, clarinetist, and flautist with the Lucky
Millinder band. Consequently, Bowen knew the arrangements and had even
done some occasional fill-in work with the quartet as a substitute singer.

Thus the Gale Agency found him a natural when the need developed. On wax, Bowen's debut with the group was at the February 26, 1945, session. He can be heard singing lead on the 1946 tunes "I Get The Blues When It Rains" and "I Never Had A Dream Come True."[10]

Bowen's arrival wasn't the end of the upheavals, however. Following the Howard Theatre engagement, their next appearance was at New York's Cafe Zanzibar. At this time, accompanist Bill Doggett lost his job over an arrangement. Morty Howard, the Spots' vocal arranger, was sitting at the piano, and gave the group a chord for "I'll Get By." It didn't sound right to Doggett, and he came over and suggested a different one. This must have hit a sour note somewhere; four days later he was fired.

Bill Doggett then returned to Lucky Millinder's orchestra, where he stayed for several months. In 1945 he had his own band again, the Bill Doggett Octet, and a permanent engagement at the Club Sudan in Harlem. He went on to work with Johnny Otis, Illinois Jacquet, Emmett Berry, Wynonie Harris, Willie Bryant, Doc Pomus, and Buddy Tate. In 1949 Doggett joined Louis Jordan's Tympany Five, replacing Wild Bill Davis.[11] A piano player up to this point, he took up the Hammond organ, since Davis had been experimenting with it. Then there were recordings with Ella Fitzgerald, Jesse Powell, Tyree Glenn, Jimmy Rushing, Coleman Hawkins, Eddie Davis, and Vic Dickenson. In 1952 Bill had his own unit again, the Bill Doggett Trio. The trio became a quintet, and in 1956, he came to national prominence with his instrumental hit, "Honky Tonk." In fact, after Bill Kenny, Doggett's is probably the most famous name of any Ink Spot (even though he's not usually even associated with the group). Bill Doggett died in November 1996, of a massive heart attack, at the age of 80.

Doggett's job passed to Ray "Tuny" Tunia, who had been with the Lucky Millinder and Tab Smith orchestras. Since both units had toured with the Ink Spots, it was once again a case of the newest arrival already knowing the arrangements.[12]

Unfortunately, the worst was yet to come. Just a couple of days after Ray Tunia joined, on October 18, 1944, Hoppy Jones collapsed on stage, dying after being taken home. He was 39. It turned out that he had been having cerebral hemorrhages for over a year. At Jones' funeral in Manhattan, Bill Doggett and Deek Watson appeared, and paid their respects by joining the rest of the group for a somber rendition of "We'll Meet Again." Strangely, *Billboard* reported that Jones was the "last of the original Ink Spots."[13]

October 1944: Billy Bowen, Bill Kenny, Hoppy Jones, Bernie Mackey. (One of the last photos of Hoppy.)

Bill Doggett (in the 1950s).

The immediate replacement bass and bassist came, once again, from Moe Gale: Cliff Givens from the Golden Gate Quartet (and, prior to that, the Southern Sons).[14] Although Givens was with them for about six months, he was only on a single session (in February 1945), which didn't use the talking-bass gimmick. Thus, he's never actually heard on record.

In October, Decca issued one of the Spots' biggest double-sided hits: "I'm Making Believe" backed with "Into Each Life Some Rain Must Fall." Both sides were pairings with Ella Fitzgerald. The very next week, after having been reviewed in *Billboard*, "Rain" was Number 2 on the Harlem Hit Parade (behind the King Cole Trio's "Gee Baby, Ain't I Good To You?"). It eventually went on to Number 1 on the Most Played Juke Box Records chart, and peaked at Number 5 on the National charts in December.

Meanwhile, "I'm Making Believe" entered the National charts at the end of November at the Number 4 position; it subsequently made it to the Number 1 slot. "Rain" reached Number 1 on the Harlem Hit Parade chart and remained at that rarefied position until the end of January 1945 (at which time it was toppled by Cootie Williams' "Somebody's Gotta Go").

Since the war was winding down (the papers were full of talk about what life was going to be like after the war; as far as they were concerned, we'd won it in 1943), it was also time for the AFM recording ban to come to a conclusion. It had gotten to the point where the War Labor Board had demanded that AFM members resume recording. Petrillo refused. Finally, President Roosevelt got involved, urging the musicians to go back to work, and Petrillo to sit down and arbitrate with the WLB to end the strike.[15] Victor and Columbia, the last holdouts, signed with the AFM on November 11 (symbolically Armistice Day). The next day, at 1:00 p.m., Victor started recording Vaughn Monroe's "The Trolley Song" (it was in the can by 1:34). Columbia was tardier, waiting until 7:30 that evening to cut Andre Kostelanetz (the score from "Oklahoma"). There was (almost) "peace in our time."

At the end of October, Deek Watson tried to return to the Ink Spots; Bill Kenny refused to allow him back on stage. This triggered a complex array of legal machinations which unfolded throughout late 1944 (and paved the way for lawsuits throughout the '50s). Suits and countersuits followed, and courtrooms became the place for memorable, albeit nonmusical, performances.

Starting in early November 1944, there was a bitter court battle involving Deek Watson and Charlie Fuqua on one hand, Bill Kenny on the other, and Moe Gale on the third:

WISH IT WERE TRUE – BUT WE HAVE TO MAKE <u>MAKE</u> DECCA RECORDS

No, they don't grow on trees. We have to manufacture these DECCA hits that everybody wants. And under today's conditions, that means we can't turn out all we'd like to —all *you'd* like us to.

But we *can* promise you this. DECCA will continue to give you big-name orchestras and artists—the best in the business. We'll make all we can of these hits. Then we'll distribute the supply just as evenly as we know how.

So, even if you can't get all the DECCA records you want, you can be absolutely sure that you're getting your fair share—that's DECCA'S promise to every coin machine operator.

DECCA
DISTRIBUTING CORPORATION

1. Watson and Fuqua sued Kenny for $250,000 and the right to get back into the group, as well as to deny Kenny the right to use the name "Ink Spots" until they were reinstated[16]—that battle they lost almost immediately.[17] Even though Fuqua was still in the army (stateside), he sued to be allowed back into the group upon his discharge, as well as to be declared a full partner in the Ink Spots. Both Watson and Fuqua wanted to deny Kenny the right to represent himself as the sole owner of the Ink Spots name.[18]

2. Kenny sued Gale for an accounting, charging that Gale took a 50% cut out of the group's earnings, as well as his 10% commission. (Gale said that he paid a lot of the group's expenses, such as advertising, arrangements, publicity, and half their transportation.)[19] Kenny also countered that they had signed a new 5-year contract with him just the prior year, indicating that they were satisfied with his services.

3. Gale sided with Deek Watson, and sued to deny Kenny the right to use the "Ink Spots" name if he wouldn't use Watson in the group.

The suits kept everyone in court and cost the Ink Spots several bookings, including the New York Paramount for Christmas (Woody Herman was hurriedly booked in their place). They also lost bookings in Minneapolis and Detroit. Although they were still appearing at the Cafe Zanzibar, Kenny, not Gale, was now collecting the money. It was finally decided to roll all the lawsuits into a single trial, which began in December 1944.[20] Note that through all this, Bernie Mackey kept a very low profile; he only remained in the group as a personal favor to Charlie Fuqua.[21]

SONGS RECORDED

01/06/44	71620	Someday I'll Meet You Again
08/23/44	72357	I Hope To Die If I Told A Lie (U)
08/29/44	72368	I Hope To Die If I Told A Lie
	72369	Maybe It's All For The Best
08/30/44	72370	Into Each Life Some Rain Must Fall (EF)
	72371	I'm Making Believe (EF)

NOTE: (U) indicates an unreleased version of a song. (EF) indicates Ella Fitzgerald and the Ink Spots.

RECORDS RELEASED

DECCA

18583	Don't Believe Everything You Dream	11/17/43	71514		01/44
	A Lovely Way To Spend An Evening	12/22/43	71609		
18587	Cow-Cow Boogie (EF)	11/03/43	71482		02/44
	When My Sugar Walks Down The				
	Street (Ella only, no group)			DLA2609A	
18579	I'll Get By	12/22/43	71610		04/44
	Someday I'll Meet You Again	01/06/44	71620		
23356	Into Each Life Some Rain				
	Must Fall (EF)	08/30/44	72370		10/44
	I'm Making Believe (EF)	08/30/44	72371		

AFRS

78	If I Didn't Care	INK-1	—/44
	Java Jive	INK-2	
	A Lovely Way To Spend An Evening	INK-3	

Armed Forces Radio Service pressings. Recorded in Hollywood on May 1, 1944.

V-Disc

205-A	We'll Meet Again	06/44
-B	(Down By The Old Mill Stream—B. Goodman)	
	(Jumping At The Woodside—B. Goodman)	
118-A	We'll Meet Again	12/44
-B	(Blues In The Night—Loumell Morgan Trio)	
	(Them There Eyes—Loumell Morgan Trio)	

V (for Victory)-Discs were recorded by many of the big-name acts of the day to be sent to servicemen in war zones as a morale booster, as a way of keeping them in touch with musical trends at home, and because there just weren't that many USO shows.

For your autograph collection (from September 1944).

RECORD REVIEWS

COW-COW BOOGIE/WHEN MY SUGAR WALKS DOWN THE STREET
The combination of Ella Fitzgerald and the Ink Spots for the classic *Cow-Cow Boogie* stacks up as a natural on label. But in the actual spinning, it's mostly a good intention that was never meant to be. Comparisons with Ella Mae Morse, who skyrocketed with the boogie-woogie Western and carried the Capitol record label along with it, are odious. Both singers are highly individualized stylists, and both at the head of their own respective classes. For that matter, so are the Ink Spots. But in pairing Miss Ella with the foursome, the mixture fails to jell, save for the fact that such a blend must have immediate sales appeal, particularly among the Harlem folk. Miss Ella is quite at home in singing the song, but the support from the Ink Spots is not ample to frame her sultry pipes. Plattermate [which doesn't have the Ink Spots] dates back to the days when Miss Ella hit out with a band of her own, and the musical accompaniment provided here by her own orchestra for *When My Baby* [sic] *Walks Down The Street*, hit ditty of a generation ago, makes it easier to understand why Miss Ella junked the band career, and why the record company saw fit not to issue the side originally. (*Billboard*, 3/11/44)

DON'T BELIEVE EVERYTHING YOU DREAM/
A LOVELY WAY TO SPEND AN EVENING
Following the past formula that always paid off fat dividends for their disks and otherwise, the Ink Spots take both of these star-studded ballads in familiar stride. In each instance, it's the solo tenor-soprano singing, bridged by the gravel-voiced philosophizing for the song's lyric. Aided and abetted by such excellent song material, both faces of the platter shape up on the stronger side for the Ink Spots. Both ballads are from screen source, and both the composition of Jimmy McHugh and Harold Adamson, with "Don't Believe Everything You Dream" stemming from "Around the World" and "A Lovely Way To Spend An Evening" from "Higher and Higher." (*Billboard*, 2/12/44)

I'LL GET BY/SOMEDAY I'LL MEET YOU AGAIN

A new burst of popularity will undoubtedly attend the Ink Spots with the spinning of these two sides. Taking two of the more important picture ballads in stride, it's their characteristic singing all the way. "I'll Get By" is the familiar ballad favorite of an earlier year getting a new lease on popularity on the strength of its revival in the "A Guy Named Joe" movie. The Ink Spotters in their rendition should help loads in getting the song on again. Max Steiner's and Ned Washington's "Someday I'll Meet You Again" is also a lush lullaby tailored to the singing talents of this group. A fetching love ballad from the "Passage to Marseilles" movie, the plaintive singing of the foursome makes it all the more appealing. Both ballads taken at a slow tempo, with the talking interludes interspersing the solo singing pitched against the sustained vocal harmonies. (*Billboard*, 4/29/44)

INTO EACH LIFE SOME RAIN MUST FALL/I'M MAKING BELIEVE

The combined vocal talents of the Ink Spots and Ella Fitzgerald have hit the proper formula in this pairing, with the result that their efforts should enjoy a highly enthusiastic response from the disk fans. In both the selection of song and in its singing, the combination is definitely a winning one. Jimmy Monaco's and Mack Gordon's lovely torch ballad, "I'm Making Believe," from the movie "Sweet and Low-Down," finds Miss Ella and the foursome doing some excellent vocal believing with each retaining identity of style and talents. Taken at a moderate tempo, it's the stylized solo singing against a soft bank of sustained harmonies for the Ink Spots, alternating with the individual throatings of la Ella, with both lead voices joining forces on the out-chorus to polish off the platter. "Into Each Life Some Rain Must Fall," a sentimental rain ballad by Allan Roberts and Doris Fisher, is particularly suited to their singing talents. Stepping up the tempo to even brighter proportions, la Ella provides an infectious lilt to the lyrics, with the Ink Spots characteristic even more pronounced in providing a half stanza for the song story in talk and again the dandy dueting to make the couplet all the more complete. (*Billboard*, 10/28/44)

Ella redeems the first side with her wonderful chorus; without this, reduced to the passages by the soprano and bass members of the Ink Spots, it would have been at best a C Minus side [it received a B- in this review]. The tune is a real corny tear-jerker which, like so many others recently, will probably make a small fortune for Doris Fisher, who wrote it. (*Metronome*, 12/44)

PERFORMANCE REVIEWS

Albee (Cincinnati)

It's the first sepia show to play the Albee, and the response is terrific, heavy play coming from sepia trade.

Ink Spots have a record, radio and screen rep. Deke [sic] Watson, Bill Kenny, Hoppy Jones, Bernie Mackey on guitar. Bowing Bill Doggett at the piano gives off on "Put Your Arms Around Me," "Lovely Way to Spend an Evening," "Shoo-Shoo Baby," "My Heart Tells Me," and "If I Didn't Care." Look for their "Lovely Way to Spend an Evening" to let the record rooters forget about "If I Didn't Care." (*Variety*, 1/19/44)

Orpheum (Minneapolis)

An all-Negro show, headed by the rejuvenated Ink Spots, has everything it takes to be a top entertainment piece. The Spots, making their periodic visit here, were never better.

Ella Fitzgerald takes second billing to the Ink Spots, but more than holds up her end with *I've Got Rhythm, Do Nothin' Till You Hear From Me* and the oldie, *Tisket-a-Tasket*. Stopped show and had to beg off with *Five Guys Named Moe*.

Ink Spots come on with *Shoo-Shoo Baby*, ["Cow-Cow Boogie"?] followed by *Lovely Way to Spend An Evening* and *Don't Sweetheart Me*. Encore with *My Heart Tells Me* and beg off to thunderous hand with the inevitable *If I Didn't Care*. (*Billboard*, 2/26/44)

Cafe Zanzibar (New York)

The Zanzibar, removed from its old quarters to the site of the former Hurricane at 49th and Broadway, is a luxuriant spot providing New York's best setting for a colored show.

The Ink Spots did one number that I've always liked, *Your Feet's Too Big*. The rest of their act seemed to me to be musically as offensive as ever. The success of Billy Kenny is a mystery that I shall never understand. However, he and the Spots got an enormous hand, which proves something, perhaps. (*Metronome*, 12/44—review by jazz critic Leonard Feather)

Intermezzo II:
Hoppy Jones

Orville "Hoppy" Jones was the elder statesman of the Ink Spots. As such, and because he was simply a nice man, the others looked up to him. This helped keep the group together far longer than would have been possible: Deek and Bill would have fought the Ink Spots into extinction, had it not been for Hoppy's constant mediation.

Because Hoppy was part Cherokee, he was so light-skinned that he used a good deal of makeup to look darker.

One of the more interesting honors won by a member of the Ink Spots was Hoppy's receipt of a solid gold diaper pin. In a ceremony at the Savoy Ballroom, he was named "typical Harlem father" for 1939. At the time, Hoppy had seven children (including four from his wife's first marriage). As usual, press reports differ: an article about Moe Gale, in 1941, quotes him as saying that Hoppy had nine children, including three pairs of twins.[1] However, the final count was eight, with two sets of twins (although there could also have been another child from a possible first marriage). Considering that his wife, Esther Golden, was both white and Jewish, it's difficult to see how this made Hoppy a "typical Harlem father."

Certainly not the deepest or most tuneful bass ever, Hoppy still had a tremendous warmth that he projected to the vast audience of Ink Spots fans. His funeral attracted thousands of mourners, and floral arrangements arrived in the shape of instruments. On an equally somber note, during the funeral, thieves broke into Hoppy's house in Queens, New York, and stole over $10,000 worth of jewelry. With his usual gift of hyperbole, Deek claims in his book that the amount was $150,000.

Said Bill Kenny many years later:

> Everything I learned about show business, I learned from Hoppy. Hoppy was a very wise and kind person. When he died in 1945 [sic], of a cerebral hemorrhage, it was a big upset to all of us personally. And as for the group, we never did find a really adequate replacement.[2]

(While this shows that Bill thought highly of Hoppy, the statement certainly has to be an insult to Bill's own brother, Herb, who, in the following year, would become the bass of the group and hold that position for six years.)

Hoppy addresses his "Honey Chile": Bill, Deek, Hoppy, Charlie.

1945

Yalta Conference. FDR dies. Hitler a suicide. Germany surrenders. Battles for Iwo Jima and Okinawa. Kamikaze pilots attack American ships. Atomic bombs dropped on Hiroshima and Nagasaki force Japan's surrender. Final count: about 45 million dead in World War II. U.N. Charter signed. Fluoride added to the water in Grand Rapids, Michigan.

The competition: Ac-Cent-Tchu-Ate The Positive, Candy, Dream, If I Loved You, I'm Beginning To See The Light, It Might As Well Be Spring, It's Been A Long Long Time, Laura, My Funny Valentine, My Heart Sings, On The Atchison Topeka And The Santa Fe, Saturday Night Is The Loneliest Night In The Week, Sentimental Journey, There I've Said It Again, There Must Be A Way, Till The End Of Time.

On January 8, 1945, the entire litigation mess was settled out of court. As it turned out, Deek was the one who was denied the name; clubs were barred from booking any Ink Spots group not containing Bill Kenny. Watson countered that he was going to form a new group based "on a completely new idea"[1] (see Intermezzo III on the Brown Dots). Gale was to remain as Kenny's manager (his contract had four and a half years to go). Watson and Fuqua retained a financial interest in Bill Kenny's earnings (with Fuqua

Some newcomers: Cliff Givens, Bill Kenny, Bernie Mackey, Billy Bowen (in front).

More new faces: Huey Long, Billy Bowen, Herb Kenny, Bill Kenny (in front).

being paid a weekly salary even though in the army).[2] Finally, Kenny dropped his suit against Gale.

Bill thought that one way to prevent future unpleasantness was to buy out Deek's share. For the sum of $10,000 (some sources said $20,000), Deek promised never to use the name again.[3] It was a valiant attempt on Bill's part, but we'll see later how it all turned out. Additionally, for several years, Bill generously continued to pay a share to Hoppy's widow.

One of the more interesting side effects of the breakup was the loss of the hotel that the group owned: Gordon's Rest, in Patchogue, New York. This investment was sold as a direct result of the split.

1944 had been a banner year for the Gale Agency. It was reported that the "Big Three" (the Ink Spots, Cootie Williams, and Ella Fitzgerald) grossed over $500,000 for the year.[4] (The same article stated: ". . . the Brown Dots [Deek's 1945 group], handled by Moe Gale, . . . asking $2,000 a week on opening dates.")

In March, Decca released "I Hope To Die If I Told A Lie"/"Maybe It's All For The Best," interesting titles in light of all the litigation. However, the public wasn't amused and the disk didn't chart at all (nor was it even reviewed in *Billboard*). In the same month they also released "I'm Beginning To See The Light," another outing with Ella Fitzgerald. This did take off, making it into the top ten. But judging from the reviews, it was Ella's talent that made the song. Even *Billboard*, normally sympathetic to the Ink Spots' formula, said that ". . . you don't become really enthusiastic until Miss Ella takes over." The other magazines were not *that* charitable. (See the full reviews at the end of this chapter.)

Although it seemed that the lawsuits should have vanished, Bill took Moe Gale back to court, where the judge ruled that Gale was working for the Ink Spots, not the other way around.[5] Thus he was only entitled to a 10% fee.

In May the Ink Spots kind of switched from the Gale Agency to Universal Attractions (a partnership between Ben Bart and Harry Lenetzka).

> Newest indie disking outfit is Hub Recording Company, race disking org headed by Ben Bart, now treasurer with Moe Gale Agency [translation: Ben Bart set up an independent rhythm and blues label called Hub]. . . . Bart recently formed combine with Harry Lenetzka, formerly with Gale office, to supervise

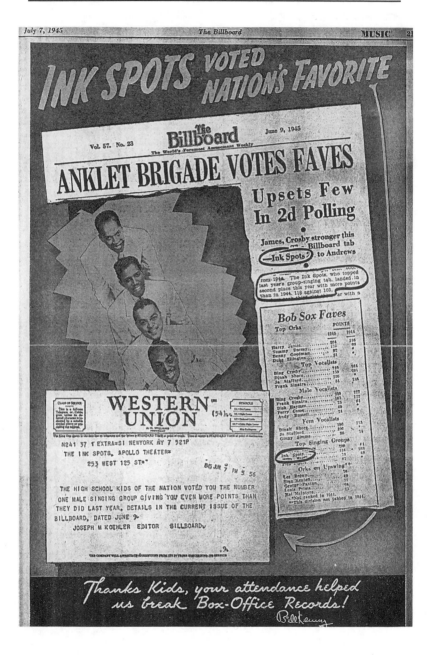

bookings of the Ink Spots altho act is booked by Gale office and personally managed by Gale.[6]

This doesn't make a whole lot of sense. Universal Attractions (the name of the "combine" mentioned) will supervise bookings and Gale will book! Also:

> Ben Bart, head one-nighter booker at the Moe Gale agency, left Gale recently to open a booking office in partnership with Harry Lenetzka, another ex-Galer who left the agency several weeks ago. The new Bart-Lenetzka office will offer both personal management and booking facilities to their clients, the biggest of whom are the Ink Spots. . . . Unusual situation exists in that new combine will oversee the bookings of the Spots, while Gale will continue to book the act for another year and a half. Gale's personal management contract with the Spots runs for another four and a half years. New set-up calls for Bart and Lenetzka to go on salary paid by Kenny.[7]

During the summer, Gale was still booking them. It's probable that at some point Bart bought him out, although the group would come back to Gale two years later.[8] Part of the problem was Kenny's insistence on picking 50% of all the tunes the Ink Spots recorded for Decca. Dave Kapp (Decca's Artist and Repertoire vice president) wanted to negotiate with Gale, not Kenny, which may have led Kenny to abandon Gale.[9]

Without Deek Watson, the Ink Spots did virtually nothing except ballads. This baffled trade paper reviewers because the public continued to buy recordings which seemed identical to one another. At times it seemed the Ink Spots were performing little more than a parody of themselves.

In July high school students voted the Ink Spots the most popular male singing group, with 118 votes. (The category, however, was "Top Singing Combos," and the clear winners were the incredibly popular Andrews Sisters, with 200 votes.)[10] In August the Ink Spots once again made the cover of *Billboard*.

In the spring of 1945, more personnel changes occurred. Around April, Bernie Mackey departed. Remember that Bernie got the job in the first place because he and Charlie were friends. Charlie would return from the army one day, and Bernie knew that Bill didn't really want to let him back in.

Not wanting to be caught in the middle, Bernie left to join Milt Buckner's orchestra.

Bernie Mackey was replaced by jazz guitarist Huey Long, who remained with the Spots for nearly a year—he was present on the October 2 and 3, 1945, sessions.[11]

Huey Long was born in Sealy, Texas, in 1904. Originally a banjo player, he was with Frank Davis' Louisiana Jazz Band in 1925. By the mid-1930s he had switched to the guitar and had joined Jesse Stone's orchestra. In the early '40s, he was with Johnny Long's band and then Fletcher Henderson's. He came to New York to play a single Apollo Theater gig with Henderson, then took his bus fare home and banked it instead, joining Earl "Fatha" Hines' orchestra (along with Dizzy Gillespie, Bennie Green, Charlie Parker, and Sarah Vaughan). He later formed the Huey Long Trio, which played at the Three Deuces Cafe in Manhattan.

What others might consider a big break came when Bill Kenny asked him to join the Ink Spots to replace departing Bernie Mackey. Even though the Spots were at their peak, Huey said: "It was just a passing thing with me; just a business deal; a gig."[12] He went on to state: "Even though my bag was a jazz musician, as the years went by, I found out that people want to know more about the Ink Spots than all the rest."[13]

The next desertion happened during one of those times that the Ink Spots were playing a double engagement. Halfway through their four-week stint at the Paramount, the group also took over the two weeks remaining on Bill "Bojangles" Robinson's Zanzibar gig (Robinson had to leave for Hollywood to film *The Hot Mikado*). During this hectic time, bass Cliff Givens left, apparently to rejoin the Golden Gate Quartet.[14] (He couldn't have been with them long, however, for in the fall of 1946, *Billboard* carried an advertisement promoting the new Haven label, an independent with artists such as Arthur Prysock, Mahalia Jackson, the Southern Sons, and Clifford Givens and His Four Flames.) Again in need of a bass, the Ink Spots began auditioning potential replacements.

During one of those audition sessions, Bill Kenny's fraternal twin brother, Herb, stopped by to inform him that he and his new group, the Melodeers, were leaving for an engagement at the Plantation Club in St. Louis. During this farewell, Herb heard someone auditioning, and went over to show how it *should* be done. Apparently his demonstration was a good one; both road manager Murray Nadel (a CPA from the Gale office) and Bill persuaded *him* to become the new bass and do the "talking parts," which is how Herb

Three discographers @ IAJRC 11/00

referred to his role. He went so far as to say he "gave up singing" to join the Ink Spots (except for live shows when Bill was sick; then Herb, having a 2½-octave range, would do both the lead and the talking parts).[15] Herb said that on the day that he joined, the lineup was Bill Kenny, Billy Bowen, Huey Long, and accompanist Ray Tunia. (Of course, this was the demise of Herb's Melodeers, leaving their bass, Jimmy Ricks, free to form his own group, the Ravens, with which he'd become the most famous, respected, and imitated bass singer in the rhythm and blues field. Herb subsequently introduced Ricks to Ben Bart, and the first Ravens records were issued on Bart's Hub label.)

Who knows, though, it *might* have happened this way:

> The years have changed many things for the Ink Spots but the greatest and most tragic was the death of Hoppy Jones, who did the deep voiced narration for their songs. After Hoppy died, Bill and the boys were sure the Ink Spots were finished. Then one day they heard about a young singer who was appearing at the Apollo Theatre, in N.Y., who might be the right man for the bass part. They went up and Bill Kenny was surprised to find that the man was his own brother Herb who had changed his name for the appearance.[16]

When Herb joined, he brought Adriel McDonald along as a valet. Both Herb and Adriel had previously sung with Bill Westbrook's Cabineers (although not on any of their recordings).[17] At this time, Marcus Coleman was the Spots' main valet; Herb claimed that McDonald subsequently connived to get him fired.[18] More about Adriel McDonald later.

Fortunately, the Ink Spots' popularity survived all these personnel upheavals. An ad placed by Universal Attractions in the August 15, 1945, issue of *Variety* claims that the Ink Spots were voted the Number One Quartette of 1945, and shows two charts to prove it: "Bob Sox Faves" and "G.I. Faves." On both of these, the Ink Spots' name is heavily circled so you won't miss it. However, the heavy circle "accidentally" obscures the name of the *actual* Number One favorite on both charts: the Andrews Sisters. Of course, you *could* argue that the Andrews Sisters weren't a quartet. The Spots did, however, beat out the Sisters on the "College Faves" chart.[19]

With the end of the war, things got back to normal in the United States. Or did they? One of the victims of World War II was big band music. While the bands had fronted singers for years, it now turned out that the nation was more interested in the singers than the bands behind them. Additionally, many ballrooms all over the country had closed down due to the war: gas rationing, women who were too tired after the swing shift (and who didn't have many men to dance with anyway), and the 20% tax on dance halls had all contributed to a decline in bands' popularity. Big band dance music was shifting to pop vocals.

In September, Decca dipped deep into its archives and released "I'd Climb The Highest Mountain" and "Thoughtless," both several years old, although previously unissued. Once again, *Billboard* didn't review the disk, nor did it make the charts. However, Decca ads were hyping the song, and even ran a photo of the old group with Hoppy and Deek!

Also in September, RCA-Victor released its first vinyl plastic record. On the Red Seal (classical) label, it was translucent red and unbreakable (not easy to say about 78s). Although these had been developed in Germany in 1928, the cost had been prohibitive; even now Victor was charging $2 per disk.

And here's an amazing revelation, which recalls the day you found out the Easter Bunny was only a myth:

> The Negro AFM here [Chicago] tried to bring another member here this week, but the move back-fired when Herb Kenny, bass with the Ink Spots, proved to their satisfaction that he's no musician and is only using the cello in the act as a stage prop.
>
> Confusion over whether or not Kenny should be an AFM member came this week when a biz agent of the local recalled that the late Hoppy Jones was a member in good standing of the musicians' union. Jones, however, was a qualified musician and plucked the quarter-sized bass during the Spots' vocalizing.
>
> Herb Kenny, brother of tenor Bill, who leads the Spots, only makes believe he's plucking the cello to keep the Jones legend alive.[20]

SONGS RECORDED

02/26/45	72746	I'm Beginning To See The Light (EF)
	72747	That's The Way It Is (EF)
10/02/45	73057	I'm Gonna Turn Off The Teardrops
	73058	I'll Lose A Friend Tomorrow
10/03/45	73061	The Sweetest Dream
	73062	Keep On The Sunny Side (U)
	73063	Just For Me

NOTE: (EF) indicates Ella Fitzgerald and the Ink Spots. (U) indicates an unreleased song.

RECORDS RELEASED

DECCA

18657	I Hope To Die If I Told A Lie	08/29/44	72368	03/45
	Maybe It's All For The Best	08/29/44	72369	
23399	I'm Beginning To See The			
	Light (EF)	02/26/45	72746	03/45
	That's The Way It Is (EF)	02/26/45	72747	
18711	I'd Climb The Highest Mountain	12/30/40	68540	09/45
	Thoughtless	10/06/39	66737	

AFRS

100	I'll Get By	INK-4	02/45
	Someday I'll Meet You Again	INK-5	
P-167	If I Didn't Care		ca. 45
	Java Jive		
	A Lovely Way To Spend An Evening		
P-168	(All sides by Stan Kenton and his Orchestra)		

Armed Forces Radio Service pressings (the P series had a different record number on each side).

V-Disc

365-A	Into Each Life Some Rain		
	Must Fall (EF)	08/30/44	02/45
	(It Don't Mean A Thing—Mills Brothers)		
-B	(Embraceable You—King Cole Trio)		
	(What Is This Thing Called Love?—King Cole Trio)		

RECORD REVIEWS

I'M BEGINNING TO SEE THE LIGHT/THAT'S THE WAY IT IS

The combination of Ella Fitzgerald and the Ink Spots brings together the best of the ballad song sellers. And when it comes to Joan Whitney and Alex Kramer's "That's The Way It Is," a "my man" song tailor-made for Miss Ella's talents, the gal once again shows her capabilities as one of the best lyric projectionists in the business. Shares the side with the Spotters' Bill Kenny. And while it is a grand song, you don't become really enthusiastic until Miss Ella takes over. The same pattern is applied to "I'm Beginning To See The Light," with Miss Ella adding an original lilt to the lyric for her stanza. (*Billboard*, 4/28/45)

Play the last half of these, Ella's part, and they'll be worth the price. *Beginning* definitely is, even with Bill Kenny's falsetto grating on your nerves. Ella really tears this one apart; she's never done anything quite like it and her vocal is actually thrilling. *That's The Way* follows same pattern. Kenny, Ella and then the entire group on out. This she sings more subdued and it's not quite as fine. *Beginning* is definitely it! (*Down Beat*, 5/1/45)

Taking the second chorus on both sides, Ella does some of the most delightful work of her career. Her melodic variations on *Light*, on the second and last eight, are a treat for musicians, as is her treatment of the descending sevenths in the release. It's tragic that Ella has to be teamed up on wax with the revolting vocal posturing of Billy Kenny, who wastes half the space on each number. (*Metronome*, 5/45)

I'D CLIMB THE HIGHEST MOUNTAIN/THOUGHTLESS

Having ironed out their internal differences, the Ink Spots return to the disks, and with Bill Kenny's soprano-scaled pipes still ringing true, the foursome should continue from where they left off. For both of these sides, following the identical winning pattern, are designed to spot the Spots in warm hearts. With the talking sequence to bridge his song, Kenny carries the lead all the way, selling both ballads like a million. "I'd Climb The Highest Mountain" is the Lew Brow-Sidney Clare classic of a couple of decades ago and ripe to start a revival of interest. And there should be just as much enthusiasm for Jerry Livingston and Mack David's sentimental song, "Thoughtless." (*Billboard*, 10/20/45)

PERFORMANCE REVIEWS

Paramount (New York)

Ink Spots, with only Billy Kenny as the lone survivor of the original group (incidentally, he gets personal billing outside for the first time), work well too, although they do miss the spark of Deke [sic] Watson's by-play. Kenny carries the turn almost alone. Start out with "How Many Hearts" (a bit aged); "I'm Making Believe," then "If I Didn't Care," finishing, with Ella Fitzgerald added, on "Into Each Life Some Rain Must Fall," a crack item she recorded with them for Decca. Watson, incidentally, is breaking in a new act called the Brown Dots, this week at the Apollo Theatre. (*Variety*, 2/21/45)

Paramount (New York)

This is their first vaude here since squabble about management, and altho group has new members, it's still Kenny that sells all the songs. Guy has catchy voice, but there's a flaw that's creeping into his work. He's a little on the hammy side, and never lets up with mannerisms or vocalisms that prove annoying when done over and over again. He should go light on that stuff. (*Billboard*, 3/17/45)

Stanley Theatre (Philadelphia)

Only Billy Kenny, the tall, lanky tenor, remains of the original Ink Spots and the new quartet still doesn't have either the class or the distinctive style of the old one. It's pretty much of a one-man foursome now, with Kenny in front most of the time, of course, and while his current partners have been picked with an eye for approximating both the looks and particular accomplishments of the previous Ink Spotters, they still don't come close. Maybe time will correct that. (*Variety*, 5/9/45)

Adams (Newark)

Particular stars are the Ink Spots, coming up with a new routine after years of settled prosperity with stylized high jinks. In current pattern, Billy Kenny is the works. He warms up to the mike and does most of the song pitches solo style. Other members, paling into the background, have less to do than former Spots. The reception was uproarious, especially when Ella Fitzgerald teams with the boys for solid sending with "Into Each Life Some Rain Must Fall." On their own the Spots warble "I'm Making Believe," "I Don't Care Who Knows It" and "I Lose A Friend Tomorrow." (*Variety*, 9/12/45)

A new pianist: Bill, Ray Tunia, Billy, Charlie, Herb.

Intermezzo III:
The Brown Dots

Around November 1944, Deek started appearing with a new group, which he called the "Ink Spots." When he announced (in the January 1945 settlement of the lawsuits) that he would form a new group based "on a completely new idea,"[1] he simply changed their name to the "Brown Dots" (the name does sound somewhat familiar, doesn't it?). As it turned out, the "new idea" was to sound as much like the Ink Spots as possible. One real difference was that the Brown Dots relied more on harmony than the Ink Spots, who were more individualists. (Actually, even after the settlement, the Brown Dots occasionally appeared as the Ink Spots. Since the Brown Dots were also managed by Moe Gale, we know who the hands-down winner in *this* contest was.)[2] By February 1, 1945, the Brown Dots were appearing at the Plantation Club in St. Louis.[3]

The Brown Dots—Deek Watson (second tenor), Joe King (first tenor), Pat Best (baritone), Jimmy Gordon (bass)—were a wonderful group in their own right, recording for Manor from mid-1945 to late 1946.[3] Their most enduring legacy was a song penned by Deek and Pat Best: "For Sentimental Reasons."

A *Variety* review of the Brown Dots, when they played the Apollo Theatre at the start of their career, was somewhat mixed:

The early Brown Dots (1945): (top) Deek Watson, Joe King, Jimmy Gordon; (bottom) Pat Best.

This is the first theatre date of the new quartet formed by Deke [sic] Watson, one of the original members of the Ink Spots, who bowed out of that combo last fall after drawn-out litigation. One of the sparkplugs of the Spots, Watson is doing a man-sized job of carrying the new group in its early stages. And the result is that the quartet, as it works here, shows very good possibilities.

When caught, the Dots were still a long distance from big time, however. Their harmony was a bit ragged, the tenor voice [Joe King's] was inaccurate and badly controlled (due to illness, it's said), and their selection of tunes ("Little on Lonely Side," "I'm Making Believe," "Java Jive") wasn't good in view of Watson's past association with the Ink Spots.

However, as cited above, the very animation of Watson and brief flashes in the combo's work seems to indicate future strength.

When laid out several months ago, it was said Watson's idea was completely different from the Ink Spots pattern. It isn't, and the similarity to the Spots isn't wise. Watson uses a high tenor much in the way Billy Kenny works with the former act. This isn't as bad as the insertion of a spoken bridge in one song, a chore handled for the Spots by the late Hoppy Jones, whose voice and delivery is difficult to copy. It shouldn't even be attempted.[5]

Sometime in the spring of 1945, tenor Jimmie Nabbie replaced Joe King; then the Brown Dots' career started to take off. First they received an offer of a recording contract from Manor Records' Irvin Berman. Then, by mid-1946, they had *two* radio programs on the American Broadcasting System network—one at 10:15 Saturday mornings and the other at 6:30 on Sunday evenings.[6] In October 1946, they were recruited to replace the ailing Marva Louis in the movie *Boy! What A Girl* (in which they sang "Satchelmouth Baby" and "Just In Case You Change Your Mind").[7] They also appeared in *Sepia Cinderella* that same year (doing "Long Legged Lizzie" and "Is It Right?"). Deek mugged his way through both movies, and even had a speaking part in *Sepia Cinderella*.

Somehow, though, Deek was always having personality clashes, and this group was no exception. In late 1946, things got so bad that the other

The later Brown Dots (1946): Deek Watson, Pat Best, Jimmy Gordon, Jimmie Nabbie.

The Four Tunes (ca. 1950): (top) Jimmy Gordon, Jimmie Nabbie, Danny Owens; (bottom) Pat Best.

three Brown Dots recruited a fourth member, Danny Owens. (Owens had been with the Colemanaires, and also with former Ink Spot Cliff Givens, in the Southern Sons/Melody Masters, who had recorded for Apollo in 1946.) Calling themselves the Sentimentalists, they started recording for Manor also. The one thing they neglected to do was tell Deek; they first wanted to see if they could make it on their own.

When Deek finally found out, he formed another Brown Dots group, about which little is known. They recorded for Majestic (1948), Varsity (1949), and Manor (1949). There's also a record by "Deek Watson and the 4 Dots" on the Castle label; it was probably done with the same group, in 1948.

The Sentimentalists developed a problem reminiscent of the Ink Spots back in 1933: bandleader Tommy Dorsey contacted them and asked them to stop calling themselves the "Sentimentalists," since he had recently had a vocal group by that name. (They had left Dorsey in April 1946 and were now on radio as the Clark Sisters, so Nabbie felt justified in using it.) But Dorsey was nice about it, so the guys decided to honor his request. Since all they had left were four tunes that they hadn't yet recorded, they changed their name to the "Four Tunes." (Although this story sounds like one of the apocryphal tales of the Ink Spots, Nabbie swore to its authenticity.)[8] All their Sentimentalists recordings were reissued by Manor as by the Four Tunes.

But this is a much more interesting version of their origin (under the title of "Here's an Unusual Story!"):

> Here's the story of how Pat Best, who wrote the hit song "For Sentimental Reasons," became a member of The Four Tunes (Manor and Columbia recording artists).
>
> Best worked in a tailor shop just a few years back which helped outfit the Tunes when they were a struggling quartet. He became very friendly with the boys just about the time they garnered a Manor disk contract. While the boys were being fitted for their outfits, Pat used to join the foursome in impromptu song sessions. The day they scheduled to make their first platter, one of the Tunes took sick and couldn't make it. Margaret Gordon, the vocal group's manager, phoned Pat at the tailor shop and told him to hurry right down to the Manor studios for the recording session.

Best asked his very busy employer for time off. "The Tunes need me," he explained, "to cut records."

"And I need you to cut suits," ultimated the boss, "take your choice."[9]

Both on their own and behind Savannah Churchill, the Four Tunes became one of the hottest groups of the late '40s and early '50s, really hitting their stride when they switched over to RCA Victor, and then Jubilee, where they had back-to-back hits with "Marie" and "I Understand (Just How You Feel)."

It almost goes without saying that, when interviewed in 1974, Jimmie Nabbie had become the lead of an Ink Spots group; he was with them until his death, after double bypass surgery, in September 1992.

Is there a singer in the house? (ca. 1949): (standing) Jimmie Nabbie, Danny Owens, Bill Kenny, Jimmy Gordon, Herb Kenny; (seated) Pat Best, Johnny Moore (of the Three Blazers), Savannah Churchill, Oscar Moore (brother of Johnny, former guitarist with the King Cole Trio, now with the Three Blazers).

The First Brown Dots Group

MANOR

1005	Let's Give Love Another Chance	E-1264	05/45
	Thirty-One Miles For A Nickel	E-1265	
1009	You're Heaven Sent	E-1265	—/45
	For Sentimental Reasons	E-1263	
1015	Just In Case You Change Your Mind	S-1288	11/45
	You're A Heartache To Me	S-1290	
1016	That's What She Gets	I-1315	01/46
	Escuchame	I-1317	
1017	Patience And Fortitude	I-1316	02/46
	Is It Right	S-1289	
1026	Satchelmouth Baby	I-1212	—/46
	Surrender	I-1330	
1027	If I Can't Have You	I-1332	—/46
	I'm Loving You For You	I-1331	
1032	Well Natch	I-1334	08/46
	Please Give A Broken Heart A Break	I-1335	
1040	Rumors Are Flying	I-1351	09/46
	You Took All My Love	I-1353	
1041	For Sentimental Reasons	I-1263	09/46
	It's A Pity To Say Goodnight	I-1358	
1044	How Can You Say I Don't Care	S-1287	12/46
	Long Legged Lizzie	I-1350	
1057	I Don't Know From Nothing Baby	I-1336	02/47
	Shout, Brother, Shout	I-1352	
1075	That's What She Gets	I-1315	07/47
	(Why You No Knock—Benny Davis)		

The Second Brown Dots Group

MAJESTIC

1244	I've Got The Situation Well In Hand	T-1552	03/48
	Pray For The Lights To Go Out	T-1553	

CASTLE

2006	Strange As It Seems	CA 2006A	ca. 48
	Saturday Night Function	CA 2006B	
	(as by "DEEK WATSON & 4 DOTS")		

MANOR

1163	Let's Give Love Another Chance	S-1264	02/49
	Just In Case You Change Your Mind	S-1288	
1166	As Tho You Don't Know	F-1746	02/49
	Darktown Strutters Ball	F-1748	
1170	Bow-wow-wow	F-1754	03/49
	At Our Fireplace	F-1747	
1171	After Awhile	F-1762	04/49
	If I Could Be With You	F-1761	
	(Backing Gwenn Bell on both sides)		
1179	My Bonnie Lies Over The Ocean	F-1749	05/49
	You Better Think Twice	F-1753	

VARSITY

5015	I've Got The Situation Well In Hand	—/49
	The Devil Was Beatin' His Wife	

1946

Nuremberg trials. Philippines become independent. Juan Peron comes to power in Argentina. Mine workers strike. ENIAC ushers in the Age of Computers. First drive-thru bank opens in Chicago.

The competition: Come Rain Or Come Shine, Doin' What Comes Naturally, For Sentimental Reasons, The Girl That I Marry, Let It Snow Let It Snow Let It Snow, Ole Buttermilk Sky, Prisoner Of Love, Rumors Are Flying, Shoo Fly Pie And Apple Pan Dowdy, Sioux City Sue.

Just when you thought it was safe to start mass-producing records again, the record companies were hit with another kind of shortage. In February there was a shortage of the kraft paper used to make the sleeves for album sets (remember that in those days an album was just that; it looked a bit like a photo album with several sleeves inside holding the 78 rpm records that made up the set). Since record production was up, the few companies that made the albums and sleeves were swamped.

In April, the *Chicago Defender* held a popularity contest. In the "Specialty Artists" category, the King Cole Trio barely edged out the Ink Spots by a vote of 106,653 to 47,287. On the other hand, the Spots far outclassed the Mills Brothers, who could only muster 47,187 votes.[1]

When Charlie Fuqua returned from his army stint in late 1945 (or early 1946), there was a small (for the Ink Spots) amount of fighting, and Huey Long found himself out of a job. Huey then worked with Eddie "Lockjaw" Davis, Sonny Thompson, and Snub Mosely. He once again formed the Huey Long Trio in the '50s, and (of course) had his own Ink Spots, with Adriel McDonald and Orlando Roberson in the early '60s. In 1992, at age 88, Huey was still active, occasionally playing, teaching, and publishing his musical works.

In spite of all the problems and changes the Spots had weathered, the Bill Kenny-Herb Kenny-Billy Bowen-Charlie Fuqua quartet now produced the biggest hit of the Ink Spots' career: "The Gypsy," recorded in February 1946. This Billy Reid tune was typical of Kenny-led ballads, with Herb taking the talking bridge. It spent thirteen weeks at the Number 1 spot in "Most Played Juke Box Records" and ten weeks at Number 1 in "Best Selling Popular Retail Records." It only made it to Number 1 in "Records Most Played on the Air" for a single week, however, finally driving out Dinah Shore's version (there was also a single week in which the two versions were tied for Number 1). In fact, there were at least ten versions of the song vying for top positions. The others were by Sammy Kaye (vocal by Mary Marlow), Hildegarde (with the Guy Lombardo Orchestra), Hal McIntyre, Louis Prima, Phil Brito, Jan Garber, Gail Meredith, Freddie Stewart, and Betty Bradley. Only Kaye, Hildegarde, and McIntyre also made the charts. (In those days, audiences liked the song itself as much as an artist's interpretation, so it wasn't unusual for several versions to be on the charts concurrently.) At the end of this chapter, we'll chart the progress of this, the Ink Spots' biggest hit. (In December 1946, the Spots would receive the *Cash Box* award for making "Gypsy" the largest money-maker of the year.)[2]

It has been stated that there was some prejudice against playing the Ink Spots' version on the radio (in all but a handful of weeks, Dinah Shore's waxing beat out the Ink Spots on the air). But there certainly was no lack of airtime allocated to the Ink Spots; Dinah simply got more. And, on the other side of the coin, the white record-buying public appreciated genuine talent by making stars out of the Ink Spots, the Mills Brothers, Nat "King" Cole, Louis Armstrong, Fats Waller, Lena Horne, Ella Fitzgerald, Cab Calloway, and Louis Jordan, among others.

There's also a third side to the coin: at some point, certain acts changed over from "Negro" to "white" singing. The pre-"If I Didn't Care" jive/swing sounds of the Ink Spots were not meant to attract much of a white audience;

once they started singing smooth ballads, they were "in like Flynn." The same can be said of the Mills Brothers: the more "supper-clubbish" they became, the more acceptable they were to white audiences. Nat "King" Cole was a more sophisticated entertainer from the start, and Louis Jordan never tried to be anything but black (and managed to get a fair amount of acceptance by the white public anyway). Fats Waller sounded black, but also sounded like he knew something you didn't: that life was *supposed* to be fun!

In mid-1946, Ray Tunia left to become Ella Fitzgerald's arranger. Two years later he went with Pearl Bailey, and three years after that it was back to Ella again. He would also be a part of Charlie Fuqua's Ink Spots for a while in the '50s.[3] Ray's bench was filled by Harold Francis, who holds the distinction of being with the Spots longer than any other arranger—about seven years.

In July the Ink Spots topped the list of "Favorite Singing Groups" in a *Billboard* college poll. They received 322 votes, to beat out the King Cole Trio and the Pied Pipers, tied for second place, with 238 votes.

In September, the Spots' version of "To Each His Own" made it to Number 1 on the "Best Selling Retail Records" chart, beating out versions by Eddy Howard, Freddy Martin, Tony Martin, the Modernaires, the Opie Cates Orchestra, the Fiesta Four, Marie Greene, and the Don Byas Quartet. However, Eddy Howard was the clear hitmaker with this song, in terms of retail sales and jukebox plays.

In November the unthinkable happened: jukeboxes, which had been a nickel a play for as long as anyone could remember, were raised to a dime (three plays for a quarter).

In January 1947, *Billboard* presented a ranking of all the hitmakers of 1946. These are the results:[4]

Top Tune: The Gypsy (all versions)
Top Sheet Music Seller: The Gypsy
Top Disk Jockey Record: The Gypsy
    (Dinah Shore #3)
    (Ink Spots #8)
    (Sammy Kaye #25)
Top Popular Retail Record Sellers:
    #1 Prisoner Of Love (Perry Como)
    #2 To Each His Own (Eddy Howard)
    #3 The Gypsy (Ink Spots)
Top Selling Singing and Instrumental Group:
    #1 The Ink Spots
    #2 The Andrews Sisters
    #3 The Pied Pipers
Top Selling Popular Record Albums:
    #3 The Ink Spots (*The Ink Spots*)
Top Singing & Instrumental Groups on Disk Jockey Shows:
    #4 The Ink Spots
Most Played Record on Nation's Juke Boxes:
    #1 To Each His Own (Eddy Howard)
    #2 The Gypsy (Ink Spots)
Top Singing & Instrumental Groups on the Nation's Juke Boxes:
    #1 The Ink Spots
Top Singing & Instrumental Groups on Race Records in the Nation's Juke Boxes:
    #1 The Ink Spots
    #2 Johnny Moore's Three Blazers
    #3 King Cole Trio
        [A triumph for the Moore family; Nat King Cole's guitar player, Oscar Moore, was Johnny Moore's brother.]

Anatomy of a Hit—Charting "The Gypsy"

Date	Records Most Played on the Air Artist/Position	Most Played Jukebox Records Artist/Position	Best Selling Popular Retail Records Artist/Position
5/4/46	Shore/4	**Spots/15**	—
5/11/46	Shore/2	**Spots/7** Hildegarde/7 Shore/9 Kaye/10	**Spots/6** Shore/8
5/18/46	Shore/1 **Spots/8** Kaye/11 Hildegarde/13	**Spots/5** Shore/9 Hildegarde/11 Kaye/12	**Spots/2** Shore/8 Kaye/10
5/25/46	Shore/1 **Spots/2** Kaye/13	**Spots/2** Kaye/6 Shore/7 Hildegarde/8	**Spots/1** Shore/5 Kaye/7
6/1/46	Shore/2 **Spots/3** Kaye/6 Hildegarde/11 McIntyre/13	**Spots/1** Kaye/6 Hildegarde/8 Shore/9	**Spots/1** Shore/3 Kaye/8
6/8/46	Shore/1 **Spots/2** Kaye/4 Hildegarde/11	**Spots/1** Shore/4 Kaye/6 Hildegarde/8	**Spots/1** Shore/2 Kaye/6
6/15/46	Shore/1 **Spots/2** Kaye/5 McIntyre/13	**Spots/1** Kaye/4 Shore/5 Hildegarde/9	**Spots/1** Shore/2 Kaye/6

	Records Most Played on the Air	Most Played Jukebox Records	Best Selling Popular Retail Records
6/22/46	Shore/1 **Spots/1** (tie) Kaye/3 McIntyre/8	**Spots/1** Shore/3 Kaye/5 Hildegarde/10	**Spots/1** Shore/3 Kaye/4
6/29/46	Shore/1 **Spots/2** Kaye/9 McIntyre/12	**Spots/1** Shore/4 Kaye/5 Hildegarde/14	**Spots/1** Shore/3 Kaye/5
7/6/46	**Spots/1** Shore/2 Kaye/9 Hildegarde/15	**Spots/1** Kaye/3 Shore/4 Hildegarde/13	**Spots/1** Shore/2 Kaye/4
7/13/46	Shore/1 **Spots/3** Kaye/7	**Spots/1** Kaye/5 Shore/7 Hildegarde/14	**Spots/1** Shore/3 Kaye/4
7/20/46	Shore/3 **Spots/5** Kaye/13	**Spots/1** Shore/3 Kaye/7 Hildegarde/14	**Spots/1** Shore/5 Kaye/7
7/27/46	Shore/1 **Spots/6** Kaye/8	**Spots/1** Shore/5 Kaye/8 Hildegarde/11	**Spots/1** Shore/4
8/3/46	Shore/4 **Spots/6**	**Spots/1** Shore/7 Kaye/8 Hildegarde/15	**Spots/2** Shore/3

	Records Most Played on the Air	Most Played Jukebox Records	Best Selling Popular Retail Records
8/10/46	**Shore**/2 **Spots**/6	**Spots**/1 Shore/6 Kaye/7 Hildegarde/14	**Spots**/3 Shore/7
8/17/46	Shore/5 **Spots**/7	**Spots**/1 Shore/7 Kaye/12	**Spots**/4 Shore/10
8/24/46	**Spots**/3 Shore/4	**Spots**/1 Shore/10	**Spots**/5
8/31/46	**Spots**/10 Kaye/10	**Spots**/4 Shore/10 Kaye/13	**Spots**/8
9/7/46	—	**Spots**/4 Kaye/14 Shore/14	**Spots**/10
9/14/46	Shore/10	**Spots**/7 Shore/13	—
9/21/46	—	**Spots**/9	—
9/28/46	—	**Spots**/15 Shore/17	—
10/5/46	—	**Spots**/17	—

Bill, Herb, Charlie, Billy.

INK SPOTS

THE GYPSY

Vocal with Instrumental Accompaniment

EVERYONE IS SAYING HELLO AGAIN
(Why must we say goodbye?)

Vocal with Instrumental Accompaniment

DECCA RECORD
NO. 18817 . . 50¢

(Top) Billy, Cliff, Bernie; (bottom) Bill (an old photo from the prior year).

SONGS RECORDED

02/19/46	73387	The Gypsy
02/21/46	73390	Everyone Is Saying Hello Again
03/18/46	73448	Prisoner Of Love
	73449	I Never Had A Dream Come True
	73450	(master not by the Ink Spots)
	73451	(master not by the Ink Spots)
	73452	(master not by the Ink Spots)
	73453	I Cover The Waterfront
	73454	I Wasn't Made For Love
07/08/46	L 4225	I Get The Blues When It Rains
07/08/46	L 4226	To Each His Own
09/10/46	73677	Either It's Love Or It Isn't
11/07/46	73738	That's Where I Came In
	73739	When You Come To The End Of The Day
	73740	You Can't See The Sun When You're Crying
	73741	My Baby Didn't Even Say Goodbye

NOTE: Master numbers with an "L" prefix were recorded in Los Angeles.

RECORDS RELEASED

DECCA

18755	I'm Gonna Turn Off The Teardrops	10/02/45	73057	01/46
	The Sweetest Dream	10/03/45	73061	
18817	The Gypsy	02/19/46	73387	04/46
	Everyone Is Saying Hello Again	02/21/46	73390	
18864	Prisoner Of Love	03/18/46	73448	04/46
	I Cover The Waterfront	03/18/46	73453	
23615	To Each His Own	07/08/46	L 4226	08/46
	I Never Had A Dream Come True	03/18/46	73449	
23632	If I Didn't Care	01/12/39	64891	08/46
	Whispering Grass	06/11/40	67862	
23633	Do I Worry?	08/08/40	67970	08/46
	Java Jive	07/16/40	67931	
23634	We Three	07/16/40	67928	08/46
	Maybe	06/11/40	67863	
23635	I'll Never Smile Again	08/08/40	67968	08/46
	Until The Real Thing Comes Along	07/25/41	69566	

23695	I Get The Blues When It Rains	07/08/46	L 4225	10/46
	Either It's Love Or It Isn't	09/10/46	73677	
23757	Bless You (For Being An Angel)	10/11/39	66753	12/46
	Address Unknown	08/17/39	66120	

RECORD REVIEWS

I'M GONNA TURN OFF THE TEARDROPS/THE SWEETEST DREAM

The Ink Spots could just as well have failed to appear as scheduled at the Decca studios, as they did for their Army V-Disc dates. The slight semblance of jump on the first side is the only saving grace. (*Metronome*, 3/46)

THE GYPSY/EVERYONE IS SAYING HELLO AGAIN

Tune definitely looks like it is headed for the top, having been jumped onto the sheet music racks in the past weeks and the Ink Spots treatment of it adds up to the best etching the quartet has turned in, in a long time. Retailers, juke ops and disk jockeys can all go to town on this one, without taking any chances at all. Reverse is a nice job on cute twist ballad "Everyone Is Saying Hello Again (Why Must We Say Goodbye?)" (*Billboard*, 4/13/46)

PRISONER OF LOVE/I COVER THE WATERFRONT

Bill Kenny takes the lead on "Prisoner Of Love," the ballad enjoying a revival this season, and does well by it. He's in evidence again for "I Cover The Waterfront," the Johnny Greene oldie and makes it a good side. (*Billboard*, 6/1/46, page 31)

Formulas are a very fine thing, and if you have a successful one, it's probably best to stick to it—and how the Ink Spots glue on to theirs! Theirs discs are practically a series of recitations set to music. (*Down Beat*, 6/3/46)

TO EACH HIS OWN/I NEVER HAD A DREAM COME TRUE

Already the top tune of the day, the Ink Spots, with Billy Kenny for the solo singing, wrap it up handily for "To Each His Own." Lending itself to the Ink Spot treatment, it's tailor made plattering. Also designed for their dittying is Allan Roberts' and Doris Fisher's "I Never Had A Dream Come True" from the movie "Talk About A Lady." Kenny kicks it off in the slow ballad tempo, and the other lads pick it up for the second stanza in contrasting rhythm style, with the spinning selling strong all the way. (*Billboard*, 8/31/46)

PERFORMANCE REVIEWS

Million Dollar (Los Angeles)

In the last slot, Ink Spots provide ample proof that they're still straddling the top rung on the voice-blender ladder with their sugary singing of *I'll Climb The Highest Mountain, The Gypsy* (their most recent disk hit), *I Don't Care Who Knows It* (a rhythm ditty) and *If I Didn't Care*. Foursome's easy stage manner plus sock song stylings had customers clamoring for more. (*Billboard*, 6/22/46)

Oriental (Chicago)

Ink Spots illustrated during their 51 minutes' worth that altho they are much imitated, they are still in a class all their own. First four offerings consisted of *I'd Climb The Highest Mountain, Gypsy, Prisoner Of Love*, and *If I Didn't Care*. After each they drew a solid mitt [round of applause]. All they had to do was sing the songs the aisle sitters identified them with. (*Billboard*, 9/14/46)

Zanzibar (New York)

The Ink Spots, still tops, don't have to do much selling. They're sold before they reach the mike, with mention of their name bringing a roar of applause. Quartet offers a nice mixture of new pops and oldies, opening with *The Gypsy*, followed by *I Never Had A Dream Come True* and ending with *Prisoner Of Love*. Trio of ditties brought several must recalls—*To Each His Own* and the inevitable *If I Didn't Care*—which stopped the show cold. (*Billboard*, 10/5/46)

Once again, Decca used an old photo with Bernie and Cliff.

1947

Civil war in Greece. India and Pakistan become independent. Goodrich Tire Company produces the first tubeless tires. Chuck Yeager flies faster than the speed of sound. Jackie Robinson becomes the first black major league ball player in the 20th century (we mustn't forget Moses Fleetwood Walker, who played for the Toledo Blue Stockings in 1884, a major league team back then).

The competition: Chi-Baba Chi-Baba, Heartaches, How Are Things In Glocca Morra, Linda, Mam'selle, Managua Nicaragua, Miserlou, Open The Door Richard, Papa Won't You Dance With Me, Peg O' My Heart, Smoke Smoke Smoke That Cigarette, Tenderly, Too Fat Polka, Zip A Dee Doo Dah.

By 1947 the Ink Spots' recordings were still selling, but their sound had become a formula: an overly slick, bland formula, having too much of everything except spontaneity.

The same thing had brought down the creativity level of such big bands as the Dorsey Brothers' and Glenn Miller's: instead of rebelling against the music establishment, as they had done while they were "swing" artists in the '30s, they had *become* the music establishment of the early postwar years. Some artists, such as Benny Goodman, could see the stagnation setting in,

The Ink Spots "sailing" off to England in September 1947 (a posed picture—they actually ended up flying): Billy, Herb, Charlie, Bill, road manager Murray Nadel.

and returned to their jazz roots, where innovation was not stifled. The Ink Spots, on the other hand, dug themselves in deeper.

However, though the spontaneity was gone, they were still capable of turning out beautiful music; among their better tunes from the postwar era were "White Christmas" and "When You Come To The End Of The Day."

Although the group was still turning out a prodigious number of recordings, Decca was releasing almost as many old Ink Spots masters as newly recorded songs. In 1946, for instance, "Bless You (For Being An Angel)" was re-released in England, and became a huge British hit; it was a 1939 master.

On the strength of "Bless You," an engagement at London's Casino Theatre was arranged; it was to earn them $15,000 a week.[1] The engagement began on September 1, 1947, and they almost didn't make it. The Spots were booked on the steamship *America* (set to sail August 20), but there was a strike that caused the voyage to be canceled. Then they booked the *Queen Mary*,[2] but discovered at the last minute that it wouldn't get them there on time (although they did a photo session aboard the ship). They finally lucked out by getting a flight on American Overseas Airlines on August 29.

"Bless You" was so popular, that the group was mobbed by their British fans. This was the report of the opening night at the London Casino:

> Hours before the first show all the surrounding streets were thronged with people and it was virtually impossible for cars to get anywhere near the theater. Those who couldn't gain admission waited patiently hoping to getting [sic] a glimpse of the famous singing quartet as they left. Inside the theater they were given what must have been their biggest ovation ever. They were the last turn on an all star bill of vaudeville and if the audience had had their way, the Ink Spots would still be singing encores.[3]

Their reception was so startling that British show business promoters started clamoring for more American acts:

> ... representative names of the entertainment world here are preparing a memorandum to be submitted to the treasury [which made a mint off the tour] and the musicians' union, urging that everything be done to encourage future visits of U.S. orks

and acts to London. Showbiz reps feel that using Yank acts is the only way to attract the public to theaters.[4]

While there, however, they got into a disagreement with their London promoter, Bernard Delfont, who expected them to add additional performances with no additional remuneration. In addition, the extra performances would have resulted in four shows in three and one-half hours!

However, they resolved their differences with Delfont, and ended up with more performances and more money. Here's the extra money:

> After the storm which blew up in the third week of the Ink Spots' stay at the Casino—over doubling dates at suburban houses for which they had originally been booked—has been pacified, the boys have now made it up with Bernard Delfont of the Casino, who is retaining them for a further fortnight at $2000 a week.[5]

(Presumably they meant an *extra* $2000 a week, since the original booking was supposed to have been for $15,000 a week.) And here are the extra performances:

> Meanwhile, Leslie Posher . . . was able to get the act on three successive Sundays (when Casino is closed) at the mammoth Trocadero, Gaumont-Empire and Gaumont-Hammersmith movie houses. The appearance at the Empire tomorrow [10/12/47] will be the farewell appearance by the Ink Spots to the British public. . . . Setting a new precedent, the Ink Spots also agreed to appear Sunday afternoon and evening at the Lyceum Dance Palais.[6]

When they returned to the United States, they left Universal Attractions and re-signed with the Gale Agency. (This had the effect of breaking up the partnership between Ben Bart and Harry Lenetzka, with Bart keeping the Universal Attractions name and Lenetzka going on to manage Mahalia Jackson.) One speculation was that the switch was due to the problems in England (however, the same source claimed that the English tour had been canceled partway through).[7]

Strangely, with the tremendous success of "The Gypsy" in the prior year (and its more modest follow-up "To Each His Own"), and their current London smash, *Billboard* didn't review two Decca releases in a row. Neither "Always"/"White Christmas" nor "Just For Me"/"Just Plain Love" was written up. Could this be due to them not having had a real hit all year (a case of "what have you done lately")?

When they switched back to Gale, Bill Kenny assumed complete financial control of the unit (i.e., the Ink Spots and all the acts that appeared with them on a tour, such as Peg Leg Bates and Lena Horne). Everyone was paid fairly, but, because Gale's accountant was no longer involved, no one remembered that Bill was responsible for employer's taxes too. Well, it isn't quite true that *no one* remembered—the IRS did. Bill ended up owing Uncle Sam about $98,000 in unremitted taxes and penalties for 1947 to 1949.[8]

Just to keep the record industry from growing complacent, James C. Petrillo and his AFM decided on another strike, this one to take place January 1, 1948. Once again, manufacturers rushed everyone into the studio in order to stockpile masters (the Ink Spots had five sessions between late November and late December; they wouldn't record again for almost a year). Aside from just plain stockpiling, the manufacturers figured that whatever was recorded *now* would naturally cost less (in terms of musicians' fees) than whatever would be recorded *later*. Another wrinkle was that this time Petrillo threatened to cut off live music on the radio (beginning in February 1948). No one exactly knew what he hoped to gain by this, for it would mean that only records could be played, and Petrillo was known to be against the broadcast of "canned music." It was also feared, by those in the know, that if live music ceased, disk jockeys would gain tremendous power and become a driving force in radio. (Nah, that could never happen!)

There was speculation that it wouldn't be so easy for Petrillo this time around. After the war, there had been a proliferation of independent record manufacturers (the "indies"), which would make it much harder to police recording activities; it was suspected that bootlegging would be unstoppable. (Remember that "bootlegging" here means using union musicians without credit or under pseudonyms.) Add to this the lessened postwar popularity of bands; the new Taft-Hartley law, prohibiting secondary boycotts (i.e., sympathy strikes by other unions); and Petrillo's absence of friends in congress. Finally, in 1942 there had been a war, preventing manufacturers from importing masters from other countries. This time they could! The industry adopted a wait-and-see attitude.

"But wait!" you cry. So there's going to be an AFM strike; at least this time there isn't a shellac shortage, too. Oh yes there is! There were sharp drops in imports (773,928 pounds in September, compared with 4,290,569 in January) which were blamed on the unsettled political climate in India.[9] No one ever said the recording business was easy.

The Ink Spots' distinctive style invited imitation, and over the years many acts tried to either legitimately duplicate it or parody it. One such act was the almost unbelievable "Ming and Ling, Chinese Hillbillies" (I swear, I'm not making this up).

> Ming, the vocalist, takes off on hillbilly tunes, Scotch airs, then does a series of sock carbons [imitations] on Frank Sinatra, Crosby and the Ink Spots. Encore is an unusual item with a rendition of the Yiddish song "Eli, Eli," then with another reprise take-off on Al Jolson singing "April Showers."[10]

AFM President James C. Petrillo.

The wives sing, the husbands critique (1947): Ruthie Bowen, Hattie Fuqua, Gloria (Mrs. Herb) Kenny, Marghurite (Mrs. Bill) Kenny, Bill, Charlie, Herb, Billy. (Courtesy of Herb Kenny.)

What's more germane, the Ink Spots, proud champions of the 1946 honor roll of hitmakers, were *completely absent* from the 1947 tally;[11] remember, they hadn't had any substantial hits in 1947. *Sic transit gloria mundi* (Latin for "here today, gone tomorrow").

Billy, Cliff, Bernie, and Bill (bottom), with Ella Fitzgerald superimposed.

SONGS RECORDED

02/27/47	73802	I Want To Thank Your Folks
	73803	Can You Look Me In The Eyes
	73804	Information Please
	73805	White Christmas
	73806	Ask Anyone Who Knows
	73807	Always
03/05/47	73814	Do You Feel That Way, Too?
07/16/47	L 4469	Just Plain Love
08/18/47	74066	Home Is Where The Heart Is
	74067	Aladdin's Lamp
	74068	Sincerely Yours
11/21/47	74150	It's All Over But The Crying
	74151	I'll Make Up For Everything
	74152	Sorry You Said Goodbye (U)
11/24/47	74157	I Woke Up With A Teardrop In My Eye
	74158	Wanting You (U)
	74159	If You Had To Hurt Someone
12/22/47	74385	Where Flamingoes Fly
12/23/47	74394	Just For Now
	74395	A Knock On The Door
	74396	The Best Things In Life Are Free
	74397	Don't Be Sorry (U)
12/29/47	74454	To Remind Me Of You

NOTE: (U) indicates an unreleased song. Master numbers with an "L" prefix were recorded in Los Angeles.

RECORDS RELEASED

DECCA

23809	That's Where I Came In	11/07/46	73738	01/47
	You Can't See The Sun When You're Crying	11/07/46	73740	
25047	Cow-Cow Boogie (EF)	11/03/43	71482	01/47
	That's The Way It Is (EF)	02/26/45	72747	
23851	I Want To Thank Your Folks	02/27/47	73802	04/47
	I Wasn't Made For Love	03/18/46	73454	
23900	Ask Anyone Who Knows	02/27/47	73806	06/47
	Can You Look Me In The Eyes	02/27/47	73803	

23936	Everyone Is Saying Hello Again	02/21/46	73390	06/47
	The Gypsy	02/19/46	73387	
24111	Information Please	02/27/47	73804	08/47
	Do You Feel That Way, Too?	03/05/47	73814	
24140	Always	02/27/47	73807	09/47
	White Christmas	02/27/47	73805	
24173	Just For Me	10/03/45	73063	09/47
	Just Plain Love	07/16/47	L 4469	
25237	We'll Meet Again	02/04/41	68656	09/47
	My Greatest Mistake	08/20/40	67990	
25238	I'll Get By	12/22/43	71610	09/47
	Just For A Thrill	01/12/39	64892	
25239	I'd Climb The Highest Mountain	12/30/40	68540	09/47
	I'm Getting Sentimental Over You	10/11/39	66752	
25240	Coquette	08/17/39	66121	09/47
	When The Swallows Come Back			
	To Capistrano	05/13/40	67718	
24192	Home Is Where The Heart Is	08/18/47	74066	10/47
	Sincerely Yours	08/18/47	74068	
24261	I'll Lose A Friend Tomorrow	10/02/45	73058	11/47
	When You Come To The End Of			
	The Day	11/07/46	73739	

NOTE: (EF) indicates Ella Fitzgerald and the Ink Spots.

AFRS

P-685	Either It's Love Or It Isn't	ca. 47
	I Get The Blues When It Rains	
	(The Pencil Broke—Lionel Hampton)	
	(Tempo's Birthday—Lionel Hampton)	
P-686	(All sides by Freddy Martin and his Orchestra)	
P-742	That's Where I Came In	ca. 47
	You Can't See The Sun When You're Crying	
	That's The Way It Is (with Ella Fitzgerald)	
	(I Like 'Em Fat Like That—Louis Jordan)	
P-741	(Sides by Erskine Hawkins, Aristo Kats, and Louis Armstrong)	

Armed Forces Radio Service pressings (this series had a different record number on each side).

RECORD REVIEWS

COW-COW BOOGIE/THAT'S THE WAY IT IS

This was reissued in March and the review ended with: "Hardly any reason for this revival." (*Billboard*, 3/8/47)

I WANT TO THANK YOUR FOLKS/I WASN'T MADE FOR LOVE

It's the usual Ink Spots pattern for both of these slow ballads, with Bill Kenny's soulful singing for the song selling taking time out only for the deep-voiced talking patter. And in their way make it a winner for both *Thank Your Folks* and for the torchy *I Wasn't Made For Love*. [Sometimes these reviews are barely in English.] (*Billboard*, 4/19/47)

ASK ANYONE WHO KNOWS/CAN YOU LOOK ME IN THE EYES

It's the pat pattern and wearing thin on wax, that has Bill Kenny carrying the chant for both of these slow ballads. It's the talking interlude sandwiched in for "Ask Anyone Who Knows," while the tempo is picked up for solo rather than harmony singing that spaces Kenny's slow and soulful singing for the more tuneful "Can You Look Me In The Eyes?." Accompanying piano and guitar rhythms as thin as the singing. (*Billboard*, 5/24/47)

THAT'S WHERE I CAME IN/
YOU CAN'T SEE THE SUN WHEN YOU'RE CRYING

There's no deviation from the Ink Spots norm in this needling ["needling" is a record]. The lads judiciously stick to their own winning pattern of BILL KENNY's solo and soulful singing, banked by the sustained hums of the other Spots, and interspersed with the ubiquitous lyrical recitation. The familiar pattern lends itself to all the sentimental wordage contained in these two waxings, save for the "Bless You" side [this review also covered a re-release of "Bless You" backed with "Address Unknown"], where the speed-up tempo has Kenny losing much of his expressive qualities. (*Billboard*, 6/7/47)

DO YOU FEEL THAT WAY, TOO?/INFORMATION PLEASE

It's the familiar Ink Spots pattern for these sides with Bill Kenny carrying it entirely for the slow "Feel That Way" ballad and a welcome contrast in giving a bit of harmony treatment as they sing the familiar "Information Please" at a brighter tempo. Only for the Ink Spots fans, who will side with Bill Kenny's solo singing. (*Billboard*, 9/6/47)

HOME IS WHERE THE HEART IS/SINCERELY YOURS
The familiar Ink Spots pattern, never deviating from Bill Kenny's lyrical singing in a solo frame spaced by the song recitation, carries both of these two ballads. Spin to best advantage for the more attractive *Sincerely Yours*, taken at a moderate tempo, with slow and tender treatment for the earthy *Home Is Where The Heart Is*. (*Billboard*, 11/15/47)

NOTE: From here on, *Billboard* changed its review procedures. Each side was given a one- or two-sentence review, along with a numerical rating (actually, there were several ratings and an overall one—that's the one given here). The only exception to the short rating is if the record was one of the "picks" of the week.

WHEN YOU COME TO THE END OF THE DAY
Strictly an item for the Ink Spots fans. Oldie may get juke play. (81)
I'LL LOSE A FRIEND TOMORROW
Not up to Ink Spots standards. Material poor. (69) (*Billboard*, 12/20/47)

[Note that *Billboard* can't make up it's mind here. One side is downgraded for not being up to their standards; the other side is criticized for being just that.]

PERFORMANCE REVIEWS

Paramount (New York)
Ink Spots did their usual job. Kenny, however, has cut down his finger waving, tho he's still in there mugging. Numbers included recent recordings, ending with *To Each His Own*. Kenny winds up with a new finish, saying "God bless you, and God bless America." Apparently, he figures that one of the statements is good for an extra mitt. It wasn't when caught [i.e., Bill expected an extra round of applause, but, when the reviewer saw the show, he didn't get it]. (*Billboard*, 2/15/47)

Oriental (Chicago)
The Ink Spots haven't changed their style one bit and evidently shouldn't, judging from the huge mitts given their oldies and more current Decca releases. Kenny's soaring tenor holds the spot and the spot is well deserved. Even after a quartet of ditties, the boys were forced to do two encores. (*Billboard*, 5/24/47)

1948

Berlin blockade and airlift. Organization of American States formed. Korea divided into North and South. Burma gets independence. State of Israel created. Marshall Plan passes. Kinsey Report published. Columbia Records introduces the 33 ⅓ long-playing album. Ghandi assassinated. Supreme Court abolishes religion in public schools. The Chicago Tribune *elects Thomas Dewey president of the United States; the rest of the country elects Harry S Truman.*

The competition: Ballerina, Buttons And Bows, Civilization (Bongo Bongo Bongo I Don't Want To Leave The Congo), Far Away Places, I'm Looking Over A Four-Leaf Clover, Manana, Nature Boy, Near You, On A Slow Boat To China, A Tree In The Meadow, Woody Woodpecker, You Call Everybody Darlin', You Were Only Fooling.

And so there was a strike. This time Petrillo wanted a union welfare (unemployment) fund, which was specifically prohibited by the new Taft-Hartley Act. Since this couldn't be legally done, he pulled out the musicians in the hopes that some middle ground could be found.

However, the record companies were ready. They had stockpiled as before, but now they used extensive *a cappella* (no instrumentation) sessions (the Ink Spots would use a choir behind them in October), nonunion artists, union artists under assumed names, and recording in foreign studios (England and Mexico were favorites). At least in the early stages of the ban, these methods were blatantly carried out (a headline ran: "NEW RECORDING GOES ON—By-Passing of Petrillo Ban Shaping Up").[1]

Petrillo did concede that under the Taft-Hartley Act, his work stoppage left the record companies free to record with nonunion musicians.

One unusual appearance the Ink Spots made in 1948 was in a union picture:

> Officials of the United Auto Workers were in conference with Bill Kenny and his Ink Spots here [Detroit] last week. They sought the services of the famed quartette in the making of a projected film telling the story of a modern labor organization.[2]

Billy, Bill, Herb, and Charlie.

Although the Ink Spots had all but vanished from the charts in 1947, *Billboard*'s tenth annual College Poll still found them the third most popular group on campus (behind the King Cole Trio and the Pied Pipers).[3]

Lest we forget that the Ink Spots started on radio, they were still at it in 1948, playing the *Jack Benny Show* on April 4. Benny asks them "Do you happen to know 'If I Didn't Care'?" to which Herb replies in a gravel voice, "Do you know 'Love In Bloom'?" (Benny's theme song). They launch into "If I Didn't Care," starting it from the last stanza, and then go into Herb's talking bass, which turns into a Lucky Strike commercial: "But I *do* care, honey chile, that's why I smoke Lucky Strike." The group comes off the bridge by harmonizing the five syllables of Lucky's catchphrase "L-S-M-F-T" in place of the words "If I Didn't Care," and the audience loved it.

Finally, in May, Petrillo decided to crack down on *a cappella* waxings by banning AFM members from doing any arranging or conducting for the record companies. Since many singers held AFM union cards (some were musicians also and some were honorary members), Petrillo went after them too. This was beginning to signal desperation on his part. Some companies had been using English studios to do their recordings; in August the BMU (British Musicians Union) banned any local recording of American artists.

The really big news in May was the announcement, by Columbia, of the long playing record (LP), with a speed of 33⅓ rpm; the product was being readied for a September release. This wasn't really a new speed, Victor having dabbled with it in the early '30s, but now Columbia would produce 12-inch vinylite records with fifteen or so minutes of superior-sound music on each side. It would take the 78 nearly ten more years to die, but this (and the introduction of the 45 in 1949) signaled its demise.

Television was also becoming serious business in 1948 (*Billboard* had had a column on it going back to at least 1934; color television had been demonstrated in 1946), and Bill Kenny began dabbling in it. It was reported that he was going to put together a series of fifteen-minute Ink Spots shows, with the group singing its big hits against a backdrop of newsreels depicting the main events occurring when the songs became hits.[4] Nothing ever came of this unusual idea, but it was interesting enough so that this book is laid out in a similar fashion (although you'll have to imagine the "Movietone News" being shown in the background).

With few new recordings to offer, in August Decca re-released all the "Ella and the Ink Spots" recordings as a 78 album.

Petrillo's attempt to head off *a cappella* recordings was a dismal failure. In October it was reported that

> Decca Records this week continued to cut new wax in a cappella fashion, mainly to keep up with the blossoming hits. The diskery held at least three waxing sessions within the past 10 days. . . . Other dates had the Ink Spots turning out *Say Something Sweet To Your Sweetheart* and *You Were Only Fooling*, with assistance from a nine-voice mixed chorus. . . .[5]

Moe Gale was having his own labor problems: the Gale Agency was a partnership between Moe, his brother Tim, and Billy Shaw. Now, Shaw wanted to leave. Moe and Tim bought him out in November, and he immediately set up the competing and, ultimately, quite successful Shaw Agency. By late 1951 he would be handling a diverse clientele which included, among others, George Shearing, the Orioles, Amos Milburn, Tiny Grimes, Hot Lips Page, Sidney Bechet, the Clovers, Al Hibbler, Buddy Rich, Charlie Parker, and the 5 Keys.

The Ink Spots, meanwhile, broke into the charts with "You Were Only Fooling," which made it to Number 18 on December 4. Their days of Number 1 hits had ended in 1946 with "To Each His Own;" soon their days of Top Ten hits would vanish too.

With the announcement that a trustee had been appointed to oversee the royalties paid into a musicians' welfare fund, the end of the AFM ban was announced on December 14. When Decca President Jack Kapp was cornered in a restaurant that day and asked why he was there instead of cutting records, his reply was: "What for? There's nothing we particularly want to record."[6]

In December 1948, putting white audience acceptance of the group to the test, the Ink Spots became the first black act to play the posh Monte Carlo in Miami Beach. In spite of great trepidation, they received a fifteen-minute ovation.[7] It was subsequently reported that "cops assigned to the Ink Spots opening had nothing to do."[8]

SONGS RECORDED

09/14/48	74598	Say Something Sweet To Your Sweetheart
	74599	You Were Only Fooling
10/19/48	74608	Am I Asking Too Much
	74609	Recess In Heaven

RECORDS RELEASED

DECCA

24286	I'll Make Up For Everything	11/21/47	74151	01/48
	It's All Over But The Crying	11/21/47	74150	
24327	The Best Things In Life Are Free	12/23/47	74396	02/48
	I Woke Up With A Teardrop In My Eye	11/24/47	74157	
25344	I'm Gonna Turn Off The Teardrops	10/02/45	73057	02/48
	I'm Beginning To See The Light (EF)	02/26/45	72746	
25378	Don't Leave Now	08/21/41	69671	05/48
	Ring, Telephone, Ring	12/23/40	68533	
24461	Just For Now	12/23/47	74394	07/48
	Where Flamingoes Fly	12/22/47	74385	
18587	Cow-Cow Boogie (EF)	11/03/43	71482	08/48
	When My Sugar Walks Down The Street (Ella, no group)		DLA2609A	
23356	I'm Making Believe (EF)	08/30/44	72371	08/48
	Into Each Life Some Rain Must Fall (EF)	08/30/44	72370	
23399	I'm Beginning To See The Light (EF)	02/26/45	72746	08/48
	That's The Way It Is (EF)	02/26/45	72747	
24496	Aladdin's Lamp	08/18/47	74067	09/48
	My Baby Didn't Even Say Goodbye	11/07/46	73741	
24507	Say Something Sweet To Your Sweetheart	09/14/48	74598	10/48
	You Were Only Fooling	09/14/48	74599	
24517	Am I Asking Too Much	10/19/48	74608	11/48
	Recess In Heaven	10/19/48	74609	

NOTE: (EF) indicates Ella Fitzgerald and the Ink Spots.

AFRS

P-956   I'll Lose A Friend Tomorrow   ca. 48

        I'll Make Up For Everything

        It's All Over But The Crying

        When You Come To The End Of The Day

P-955   (All sides by Louis Jordan and his Orchestra)

Armed Forces Radio Service pressings (this series had a different record number on each side).

Billy, Bill, Herb, and Charlie.

RECORD REVIEWS

I'LL MAKE UP FOR EVERYTHING
> The old inflexible Ink Spots style. Will attract their fans but few added starters. (77)

IT'S ALL OVER BUT THE CRYING
> Good tear jerker. Up-tempo second chorus gives disk needed lift. (81) (*Billboard*, 1/24/48)

THE BEST THINGS IN LIFE ARE FREE
> Typical Ink Spots treatment. 'Nuff said. (76)

I WOKE UP WITH A TEARDROP IN MY EYE
> Mood music for a crying jag. Ideal Billy Kenny material. (82) (*Billboard*, 1/31/48)

SAY SOMETHING SWEET TO YOUR SWEETHEART
> Strong production job by Spots and nine-voice choir on the soft-shoe vaude throwback should have top impact. (90)

YOU WERE ONLY FOOLING (WHILE I WAS FALLING IN LOVE)
> Same treatment of tune the Blue Barron platter has skyrocketed, figures to make platter a two-sided sock. (81) (*Billboard*, 10/9/48)

RECESS IN HEAVEN/AM I ASKING TOO MUCH
> . . . Ink Spots remain in top form with the simple and fairly attractive tune (also recently etched for Victor by the Deep River Boys) which should follow the group's fast-moving "Say Something Sweet To Your Sweetheart" etching. Quartet is aided and abetted by additional voices, with Billy Kenny's syrupy tenor showing the way. Reverse is "Am I Asking Too Much," a tune which is currently riding high in the race lists via a Dinah Washington waxing on Mercury. Disking could firmly re-establish the Spots, who had been slipping of late in wax stakes. (*Billboard*, 10/30/48)

PERFORMANCE REVIEWS

Vogue Room (Hotel Hollenden, Cleveland)

Their novelty numbers went biggest with the capacity crowd. One was *If You Have To Hurt Someone, Why Does It Have To Be Me?*, and they attribute the authorship to fighters Joe Louis and Jersey Joe Walcott. The other humdinger is *Your Feet Too Big* [sic]. The latter, reminiscent of *Dry Bones*, builds better and hotter than the one emulated. For contrast the quartet gives out with *The Best Things In Life Are Free* and *I Woke Up With A Teardrop In My Eye*. On the beam with both hot and sweet, they never miss a chance to plug their disks, which got a bit tiresome after awhile. Also they overdid the dedications for a first night, referring constantly to the "big bosses of the hotel who are in the audience." (*Billboard*, 8/14/48)

Chicago (Chicago)

Bill Kenny and the Ink Spots have finally replaced the comedy of Deke [sic] Watson with the capers of Butterball [Billy Bowen], the hefty baritone who is now doing the little asides. The comedy spices the stellar tenoring of Kenny and the blend of the Decca foursome. They walked off to a tumultuous hand after six numbers. (*Billboard*, 11/13/48)

1949

NATO formed. Communists under Mao Tse-Tung take over China. "Tokyo Rose" tried and sentenced to ten years imprisonment. Bikini bathing suits appear. Joseph McCarthy had "a list." RCA-Victor starts releasing 45 rpm records.

The competition: "A" You're Adorable, Again, Baby It's Cold Outside, Chattanoogie Shoe Shine Boy, Cry Of The Wild Goose, Far Away Places, I've Got My Love To Keep Me Warm, Mule Train, Once In Love With Amy, Peter Cottontail, Red Roses For A Blue Lady, Riders In The Sky, Some Enchanted Evening, That Lucky Old Sun, You're Breaking My Heart.

We've had the ASCAP/BMI War, the Petrillo Ban, the Shellac Shortage, the Kraft Paper Shortage, the Other Petrillo Ban, and now, because it seems that the recording industry can only thrive on chaos, we have the great War of the Record Speeds. It went something like this:

1. In May 1948, Columbia announces the 33⅓ rpm record. The next month it's demonstrated; the process will be made available to anyone who wants it. In July the first "LPs" (long-playing records), made of vinyl, start to ship.

2. RCA parries with the 45 rpm record (announced in December 1948). They had actually produced 33⅓s themselves back in the early '30s, but abandoned them at that time. The new disks were due to ship in the spring of 1949. Just for a different touch, each series would be pressed using a different color vinyl.

3. Columbia ripostes (January 1949) with the 7-inch 33⅓ rpm microgroove record (which just happened to match the size of the 45).

4. Decca, mercifully not coming up with its own speed, announces in February that they have a vinyl 10-inch 78 capable of playing five minutes of music per side. Selling for $1 each, the first release was Ray Bolger's "Once In Love With Amy."

5. Fearing that the 78 is going to go the way of the dodo, and not wanting to be stuck with a lot of excess stock on hand, dealers begin cutting prices on their 78 rpm stock in March.

6. That same month, Tempo Records of Hollywood becomes the first company to announce that it will issue records in all three speeds. The first major to do so would be Capitol, in July.

7. Decca reduces its prices on 78s and begins a 45 rpm campaign (July). The next month they'll also announce 33⅓ rpm disks.

8. Victor, Columbia, and Decca executives hold a meeting in July to determine what could be done about the various speeds. The talks break off almost immediately.

9. Victor says (August) it will only push 45s and 78s. Columbia says it will make records in any speed that the public wants (so far, strangely enough, they've only been asked for 78s and 33⅓s).

10. In September, Seeburg announces that it's bringing out a line of juke boxes that will take 45s.

11. Victor announces in February 1950 that it will soon produce 33⅓ LPs.

Still, after all the plans and schemes of the recording industry, 78s remained standard production items (by the "indies") until around 1957. The majors, however, stopped shipping 78s to DJs in July 1954.

In late March, Decca President Jack Kapp died suddenly at age 47, from a cerebral hemorrhage. Just weeks before his death, Kapp had been the subject of an article in *Life*, and had also been praised on the floor of congress as representing the rags-to-riches American dream. Probably as a result of his death, British and American Decca drew up some contracts to go their separate ways (in June). Kapp's brother, Dave, remained at Decca as Vice President of Artists and Repertoire; another brother, Paul, would end up managing many acts well into the '50s.

In June, *Billboard* came out with its annual College Music Poll. In the "Groups" category, the Ink Spots placed fourth, behind the Pied Pipers, the King Cole Trio, and the Mills Brothers; the Ravens placed fifth.

A *Cleveland Call And Post* headline shouted: "Ink Spots Make Secret Waxings."

> Before anyone knew what they were up to, the Ink Spots planed from Pittsburgh to New York and back again secretly recording two new tunes for Decca Records. The super-secret mission took place last weekend at the Decca Studios on 57th Street in New York City and was held at night so that not even members of the Decca staff knew what songs the famed quartet were waxing.[1]

Presumably this was the June 27 session (which was a Monday, not a weekend). With all the secrecy, the *five* tunes recorded produced a single hit, "You're Breaking My Heart," which only rose to Number 9. The reason for the secrecy? This was the first time that Decca had recorded the Ink Spots with a full orchestra (although they were usually backed by one at live appearances). Actually, "You're Breaking My Heart" was memorable in another respect: it was the end of the chart-topping road for the Ink Spots; they would never again have a Top Ten hit.

An interesting aspect of Ink Spots' life was detailed in an article about Billy Bowen's wife, Ruthie:

> The Ink Spots travel by automobile. Each one of them owns his own car and either he or his wife drives from one engagement to another. There is also a truck which carries the uniforms and baggage and the car of manager Murray Mandel [should be Nadel] completing the caravan.
>
> . . . The quartet and the manager usually start out in a convoy together, but, according to Ruthie, there are some members of the quartet "who just can't drive under 70" and the group usually gets split up, meeting at a pre-arranged spot in the town to be played.[2]

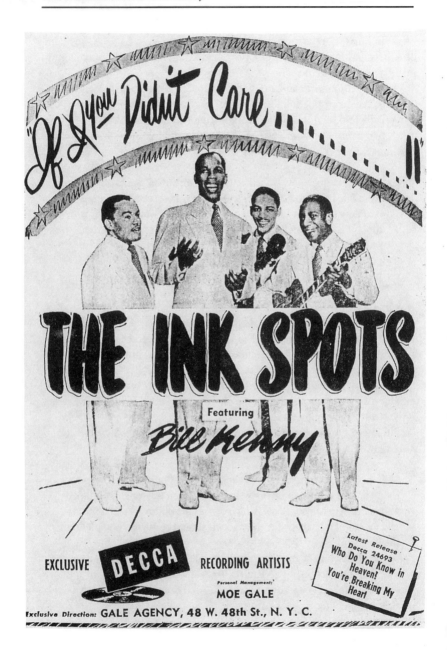

The same article went on to talk about the Ink Spots' upcoming four-month tour of England, which would start in August 1949:

> Among those who will make the trip are Bill Kenny, the top vocalist, Mrs. Kenny, his newlywed French Canadian wife [Audrey], Ruth and Billy [Bowen], Bill's brother Herb Kenny and his wife, Gloria of Philadelphia, and Charles Fuqua and his wife, Hattie of Buffalo.[3]

The Spots did jolly well on their London tour:

> ... the singers are the sensation of London with their performance at the Palladium. Tickets for their shows are as difficult to obtain in London as are tickets for "South Pacific" in New York. Despite the efforts of the management, speculators are selling tickets for double or more. American bookers continue to invest money in transatlantic calls to the Ink Spots to get in line for 1950 bookings.[4]

One who called was Milton Berle:

> While a host of television producers tear at their already thinning hair, Milton Berle, fast-thinking video headliner, this week grabbed the services of the Ink Spots, who are currently clicking in England, for an appearance on his program the day after they arrive in the United States on December 13 [they actually seem to have flown back on November 28]. The famed comic anticipated the flood of offers which the quartet have received through their New York office and cabled them direct in London inviting them to make their "Welcome Home" debut on his TV show.[5]

While reviewers in 1934 noted the dance portion of the Ink Spots' act, we don't usually think of the Spots as doing anything but singing. However, photos show Bill and Deek (later Herb) doing jitterbug routines; reviews state that it was a popular part of their act.

In *Billboard*'s 1949 DJ poll, the Ink Spots placed a dismal #6 (although the Andrews Sisters had plummeted to #8). The front-runners were the Pied

Pipers, the Starlighters, the King Cole Trio, the Mills Brothers, and the Modernaires.[6]

While the Spots were abroad, an article reported Herb leaving the group:

> Herb Kenny, brother of Bill Kenny and singing member of the Ink Spots, will leave the act in November to go under the banner of Jolly Joyce, local booking agency.
>
> Currently in England with the singing combo, Herb, it is understood, has signed a three-year contract with Joyce, who plans to build a small musical unit around the singer.[7]

Stay tuned to 1950, and we'll see what this is all about.

SONGS RECORDED

01/19/49	74697	No Orchids For My Lady
	74698	As You Desire Me
	74699	Bewildered
02/07/49	74747	It Only Happens Once
	74748	A Kiss And A Rose
06/27/49	75026	Land Of Love
	75027	Who Do You Know In Heaven
	75028	You're Breaking My Heart
	75029	Echoes

RECORDS RELEASED

DECCA

24566	Bewildered	01/19/49	74699	02/49
	No Orchids For My Lady	01/19/49	74697	
24585	It Only Happens Once	02/07/49	74747	03/49
	As You Desire Me	01/19/49	74698	
24611	A Kiss And A Rose	02/07/49	74748	04/49
	A Knock On The Door	12/23/47	74395	
25431	I Don't Want To Set The World On Fire	08/21/41	69660	06/49
	Someone's Rocking My Dream Boat	10/13/41	69807	
24672	If You Had To Hurt Someone	11/24/47	74159	07/49
	To Remind Me Of You	12/29/47	74454	
24693	You're Breaking My Heart	06/27/49	75028	08/49
	Who Do You Know In Heaven	06/27/49	75027	
24741	Echoes	06/27/49	75029	09/49
	Land Of Love	06/27/49	75026	

(Ca. 1949) Billy Bowen, Harold Francis, Bill Kenny, Herb Kenny, Charlie Fuqua. (Courtesy of Herb Kenny.)

RECORD REVIEWS

BEWILDERED
> Spots are in the groove for this one. Release would be late for most other performers [i.e., since multiple versions of the song had existed for a while, most other performers would hesitate to put out a version this late] but group has faculty of scoring with already established material. (84)

NO ORCHIDS FOR MY LADY
> Boys put out, but don't convince with this type of material. (74) (*Billboard*, 2/26/49)

AS YOU DESIRE ME
> Billy Kenny sings all the way with this revival. He gets a little too dramatic at times. (74)

IT ONLY HAPPENS ONCE
> The Spots turn in an airy and light job on the Frankie Laine ballad. (82) (*Billboard*, 4/9/49)

YOU'RE BREAKING MY HEART/WHO DO YOU KNOW IN HEAVEN
> The Spots may return to disk prominence with this pairing of a couple of fast-moving ballads. The difference here is the addition of a string ork for backing for the quartet while Bill Kenny tenors superlatively and the bass-baritone does his half-chorus recitation. (*Billboard*, 7/16/49)

IF YOU HAD TO HURT SOMEONE
> The Spots handle the typical Tin Pan Alley ballad in their usual fashion. (72)

TO REMIND ME OF YOU
> Same comment. (72) (*Billboard*, 8/13/49)

LAND OF LOVE
> With string backing and bolero beat, Billy Kenny does a solo on the slowly arriving, but highly poetical eden ahbez [Alexander Aberle, who wrote "Nature Boy" and who spelled his name in lower case] tea-with-lemon tune. (76)

ECHOS
> The Benjamin-Weiss clippity-clopper again features the Ink Spot [sic] and strings. No recitation either. Tune will need a stronger rendition. (72) (*Billboard*, 11/12/49)

PERFORMANCE REVIEWS

Capitol (New York)

The Ink Spots did their usual competent job, mixing up their tunes for the best effect. Their biggest applause getter was their *If I Didn't Care* and the aforesaid *You Were Only Fooling* [backed by the Blue Barron ork, which had been reviewed in the prior paragraph]. Latter got much of its heft, however, from the Barron bits (plus the entire band), which gave it additional glee club backing. A couple of cute things in the novelty vein, one a jitter dance by Bill Kenny and his viola plucker [sic], drew appreciative laughter. [At the time of this show, Blue Barron was riding high with his "Cruising Down The River," which would subsequently reach Number 1.] (*Billboard*, 1/29/49)

Carnival Club (Minneapolis)

The Carnival Club is currently proving that perseverance and foresight pay off even in these comparatively goldless days. Months ago many of the Minneapolis supper clubs decided to snap up all the top name talent to interest their former patrons in dropping in nightly. When the news got out that the Ink Spots were available every clubowner began to think that he would like them to headline his floorshow. Instead of just thinking, the Carnival Club spent a small fortune in telephone calls and located the quartet in San Francisco where they were then appearing and signed via the long-distance telephone to a long engagement.

Ever since June 9 the Spots have been headlining the Carnival Club's show and the Minneapolis Police Department, as a result, has assigned two patrolmen to handle the long lines waiting to get into the supper spot. The response has been so impressive that the Carnival's manager has asked the Spots to pen a deal which would bring them back to Minneapolis each year for a month at—naturally—the Carnival Club. (*Cleveland Call And Post*, 6/25/49)

1950

Korean War begins as Communist North Korea invades South Korea. Brinks Robbery ($2.8 million). Hydrogen bomb production begins. United States sends thirty-five advisors to Vietnam.

The competition: All My Love, Bewitched Bothered And Bewildered, Bonaparte's Retreat, The Cry Of The Wild Goose, Diamonds Are A Girl's Best Friend, Enjoy Yourself—It's Later Than You Think, Goodnight Irene, Harbor Lights, Hoop-De-Doo, I Can Dream Can't I?, If I Knew You Were Coming I'd've Baked A Cake, La Vie En Rose, Mona Lisa, Music Music Music, My Foolish Heart, Nevertheless, Rag Mop, Rudolph The Red-Nosed Reindeer, Tenderly, Tennessee Waltz, The Thing, Third Man Theme.

Before the 1949 English tour, Herb Kenny had had thoughts about going out on his own. Learning of this, Jolly Joyce, owner of the Jolly Joyce Attractions booking agency, came around to see him. Joyce was very aggressive and, in Herb's absence, contacted Eddie Mesner, Aladdin Records' owner, about Herb's career change. When the Spots returned from England, Mesner flew in from Los Angeles and, during the group's engagement at the Capitol Theatre, visited Herb, convincing him to do some extracurricular recordings. They located some pickup musicians, got a studio, and soon thereafter a

Herb strays from the fold.

release by "Herb Kenny and His Trio" appeared.[1] Aladdin Records announced Herb's signing in December 1949. Herb was overwhelmed by these events; he didn't even have a repertoire or any arrangements. Moe Gale, Dave Kapp, and brother Bill all resented this freelancing and had to pay Joyce $800 to get Herb out of this mess (since Joyce had already set up some bookings).[2] It took a long time to get things straightened out: Herb's photo appeared in an Aladdin ad (in March) and also in one for Jolly Joyce (in September). In August it was reported that Eddie Mesner was coming to New York to cut some more tracks with Herb,[3] but by that time the pressure had been applied and Herb never again recorded for Aladdin.

In January the Ink Spots became the first act to do a stage show at the Loew's Uptown Theater (Toronto) in twenty years. The show was set up especially for the Spots. On February 12, they again did a guest spot on the Jack Benny radio show.

The middle of March saw the Spots booked for a week each at three Chicago theaters: the Chicago (March 17), the Paradise (April 7), and the North Shore (April 14). Since Chicago is such a large city, the feeling was that they wouldn't outstay their welcome, especially since the theaters were in different areas of the city.

Bill Kenny may have had an easy time singing, but he had a rough time with marriage. A 1946 article had his first wife, Zena, suing him for divorce.[4] He had been having an affair with a woman named Marghuerite Wendell, to whom he had been introduced by Joe Louis. When Marghuerite told him she was pregnant, Bill (who was still married to Zena) packed her off to Los Angeles to have the baby, continually sending her money to see her through. This caused his breakup with Zena, after which he married Marghuerite (who refused to go on a tour of England unless he married her). However, in an April 1949 interview, printed while he was in Reno seeking an annulment (Marghuerite, in turn, was seeking a divorce), Kenny said that the baby wasn't his. In fact, there *was* no baby (at least not originally). She had tricked him into marrying her (Bill said) by claiming that she was carrying his child. In the article, Bill stated that he had no way of knowing what the truth was, and that she never was pregnant at all; she simply used his money to adopt a baby in Los Angeles.[5] (Marghuerite, a model, attracted famous men; in 1956 she married Willie Mays [they were divorced in 1963]).[6] Bill married again almost immediately, this time a Canadian model named Audrey MacBurney Buchanan (an article about the Spots' impending trip to England July 1949, speaks of Bill as "newlywed"). In May 1950, Bill was sued by Audrey's ex-husband for "alienation of affection." He claimed that the divorce (which she got in the United States) would not be recognized in Canada;[7] the case was settled out of court.

Remember that Royal Crown Cola ad they did back in 1944? In 1950 the Ink Spots appeared in some newspaper ads for Manischewitz wine. While the copy varied, some of it read: "Manischewitz Kosher Wine . . . Harmonizes With Us—Sweetly!" and "Manischewitz Kosher Wine Hits the Spots." The ad features Herb, Bill, Charlie, and Billy.[8]

In April the record player manufacturers declared that the War of the Record Speeds was over. The public was buying three-speed changers and accepting *all* the speeds. Music industry executives weren't so sure; they wanted to believe that a single speed would prevail (of course, RCA believed that the 45 would reign; Columbia was betting on the 33⅓). In June, James Petrillo released some sales figures, broken down by record speed. Since December 8, 1948 (when his latest AFM ban ended), the major manufacturers had shipped the following:

177,771,476	78s
7,330,785	45s
3,332,793	33s

These totals only counted those disks for which his AFM members received payments, so figures are understated. However, it was clear that the 78 was not going to fall by the wayside so easily.

And the Ink Spots continued to pack them in: Las Vegas' Thunderbird Hotel reportedly enlarged its supper club specifically for the debut performance of the Spots on June 22. The hotel expected one of the biggest opening crowds in months.[9] However, in spite of the enthusiastic receptions they received wherever they appeared, the Spots were beginning to get lost in the shuffle at Decca. Here's one reason:

> A revitalized concept in the recording and merchandising of records is now in effect at Decca. Plattery a. and r. [artists and repertoire men matched the singers to songs] chieftain Dave Kapp told *The Billboard* that Decca henceforth is restricting and reducing the number of diskings and will stress "quality rather than quantity." In cutting down on rampant recordings, Kapp stated that pubbers [publishers] will have "to return to

The Ink Spots endorse Manischewitz Kosher Wine. (Graphic provided by Rico Tee; used courtesy of the Canandaigua Wine Company, Inc.)

the music business and work at making a tune." No longer will hits be made by freak diskings and no longer will diskers [record manufacturers] carry the pubbers' burden of making a hit via platters alone, claims Kapp. Records plus exploitation must be the new formula, according to the Decca exec.

According to Kapp, Decca has recorded furiously during the past six months as a "protective measure," but cannot afford to wax indiscriminately in the future. The multitude of releases which diskeries have been forced to issue have found disk jockeys and dealers unable to keep up with demands. A platter spinner receives as high as 100 new releases weekly and cannot possibly play them all. Many die for lack of playing time and likewise gather dust on dealers' shelves. Decca in Hollywood alone has waxed as high as 25 sides weekly with as many as three four-hour sessions held in one day. Material came from the avalanche of tunes thrust at diskers by music men.[10]

Now back to the great War of the Record Speeds. In June, Mercury Records announced a new policy in this ad, which was directed at their dealers:

For every $1.00 worth of slow moving obsolete 78 R.P.M. records you desire to return you purchase $3.00 worth of fast moving, bread and butter 33⅓ R.P.M. long playing Mercury records . . . that's it! Simple isn't it?[11]

What this meant was that if dealers sent in a dollar's worth of 78s, they'd receive a dollar credit against three dollar's worth of LPs (in effect lowering the price of the LPs to two dollars). How come? To get rid of 78s. The goal of the record manufacturers was to force the public to buy either 45s or LPs; the 78 was dead (of course the public had other ideas). Naturally RCA couldn't let this go unchallenged. They offered the same terms, with the small substitution of "45" for "33⅓." Of course, all 78s received were to be scrapped (think of all that shellac!). A couple of weeks later, Mercury raised the ante: trade for LPs *or* 45s (up to 25% of the $3 purchase could be 45s). Then London Records (a subsidiary of British Decca) entered the fray with the same terms, but taking *anyone's* 78s, not just their own. By mid-July, Mercury was saying the same. Only Columbia and Decca were silent; they didn't join in.

But Decca didn't remain silent for long; in July they announced that from then on, all pop records would be issued on both 45s and 78s. This left Columbia as the only major that wasn't releasing on all three speeds. Columbia was holding out with its 7-inch 33⅓; its motto was: "One Speed Is All You Need!" This lasted exactly one month; then Columbia caved in and announced it was issuing 45s also. The first releases were "Goodnight Irene," by Frank Sinatra, and "Sometime," by the Mariners (a mixed group, sometimes seen on the Arthur Godfrey show).

To make the War of the Record Speeds even more fun, Zenith announced the introduction of the 16 rpm record. This was derided by those in the know as being unfit for music recording (the speed was too slow to capture the fidelity of music). They were correct; the 16, when used at all, would only be used for the spoken word.

When *Billboard* announced its "Top Record Artists" poll for the first half of 1950, the Ink Spots were absent from the list of thirty-four artists. While not yet gone from charts and polls, they had begun the long slide. Later in the year, *Billboard*'s DJ poll found the Ink Spots fifth-ranked in the "Top Small Singing Groups of the Year," behind the Andrews Sisters, Ames Brothers, Mills Brothers, and King Cole Trio.[12]

A new decade, a new war. This time in Korea. Remember what happened to the record industry last time? Well hang on tight, here we go again! This time there was plenty of shellac, but the manufacturers were trying to kill the 78 anyway. Now it was feared that there would be a shortage of vinyl resins needed to make 45s and LPs. As of early August there was no problem, but the most important ingredient in vinyl is acetylene, which was, of course, an "essential war product." Naturally, to compound matters, there was a strike against the manufacturers of chlorine and chlorides, also vital ingredients in vinyl manufacture. The Bakelite Company, which shipped most of the vinyl to record manufacturers, was worried; if they were worried, the record companies were worried:

> On top of the complications in the vinyl picture in the disk industry caused by the chloride strike, record manufacturers, notably RCA Victor, were further slugged this week when the Bakelite Company cut back vinyl allotments to diskers because of critical war needs. . . . The result is a distinct and imminent possibility that disks, particularly 45 r.p.m. platters, will have to be made with fillers and vinyl, instead of pure

vinyl as formerly. There is also a strong possibility that RCA
Victor will have to drop its color identification gimmick on
the 45s [remember that each category of RCA 45 was a
different color vinyl]. Probability is that all classifications of
Victor 45s will be made black, rather than separate colors for
each musical type.[13]

On September 2, the Spots' "Sometime" broke into the charts at Number
27. It would remain for a scant two weeks before fading away. In November,
the Ink Spots were pictured atop Decca's monthly ad, which touted "Time
Out For Tears" and "Dream Awhile."

If you wanted an Ink Spots album in 1950, Decca would sell you *The
Ink Spots*, Volumes 1 and 2. For a 10-inch LP, you had to be prepared to
shell out $2.85; or you could get a 78 album (containing four records) for
$3.75.

Although the Ink Spots weren't churning out hits as in days of yore, Dave
Kapp announced, in October, that he'd renewed their contract for another
three years.

In November it was reported that vinyl was not going to be controlled
for the time being; it wasn't on the National Production Authority's list of
"priorities," which would have made it akin to shellac's rationing.[14]

That same month, Moe Gale was also back in the news:

> Gale, whose agency recently expanded its scope to include
> film, TV and radio talent as well as musical acts, has been
> gathering hand-tailored material from his properties for the
> last nine months, with Sheldon in mind. ["Sheldon" was the
> name of a publishing company he had just set up.] His first
> publishing operation, with which he is still connected, was
> Advanced Music.[15]

RCA finally did cut out most of the colored vinyl records it produced.
Only the classical Red Seal and its "kiddisk" series would remain on nonblack
vinyl (red and yellow, respectively). RCA would try to retain some of the
flavor by printing the labels in different colors. Here's the reason given:

> [VP Paul] Barkmeier, when contacted, explained that the
> reason Victor decided to eliminate the colors was to afford

the diskery an opportunity to make use of scrap vinyl. Under the multi-color system, the exec said that the scraps cut from center holes and trimmed edges could not be salvaged. By establishing the uniform black, these waste products can be converted into usable vinyl substance.

Barkmeier explained that this vinyl conservation program was an essential step since vinyl production, recovering from the effects of a lengthly [sic] chlorine manufacturers' strike and involved in production for war uses, is still at a precariously low point for the disk industry.[16]

In December costs were increasing and the supply of vinyl was decreasing. With this in mind, Decca became the first major to raise the price of a single (45 or 78) to 85¢. This occurred just at the time that retail prices were going *down* due to a price war which had broken out between Macy's department store and other New York retailers; it was expected to spread to other parts of the country. This led *Billboard* to issue a classic understatement:

The situation is unique mirroring an exceptionally complicated situation in a normally complex industry.[17]

At the end of December, the Ink Spots recorded their final two sides with Ella Fitzgerald: "Little Small Town Girl" and "I Still Feel The Same About You." Unfortunately, when released in 1951, it failed to chart. Recognizing that Miss Ella, over the years, had recorded with many groups and orchestras, Decca released an album in June 1957 entitled "Ella And Her Fellas." This spotlighted her work with the Ink Spots ("That's The Way It Is"), the Delta Rhythm Boys, and the Mills Brothers, as well as the bands of Louis Jordan, Chick Webb, Louis Armstrong, Sy Oliver, and Eddie Heywood.

SONGS RECORDED

01/16/50	75715	You Left Me Everything But You
	75716	With My Eyes Wide Open, I'm Dreaming
	75717	Lost In A Dream
	75718	My Reward
06/15/50	L 5669	I Was Dancing With Someone
	L 5670	Sometime
	L 5671	All My Life
	L 5672	Right About Now
	L 5673	The Way It Used To Be
09/27/50	76906	Stranger In The City (BK)
	76907	Our Lady Of Fatima (BK)
	76908	Time Out For Tears
	76909	Dream Awhile
10/23/50	80063	What Can You Do
	80064	Castles In The Sand
	80065	If
	80066	A Friend Of Johnny's
10/27/50	80101	Ave Maria (BK)
	80102	The Lord's Prayer (BK)
	80103	I Hear A Choir (BK)
	80104	It Is No Secret (BK)
12/20/50	80291	Little Small Town Girl (EF)
	80292	I Still Feel The Same About You (EF)

NOTE: (BK) indicates the song was credited only to Bill Kenny on the label. (EF) indicates Ella Fitzgerald and the Ink Spots. Master numbers with an "L" prefix were recorded in Los Angeles.

RECORDS RELEASED

DECCA

24887	With My Eyes Wide Open, I'm			
	Dreaming	01/16/50	75716	02/50
	Lost In A Dream	01/16/50	75717	
24933	My Reward	01/16/50	75718	03/50
	You Left Me Everything But You	01/16/50	75715	

27102	Sometime	06/15/50	L 5670	07/50
	I Was Dancing With Someone	06/15/50	L 5669	
27214	Right About Now	06/15/50	L 5672	09/50
	The Way It Used To Be	06/15/50	L 5673	
27256	Stranger In The City (BK)	09/27/50	76906	10/50
	Our Lady Of Fatima (BK)	09/27/50	76907	
27259	Time Out For Tears	09/27/50	76908	10/50
	Dream Awhile	09/27/50	76909	
14538	Ave Maria (BK)	10/27/50	80101	12/50
	The Lord's Prayer (BK)	10/27/50	80102	
27326	It Is No Secret (BK)	10/27/50	80104	12/50
	I Hear A Choir (BK)	10/27/50	80103	

RECORD REVIEWS

WITH MY EYES WIDE OPEN I'M DREAMING

Billy Kenny's wide wobbly vibrato has a ball with this revived oldie. This waxing should help shove the tune into important contention. The best Ink Spots' effort in ages. (88)

LOST IN A DREAM

Pretty ballad is done in more straightforward fashion than is usual of the Spots. A pleasant waxing. (81) (*Billboard*, 2/25/50)

MY REWARD

Intense ballad is a strong vehicle for tenor Kenny and his lads. Strings supply the backing for an especially schmaltzy side. (86)

YOU LEFT ME EVERYTHING BUT YOU

Lovely ballad gets more of the same treatment. (82) (*Billboard*, 3/25/50)

I WAS DANCING WITH SOMEONE

A strong new Henry Nemo torcher makes good grist for the Spots' mill. They weave a neat mood job with it. (84)

SOMETIME

An oldie which has shown sporadic signs of revival gets a lushly sentimental treatment that could nab shekels [convince people to part with coins]. (82) (*Billboard*, 7/22/50)

RIGHT ABOUT NOW
> The Spots apply their usual talk-and-sing treatment to a slow ballad of indifferent impact. (66)

THE WAY IT USED TO BE
> Throbber here is better suited to the group, and they get an okay side with it. (73) (*Billboard*, 10/21/50)

IT IS NO SECRET
> Kenny and the [Song] Spinners combine for a winning, moving rendition of this Stu Hamblen moralizing slice of religion. Should score in pop as well as r & b quarters. (88)

I HEAR A CHOIR
> Another ballad moralizer is done up with sincerity and warmth by the king Ink Spot and the fine choral unit. But not as potent as top side. (72) (*Billboard*, 12/2/50)

THE LORD'S PRAYER
> Kenny surprises with a legit vocal—no falsetto, but a sincere, dramatic tenor, with choir and organ. Strictly on the concert kick—no concessions to pop requirements here. (69)

AVE MARIA
> More of the same. (69) (*Billboard*, 12/23/50)

PERFORMANCE REVIEWS

Capitol (New York)
> The Ink Spots opened with *Feets Too Big* [sic] to which Kenny and Butterball did a jitter. From then on it was in the customary Ink Spot vein. *No Orchids For My Lady, Maybe*, finally ending with their perennial *If I Didn't Care*. Kenny still holds a note longer than almost any guy around and the customers love it. (*Billboard*, 1/28/50)

NOTE: This marks the end of the performance reviews. Vaudeville was clearly dying (done in by radio and finished off by television); the Palace Theater came close to closing. Very few locations were reviewed at this time, and none of them past this point feature the Ink Spots. They must have been performing *somewhere*, but not anywhere that *Billboard* sent its reviewers.

1951

Cease-fire in Korea. Arab League begins boycott of Israel. Three thousand killed in New Guinea volcanic eruption. China occupies Tibet. Kefauver's Senate investigation into organized crime broadcast on TV. "The King And I" opens on Broadway. President Truman relieves General Douglas MacArthur of his Korean command.

The competition: Aba Daba Honeymoon, Be My Love, Because Of You, Bushel And A Peck, Cold Cold Heart, Come On-a My House, Down Yonder, How High The Moon, (It's No) Sin, Jezebel, Loveliest Night Of The Year, Mister And Mississippi, My Heart Cries For You, Mockin' Bird Hill, On Top Of Old Smokey, Rose Rose I Love You, The Roving Kind, Sound Off, Sparrow In The Treetop, Sweet Violets, Too Young, You're Just In Love.

The Fourth Law of Thermodynamics states: "Everything takes longer and costs more." This was driven home when, in January, the telephone company announced that the cost of a phone call would increase to a dime; it had been a nickel since 1906!

At least the Ink Spots were still popular with college students: *Billboard*'s "College Music Poll" found them in third place in the "Small Groups" category, right behind the Mills Brothers and the Andrews Sisters.[1]

In April, Decca made the following announcement:

211

Bill, Billy, Charlie, Adriel McDonald, and pianist Harold Francis.

Bill, Adriel, Billy, and Charlie.

Decca Records' May 14 release will concentrate largely on special faith series album issue of 11 packages. The diskery has slowly been building its faith series since its inception less than a year ago. The series has made use of the star pop talent as well as specially added artists to do religious material.

The 11-album release, to be issued on three speeds, will make use of many of the single platters which already have been issued in the series. . . . The 11 participating artists are: Bing Crosby, the Andrews Sisters, Bill Kenny and the Ink Spots, the Mills Brothers, the Waring Chapel Choir, Red Foley, Ernest Tubb, Jack Owens, Felix Knight, the Hamilton Quartet, and the Cass County Boys.[2]

This would help to explain the large number of religious songs recorded by the "Ink Spots" (usually only Bill Kenny as a soloist). Between 1950 and 1952, he would cut around twenty religious and inspirational titles.

In May 1951, Herb overslept and missed a radio gig in Buffalo, New York. On the program, Bill introduced Adriel McDonald (the group's valet) as the new bass[3] (remember, he had been the bass of the Cabineers when he and Herb were members of that group back in 1945). Herb may have overslept, but he *was* listening and became somewhat angered by what sounded like an impromptu expulsion. At their next encounter, Bill and Herb engaged in some nonbrotherly combat (Bill hit Herb in the eye with his ring; Herb countered with some body blows[4]), and Herb left to try his luck as a solo artist (stopping for a while with Buddy Hawkins and the Key Notes).[5] Adriel McDonald then became the Ink Spots' official bass.

After Herb left, regardless of what the session sheets or the record labels say, there were *no* recordings by the Decca "Ink Spots." In the two years he was with the group, Adriel McDonald was not *on* a single session (although he was *at* all of them, and got paid for them). Most sessions from this period don't use a talking bass, and on those that do, it's Bill Kenny (who wanted to be a one-man quartet) doing the honors. (It's more like a talking baritone, and he sounds a bit like Deek, but in all, it isn't a bad job. Examples can be heard on "I Must Say Goodbye," "Forgetting You," and "Do You Know What It Means To Be Lonely.") Although many of these efforts were released as by the "Ink Spots," many others were released as Bill Kenny solos—most notably "It Is No Secret (What Love Can Do)" from late 1950, and "(That's

The Song Spinners.

Just My Way Of) Forgetting You," from late 1952. On most of the solos he's billed as "Bill Kenny of the Ink Spots."

This is not to say, however, that Bill's is the only voice heard on these songs. Decca brought in another of its acts, the Song Spinners, to back him up on most of the recordings. The Song Spinners, a white pop group, had come into their own in a single week in July 1943, when they had placed four songs on the survey—"You'll Never Know" (#1) and "It Can't Be Wrong" (#3) behind Dick Haymes, and "Comin' In On A Wing And A Prayer" (#2) and "Johnny Zero" (#8) on their own.

When Jack Kapp died in March 1949, he left his brother Dave as vice president in charge of Artists and Repertoire (A&R) for Decca. Now, Milton Rackmil, the new president, started to force Dave out. In May 1951, he was demoted to head of A&R only for pop records. This had the desired result; in June he quit (Decca still had to buy out his contract for about $75,000).[6] In November, Dave went to work for RCA, also as head of A&R for pop; in August 1953 he would leave them, forming Kapp Records the next year. The third brother, Paul, had formed Corona Records in 1950, although he would become better known for his managing talents; his artists included Hot Lips Page and the Delta Rhythm Boys.

While there was a sameness to the Ink Spots material in the '40s, at least they had hit after hit. In the '50s, their music suffered from sameness, but there was no excitement in it at all. Bill Kenny didn't sound youthful and vibrant anymore. Although his voice was still beautiful, it wasn't particularly interesting. There was an overabundance of violins, organs, and heavy orchestration that actually detracted from his voice. The white choruses, such as the Song Spinners, may have made him sound mainstream pop, but they detracted from the overall effect even further. The same thing would happen, over the years, to other black artists, such as Clyde McPhatter and Jackie Wilson, in the hopes of making them more salable. Their creative spark would be allowed to die and they'd be burdened with oppressive arrangements and white choruses.

Radio was once the way America learned about new songs, but in the '50s all that had changed. It became clear that television was now the medium of choice:

> The companies, the publishers and the talent agencies have
> learned by experience that appearances on TV programs can

do more toward putting over the disk, artist and tune on a national basis than anything since the days of pre-war radio.
. . . According to many of the disk manufacturers, after a key artist does a TV shot on any of the big shows, his or her current platter shows a substantial increase in sales within 24 hours.[7]

This conclusion was traced back to 1951, when Les Paul and Mary Ford's "How High The Moon" was introduced on Ed Sullivan's "Toast Of The Town" show and immediately took off. The same thing happened with Kay Starr's "Wheel Of Fortune." The preferred shows were Ed Sullivan, Jackie Gleason, and Milton Berle.

As a way of appearing on TV, the Ink Spots filmed five tunes for a company called Snader Telescriptions: "If I Didn't Care," "The Gypsy," "I'm Heading Back To Paradise," "It Is No Secret," and "You May Be The Sweetheart Of Somebody Else." The deal fell through, however, and these early music videos were never issued. "The Gypsy," however, has surfaced, and in it you can see and hear Adriel McDonald singing and Bill Kenny's wife, Audrey, playing the part of the "gypsy."

Finally, the vinyl shortage ended:

The problem of obtaining sufficient vinyl resins for record pressing needs appears to be almost completely alleviated according to local diskeries. Most manufacturers reported that for the first time in over a year orders for vinyl resins were being filled promptly and fully.[8]

The vinyl shortage had had its effect on the kind of records that the public saw: since it was in short supply, the price skyrocketed. It was estimated that you could make about ten of the 7-inch 45 rpms from a pound of vinyl, but only two or three of the 12-inch 33⅓ rpms. This meant that singles were produced in much greater quantity with correspondingly greater acceptance from the public; it took albums years to catch up.

In September, *Billboard* presented its annual DJ Poll. The Ink Spots were still there: Number 7 in the "Top Small Singing Groups of the Year" category.

Since there were so many problems besetting the recording industry, Decca, Capitol, and MGM decided to do something about it. That something was the creation, in October, of the Record Industry Association of America (RIAA). Shortly thereafter, Victor and Columbia joined, to be followed by a host of "indies." When they really got rolling, in 1952, they began by addressing what the industry could do about rampant bootlegging (counterfeiting) of records. In July 1953 they adopted a slogan: "Make Friends With Records;" it was recommended that all record manufacturers use it. Perhaps their most enduring contribution (in 1954) was the "RIAA curve," an industry standard for recording equalization:

> In effect, the decision of the RIAA means that all, or most,
> new recordings will eventually be capable of proper reproduc-
> tion without special adjustment of equalization controls now
> a fixture of most high-fidelity equipment.[9]

Over the years, Decca had been steadily growing; *Billboard* was always running articles which gave Decca's sales and dividend information. In October, Decca purchased some huge blocks of stock in Universal-International Pictures, becoming the largest shareholder (with 35% of the stock). It was rumored that the companies would merge.

Finally, in November 1951, congress acted on one of the most hated but enduring legacies of World War II: the 20% cabaret tax. Imposed during the war to force people to save on gas, for some reason the tax lingered on, even though the owners of entertainment facilities had been trying to get it repealed for years.

SONGS RECORDED

01/17/51	80394	More Of The Same Sweet You
	80395	A Fool Grows Wise (U)
	80396	The Vision Of Bernadette (BK)
	80397	Precious Memories (BK)
01/22/51	80441	A Fool Grows Wise
	80442	Tell Me You Love Me
02/15/51	80551	Sorry You Said Goodbye (BK)
	80552	And Then I Prayed
	80553	Somebody Bigger Than You And I
	80554	Do Something For Me
03/20/51	80723	His Eye Is On The Sparrow (BK)
	80724	The Gentle Carpenter Of Bethlehem (BK)
08/01/51	81324	I Don't Stand A Ghost Of A Chance With You
	81325	I'm Lucky I Have You
	81326	At The End Of The Day (BK)
	81327	I See God (BK)
09/04/51	81481	These Things Shall Pass (BK)
	81482	Keep On The Sunny Side Of Life (BK)
10/12/51	81681	My First And My Last Love (BK)
	81682	Once (BK)
	81683	Honest And Truly

NOTE: (U) indicates an unreleased song. (BK) indicates the song was credited only to Bill Kenny on the label.

RECORDS RELEASED

DECCA

27391	A Friend Of Johnny's	10/23/50	80066	01/51
	If	10/23/50	80065	
27419	Little Small Town Girl (EF)	12/20/50	80291	02/51
	I Still Feel The Same About You (EF)	12/20/50	80292	
27464	Castles In The Sand	10/23/50	80064	03/51
	Tell Me You Love Me	01/22/51	80442	
14547	The Vision Of Bernadette (BK)	01/17/51	80396	03/51
	Precious Memories (BK)	01/17/51	80397	

27493	A Fool Grows Wise	01/22/51	80441	04/51
	Do Something For Me	02/15/51	80554	
27494	And Then I Prayed	02/15/51	80552	04/51
	Somebody Bigger Than You And I	02/15/51	80553	
14548	I Hear A Choir (BK)	10/27/50	80103	05/51
	It Is No Secret (BK)	10/27/50	80104	
14549	Stranger In The City (BK)	09/27/50	76906	05/51
	Our Lady Of Fatima (BK)	09/27/50	76907	
14562	The Gentle Carpenter Of Bethlehem (BK)	03/20/51	80724	05/51
	His Eye Is On The Sparrow (BK)	03/20/51	80723	
27632	What Can You Do	10/23/50	80063	07/51
	More Of The Same Sweet You	01/17/51	80394	
14588	At The End Of The Day (BK)	08/01/51	81326	09/51
	I See God (BK)	08/01/51	81327	
27742	I Don't Stand A Ghost Of A Chance With You	08/01/51	81324	09/51
	I'm Lucky I Have You	08/01/51	81325	
14593	These Things Shall Pass (BK)	09/04/51	81481	10/51
	Keep On The Sunny Side Of Life (BK)	09/04/51	81482	
27844	Once (BK)	10/12/51	81682	11/51
	My First And My Last Love (BK)	10/12/51	81681	

NOTE: (EF) indicates Ella Fitzgerald and the Ink Spots.

RECORD REVIEWS

A FRIEND OF JOHNNY'S
> Ballad with a John Alden story serves as an opportunity for Kenny to take a solo whirl. Pleasant disking. (75)

IF
> Another Kenny solo effort as the tenor sings the new ballad with much feeling. Good competitive slicing. (82) (*Billboard*, 1/13/51)

I STILL FEEL THE SAME ABOUT YOU
> Bright, bouncy coverage disking of a ditty which is showing the signs via the Georgia Gibbs reading should grab off a sizable share of the returns on the tune. (86)

LITTLE SMALL TOWN GIRL (WITH THE BIG TOWN DREAMS)
> Warm, sensitive mood slicing of a simple homey ballad which should bring home the bacon in both pop and r & b quarters. A strong contender. (89) (*Billboard*, 1/20/51)

TELL ME YOU LOVE ME
> The "Pagliacci" adaptation draws an unusual subdued reading which lays emphasis to [sic] the pop aspects of the song; this holds right down to the traditional Spots' recitative. It's a different approach and if accepted could be a likely item. (83)

CASTLES IN THE SAND
> Kenny again carries the burden against a thin string backing with a pleasant new ballad. This side's got a recitation as well. (75) (*Billboard*, 2/24/51)

DO SOMETHING FOR ME
> The Spots, who rarely do this sort of thing, turn on a beat for an R & B blues item. [i.e., they covered a rhythm and blues song, the first outing for Clyde McPhatter and the Dominoes.] It's a fine performance which could score big in R & B sectors. (83)

A FOOL GROWS WISE
> A batch of philosophical nothings, set down judiciously by Bill Kenny, bogs down an attractive melody line. (69) (*Billboard*, 3/31/51)

HIS EYE IS ON THE SPARROW

The Ink Spots' soloist essays as a traditional sacred opus here with the Song Spinners and the Leonard Joy Ork supplying the background. Result is a fine religious ditty that bridges all markets. (78)

THE GENTLE CARPENTER OF BETHLEHEM

Pop songwriters Drake and Shirl wrote this religioso tune and Kenny's distinctive sound hands it a heartfelt reading. Again this is suitable pop material. (78) *Billboard*, 5/12/51)

WHAT CAN YOU DO

New ballad by Bob Wells and Dave Holt is deceptively simple in the Irving Berlin tradition, grows in each hearing in this typical rendition by the Spots. (83)

MORE OF THE SAME SWEET YOU

Another stand-up ballad is retentive in this pleasingly old-fashioned job by the group. (81) (*Billboard*, 6/30/51)

I DON'T STAND A GHOST OF A CHANCE WITH YOU

Tho the billing credits the Spots, this fine reading of the wonderful standard is equally divided between Bill Kenny, who sings it and trumpeter Bobby Hackett, who plays a mess of soulful obbligato. May not break down walls, but should do well. (81)

I'M LUCKY I HAVE YOU

Kenny sings from his toes a lovely new ballad to a small ork backing which sports piano solo instrumental relief. The performance could start something for this slicing. (82) (*Billboard*, 9/15/51)

ONCE

One of the most attractive of the several "big" ballads on the market at the moment is delivered strongly by Kenny. If the song hits, this excellent coverage should catch a share of the action. Kenny's backed by strings and voices. (80)

MY FIRST AND MY LAST LOVE

The newest adaptation of themes from "Scheherazade" is sung with customary dramatics by Kenny, who's one of the best song salesmen around. Not a world beating effort, tho a good one. (74) (*Billboard*, 11/10/51)

THESE THINGS SHALL PASS
>Kenny, in a country-ish band setting does a sturdy job on the new Stu Hamblen moralizer. (72)

KEEP ON THE SUNNY SIDE OF LIFE
>The same country approach is employed for the number one Ink Spot as he runs down a traditional morsel of religioso. (71) (*Billboard*, 11/10/51)

(Top) Adriel and Bill; (bottom) Charlie and Billy.

Intermezzo IV:
Herb Kenny

Herb and Bill Kenny, fraternal twins, were born in Philadelphia in 1915. When the brothers were five, the family moved to Baltimore, where the Kenny twins attended school.

When he left the Ink Spots in 1951, Herb first joined Buddy Hawkins' Key Notes, and then got together with Perry Como's white backup group to record for Federal as "Herb Kenny and the Comets." Subsequently, they recorded for MGM, with the group renamed as the "Rockets." Regardless of the name, their sound is extremely poppish.

In 1952, Herb turned down an offer to join Charlie Fuqua's group (because he wanted a percentage, not a salary). Since leaving the Ink Spots in 1951, Herb never affiliated with any Ink Spots aggregation, only singing solo. (He felt that if he used backup voices, people would think he was trying to perform as the "Ink Spots.")[1]

Over the years Herb dabbled in radio. Late 1957 found him as an announcer on Baltimore's WEBB. When he finally retired from broadcasting, in the mid-1960s, he was program director at Washington's WJMD. He then became a car salesman for several years and also had bit parts in movies, among them *All The President's Men*, *Eleanor And Franklin*, and *Airport '75*.

Although Herb was planning a tour for 1993, the plans came to a sudden end on July 11, 1992, when he died of cancer after a short illness. Herbert Cornelius Kenny was 77.

Herb Kenny (1990).

Herb Kenny and His Trio

ALADDIN
3048   Key To My Heart   02/50
        Why Do I Love You?

Herb Kenny and the Comets

FEDERAL
12083   Only You   06/52
        When The Lights Go On Again All Over The World

Herb Kenny and the Rockets

MGM
11332   My Song   09/52
        You Never Heard A Word I Said
11360   I Don't Care   11/52
        Calling You
11397   I Miss You So   01/53
        Take A Little
11487   But Always Your Friend   04/53
        Star-Spangled Dawn
11648   Don't Take My Word   12/53
        Do I Have To Tell You I'm Sorry?

Bill and Herb Kenny in 1948. (Courtesy of Herb Kenny.)

1952

"Ike" elected president. King Farouk of Egypt ousted. Revolution in Bolivia. United States tests first H-Bomb. Theater of the Absurd, with Beckett's Waiting For Godot. *Richard Nixon's "Checkers" speech.*

The competition: Anytime, Be Anything (But Be Mine), Blacksmith Blues, Blue Tango, Botch-A-Me, Cry, Delicado, Glow-Worm, Half As Much, High Noon, I'll Walk Alone, I'm Yours, I Saw Mommy Kissing Santa Claus, I Went To Your Wedding, Jambalaya, Kiss Of Fire, Lady Of Spain, Shrimp Boats, Slow Poke, Takes Two To Tango, Tell Me Why, Tenderly, Walking My Baby Back Home, Wheel Of Fortune, Wish You Were Here, Why Don't You Believe Me?, You Belong To Me.

While popular demand for the Ink Spots continued to be heavy, Bill Kenny was doing more and more solo work. The other members of the group found this increasingly intolerable, and mainstay Billy Bowen left in early 1952. Once Bowen was gone, it doesn't seem that the Ink Spots took any further posed photos; whenever a photo appeared in an ad, it was usually the group with Herb (occasionally the one with Hoppy!).

Bowen's position was filled by Teddy Williams, who had been featured on two Federal records in early 1951. The first of these was by "Teddy Williams and the Federalites" (a female group), in which Williams shows off a high tenor voice in the Bill Kenny style! The other disk has him backed by Al Cobb's Orchestra.

Kenny *did* let the Ink Spots back him at live appearances and on TV shows, such as Steve Allen's "Songs For Sale," where, on March 29, 1952, they sang "You May Be The Sweetheart Of Somebody Else."[1] This ninety-minute program was a showcase for aspiring amateur songwriters, who brought their songs for professionals to sing on the air. There were guest singers (such as the Ink Spots) and "regulars," such as Rosemary Clooney, Tony Bennett (both relatively unknown when the show started in 1950), and Peggy Lee. *Billboard* said of the show: "Even bad songs take on a professional sound. Good tunes sound like sure-fire hits."[2]

(Although the writer of "Sweetheart" proudly announced that the Ink Spots would be recording his song "next Monday," he had no way of knowing that Bill no longer used the group in the studio; it was released as a Bill Kenny solo.)

If you think that the Ink Spots got themselves into complicated legal hassles (and if you don't you soon will), here's an article about how the Andrews Sisters sued *themselves*:

> One of the neatest ways of taking money from one pocket and putting it in another had the Andrews Sisters win $157,650 from themselves here last week [May 27] by default judgment. The circumstances of the case had members of the legal profession shaking their heads as far east as New York.
>
> The details are as follows: The three gals had filed suit as individuals against the Eight-to-the-Bar Ranch Corporation, in which each of the sisters owns 25 percent of stock, serve as organization's three officers and control the disbursement of all moneys. The suit was filed to recover funds which they had given the corporation, as well as record royalties which the firm controlled.
>
> Then the three songsters served papers on Patti [Andrews], who is president of the Ranch firm. She, in turn, with the support of Maxine and Laverne in their capacities as officers and directors of the firm, failed to file an answer, thereby assuring a default judgement in favor of the thrushes as individuals.

Left holding the bag is Lou Levy, former manager of the trio, who owns the remaining 25 percent of the company. Since he controls only one-quarter of the stock, he was not legally able to file a reply. He is leaving New York immediately to try to have the decision cast aside and the case reopened.[3]

And then the Spots' troubles *really* began. In a July interview, seemingly out of the blue, Kenny claimed that he was fighting mad that Fuqua was trying to oust him from the Spots. Kenny summed up Fuqua's contribution to the Ink Spots this way:

Fuqua has been through for years at least so far as his value to the Ink Spots is concerned. His work shows no improvement, he has done nothing to keep up with the times or even to offer any worthwhile suggestions that could do the act some good. I know what I have done for the Ink Spots because, without bragging, I am the one who kept the act from being a fourth rate group of jitterbugging clowns. I'm simply talking fact. I have been the one who has fought with our booking agent for the right type of engagements and it was I who angled things to the point where we now get $17,000 a week instead of $200 or $300.[4]

In August it was again reported that there was a rift between Kenny and Fuqua, which had occurred after the closing of their engagement at Salisbury Beach, Massachusetts. (The article related that in 1945, Kenny and Fuqua had gone to the New York State Supreme Court to determine who owned what share in the Ink Spots. The ruling was that they each owned 50%.) Fuqua then announced that he was going to leave the Ink Spots in "the next few weeks" to set up "a counterpart which will also be billed as 'The Ink Spots.'"[5] This was possible, he claimed, because legally, if a partnership which only furnishes services is dissolved, each partner is allowed to keep the trade name.[6] Fuqua was planning to leave around August 17, and start appearing with the "New Ink Spots" around September 1; this has to mean that he had been planning the break for a while, since he couldn't have gotten quality singers overnight. Kenny would remain under the Gale Booking Agency, while Fuqua's new group would be under Ben Bart's Universal

Attractions. It was rumored that Herb Kenny would be part of the new group (although he never did join).[7]

Bill Kenny replaced Fuqua with Jimmy Kennedy (baritone and guitar). The Ink Spots were now Bill Kenny, Teddy Williams, Jimmy Kennedy, and Adriel McDonald, with Harold Francis as accompanist/arranger.

The union of Decca and Universal-International Pictures moved closer to reality when Decca's Milton Rackmil was first made a director of Universal and then, a few weeks later, its president.[8] However, in March 1953, he would state that there were no plans to merge the two companies. The merger finally occurred in the early '60s, and included MCA (Music Corporation of America), although Universal was later forced to divest itself of this talent agency. By the '70s, the Decca label had been retired and replaced by the MCA label.

Also closer, in July, was the demise of the 78; for the first time, combined sales of 45s and LPs surpassed those of 78s. Then RCA-Victor threw another monkey wrench into the works: the 45 EP (extended play) record. Remember that Columbia had brought out a 7-inch 33⅓; now RCA brought out a 45 that had up to eight minutes of playing time on each side (which could be used for a single classical selection or two popular songs). While they had been in existence for several months as part of 45-rpm albums, they would now be offered for sale as single units. Originally only used for classical music, by October RCA was also releasing pop records in the EP format. The increased playing time resulted from thinner "lands" (the raised portions between the grooves) and from extending the grooves farther into the "dead wax" area near the center of the record. EPs would sell for $1.40.

In September, Decca announced its new "Curtain Call" series, for the "oldies but goodies" fans. This would consist of reissues of the biggest hits by Decca's biggest artists. The first set of releases contained the following:

Ted Lewis	When My Baby Smiles At Me
	Wear A Hat With A Silver Lining
Eddie Cantor	Makin' Whoopee
	Now's The Time To Fall In Love
Jimmy Durante	Inka Dinka Doo
	Start Off Each Day With A Song
Sophie Tucker	Some Of These Days
	Life Begins At Forty
Bing Crosby	When The Blue Of The Night Meets
	The Gold Of The Day
	I Surrender Dear
Andrews Sisters	Bei Mir Bist Du Schoen
	In Apple Blossom Time
Ink Spots	If I Didn't Care
	Do I Worry?
Mills Brothers	Tiger Rag
	Paper Doll

The Ink Spots certainly found themselves in good company in this series. It also shows what high-powered talent Decca managed to attract over the years.

On December 12, the Ink Spots were part of the *Amsterdam News*' 15th Annual "Midnight Benefit Show," at the Apollo Theatre. They shared the stage with Milton Berle, Ella Fitzgerald, Red Buttons, Duke Ellington, Billy Eckstine, and Vic Damone.

SONGS RECORDED

01/03/52	82065	If I Forget You (BK)
	82066	Please Mr. Sun (BK)
	82067	I'm Heading Back To Paradise (BK)
	82068	Do You Know What It Means To Be Lonely (BK)
	82069	Did You Tell Me A Lie (U)
01/30/52	82225	I Counted On You (BK)
	82226	Don't Mind The Rain (BK)
	82227	A Bundle From Heaven (BK)
	82228	I Must Say Goodbye
04/07/52	82648	You Are Happiness (BK)
	82649	You May Be The Sweetheart Of Somebody Else (BK)
	82650	Under The Honeysuckle Vine (BK)
04/14/52	82676	A Soldier's Rosary (BK)
	82677	Just For Today (BK)
	82678	Don't Put It Off Till Sunday (BK)
	82679	The Hand Of God (BK)
09/02/52	83337	Moonlight Mystery (BK)
	83338	Forgetting You (BK)

NOTE: (U) indicates an unreleased song. (BK) indicates the song was credited only to Bill Kenny on the label.

RECORDS RELEASED

DECCA

27946	Please Mr. Sun (BK)	01/03/52	82066	01/52
	If I Forget You (BK)	01/03/52	82065	
27996	Honest And Truly	10/12/51	81683	03/52
	All My Life	06/15/50	L 5671	
28078	I Must Say Goodbye	01/30/52	82228	04/52
	I'm Heading Back To Paradise (BK)	01/03/52	82067	
28164	You May Be The Sweetheart Of Somebody Else (BK)	04/07/52	82649	05/52
	Under The Honeysuckle Vine (BK)	04/07/52	82650	
25505	It's A Sin To Tell A Lie	11/17/41	69949	05/52
	That's When Your Heartaches Begin	12/23/40	68536	

28219	A Soldier's Rosary (BK)	04/14/52	82676	06/52
	The Hand Of God (BK)	04/14/52	82679	
28289	Sorry You Said Goodbye (BK)	02/15/51	80551	07/52
	A Bundle From Heaven (BK)	01/30/52	82227	
11050	If I Didn't Care	01/12/39	64891	09/52
	Do I Worry?	08/08/40	67970	
28412	You Are Happiness (BK)	04/07/52	82648	10/52
	Moonlight Mystery (BK)	09/02/52	83337	
28462	Forgetting You (BK)	09/02/52	83338	11/52
	I Counted On You (BK)	01/30/52	82225	

RECORD REVIEWS

PLEASE MR. SUN

Top talent has climbed aboard this one fast. Here, Kenny's effective styling is framed engagingly by the appropriately scored orking to point up the sense of the ditty. It's bound to catch a good share of the business. (88)

IF I FORGET YOU

Interpretation by the lead singer of the Ink Spots is solid, with the accent on word clarity. Altogether an excellent cover waxing of the standard. (82) (*Billboard*, 2/2/52)

HONEST AND TRULY

This is one of the four disks released by Decca on the wonderful old Fred Rose standard. [Decca covered itself with four versions of this tune—more than on any song in the past. The others were by Guy Lombardo, Little Donna Hightower, and Roland Johnson.] Bill Kenny does one of his best jobs in singing the lead, while the rest of the Spots supply the background. Quartet's bass [actually Bill Kenny himself] does a recitation bit. (83)

ALL MY LIFE

Another oldie here and handled in same way except for Kenny's attempt at a legit tenor finish which fails to come off. (76) (*Billboard*, 3/22/52)

I'M HEADING BACK TO PARADISE

Kenny sells a warm vocal in this complex but pleasant item that he wrote about a guy who wants to return to his sweetheart. Ork and choral backing is fine. Could get spins. (75)

I MUST SAY GOODBYE

Bill Kenny leads the Ink Spots on this new ballad, doing a good job of lead while the boys back him warmly. Will please group's fans. (73) (*Billboard*, 4/12/52)

NOTE: The previous record is the only one released with a Bill Kenny solo on one side and an Ink Spots record on the other. However, it's all just semantics, since the Spots themselves weren't really on the group side (see the chapter for 1951). It's also the last original record released as being by the "Ink Spots."

UNDER THE HONEYSUCKLE VINE
Attractive ditty from the "Songs For Sale" TV show is given a good reading by Bill Kenny of the Ink Spots, with choral and ork backing under Sy Oliver's direction. (74)

YOU MAY BE THE SWEETHEART OF SOMEBODY ELSE
Bill Kenny again sings good lead on this new item which also came from the TV song seg, over smooth accompaniment from the Ink Spots, with one of the boys [actually Kenny himself] talking the lyrics. (72) (*Billboard*, 5/17/52)

THE HAND OF GOD
Pleasant little hymn effort receives a warm rendition from Bill Kenny (of the Ink Spots), closely supported by chorus and ork. (67)

A SOLDIER'S ROSARY
Tune about a soldier who lost his rosary is sold capably by the warbler, over big chorus and ork support. (65) (*Billboard*, 6/7/52)

SORRY YOU SAID GOODBYE
Bill Kenny gives this new ballad, that he helped pen, a smooth, warm performance with help from a vocal group and a lush ork. (73)

A BUNDLE FROM HEAVEN
The warbler sings pleasantly about his little girl on this simple, almost lullaby-ish effort. (69) (*Billboard*, 7/12/52)

MOONLIGHT MYSTERY
The pretty Benjamin-Weiss tune is warbled expressively by Kenny in a platter that evokes a good deal of romantic nostalgia. Jock spins are in store. (76)

YOU ARE HAPPINESS
Ditty has a legit sound and the lead singer of the Ink Spots projects it with warmth and sincerity. A listenable effort. (74) (*Billboard*, 10/11/52)

FORGETTING YOU
Bill Kenny leads away with his distinctive piping with Ink Spots backing and the aid of the Sy Oliver ork. It's a pleasant side that fits into the Kenny tradition. (74)

I COUNTED ON YOU
Same as the flip side. [Yes, that was the review!] (74) (*Billboard*, 11/15/52)

On The Toast Of The Town (The Ed Sullivan Show) *October 12, 1952: Sophie Tucker, her piano player, Bill Kenny, Teddy Williams, Adriel McDonald, Jimmy Kennedy, Lilli Palmer, Ed Sullivan. (Used by permission of the CBS Photo Archive.)*

Intermezzo V:
Billy Bowen

Billy Bowen was born in Birmingham, Alabama, but moved to Detroit at an early age. After having attended the Detroit Institute of Fine Arts to learn musical theory, he could play the saxophone, clarinet, and flute. In the early '30s, he became the singing bandleader of the famous McKinney's Cotton Pickers (Benny Carter, Coleman Hawkins, and Fats Waller were other alumni). When he left the Cotton Pickers, he formed a band of his own (the Rhythm Stompers), before coming to New York to appear with Roy Eldridge and then Lucky Millinder's Orchestra.

After leaving the Ink Spots, Bowen formed the Butterball Four (sometimes the Butterball Five). Columnist/songwriter Larry Douglas (of the *New York Age*) engineered a contract between Bowen and MGM Records. Aside from the singing Bowen (with his saxophone and clarinet), this group consisted of Clyde Austin (tenor), Melvin Moore (baritone and guitar), Eddie Thompson (bass), and Kelly Owens (pianist and arranger).

After a short stint at MGM, they became one of the many Ink Spots groups floating around in the '50s and '60s.[1] Billy Bowen died in September 1982, at the age of 70.

Billy Bowen

MGM (as "Billy Bowen and the Butterball Four")
11271   You Broke My Heart   07/52
         Diamond Mine In Madagascar

X-TRA (as "Billy Bowen and the Butterball Five")
101   I'll Remember   —/60
         Butterball
X-TRA (as "Billy Bowen's Ink Spots")
101   Gimmie The Key   —/60
         Boogiedoit

Note that both the X-TRA records have the same record number. All on
X-TRA except "I'll Remember" are instrumentals.

*Billy Bowen's Butterball Four (ca. 1952; later the "Ink Spots"): (front) Billy Bowen,
Eddie Thompson; (rear) Melvin Moore, Kelly Owens, Clyde Austin.*

Intermezzo VI:
Charlie Fuqua's Ink Spots

Charlie Fuqua was the quiet member of the Ink Spots, usually content with being in the background; thus, relatively little is known about him. But there came a day in 1952 when he decided that he was being pushed *too far* into the background.

Therefore, while still with Decca, Charlie formed his own competing Ink Spots aggregation. This group consisted of himself, tenor Jimmy Holmes (former vocalist for Doc Bagby), bass Harold Jackson (who had been with the bands of Duke Ellington, Hot Lips Page, and Stuff Smith), and, once again, Deek Watson.[1] Represented by Universal Attractions, the group, of course, sang all the standard Ink Spots hits, with Jimmy Holmes doing the high-tenor leads. Bill Kenny tried to challenge Fuqua in court over the rights to the Ink Spots name, but Fuqua's claim was held to be legitimate. By November 1952, they were touring with their former Gale stablemates, the Cootie Williams Orchestra, doing a series of one-nighters.

Did the press care about the split? One headline stated: "Ink Spots Start Tour *Watson, Fuqua Headliners*":

> The Ink Spots, still giving out with rhythm and song, are set for their tour triumphant that will bring about their personal appearance at leading theatres, nite clubs, etc.

Rhythmically leaders in the entertainment field, the Ink Spots will be presented in a superb setting along with the famous Cootie Williams Orchestra.

Ivory "Deek" Watson, like Fuqua, is also one of the original members of the Ink Spots and his singing, prancing, and strutting is nationally and internationally known.

Jimmy Holmes, a native of Philadelphia, as tenor of the Ink Spots takes the lead when the [The sentence was never finished.]

The celebrated Ink Spots, America's most famous quartet, will be touring the south, southwest and middle west for fifteen weeks, and then move on to the west coast.[2]

In mid-1953, Deek departed, to be replaced by "Lord" Essex Scott; a new fifth member was pianist Isaac Royal. In September they began recording for King Records. The sides they did, such as "Here In My Lonely Room" and "Stranger In Paradise," with Jimmy Holmes' powerful Broadway-stage voice, are quite good.

Unlike what would happen in the later '50s, only two of the King cuts were old Ink Spots material: "Someone's Rocking My Dreamboat" and "When You Come To The End Of The Day." Their "Melody Of Love" was the same "Why Do I Love You" recitation that Herb Kenny had done in 1950 (here spoken by Harold Jackson). "There Is Something Missing" features the Deek-like voice of Essex Scott.

After the demise of the Decca Spots (told in the chapter about 1953), Charlie's group became the "official" Ink Spots, touring most of the country, as well as internationally (they appeared in army bases in Korea as part of an early 1954 tour of the Far East). Additionally, Charlie's group appeared in a 1955 Universal Pictures movie entitled *The Ink Spots*, singing "If I Didn't Care" and "Shanty In Old Shanty Town." Others in this fifteen-minute short were the Barry Sisters, Joy Lane, and Georgie Auld and his Auld Stars.

Charlie's first group (1952). (From the top) Harold Jackson, Deek Watson, Jimmy Holmes, Charlie Fuqua.

Late 1953: Essex Scott, Jimmy Holmes, Harold Jackson; (bottom) Charlie Fuqua.

Charlie's Spots left King in 1955, after only two years. Then, in mid-1956, Charlie signed another "long-term" contract with the Gale Agency (didn't any of them ever learn?), and by September of that year they were recording for Verve. Without going into too much detail, and leaving out an unknown number of pickup singers, the Charlie Fuqua Ink Spots had these singers over the years (listed as first tenor, second tenor, and bass):

Pre-King:	Jimmy Holmes, Deek Watson, Harold Jackson
King:	Jimmy Holmes, Essex Scott, Harold Jackson
Early Verve:	Jimmy Holmes, Charlie Owens, Harold Jackson
Late Verve:	Joe Skyles, Leon Antoine, David McNeil
Early '60s:	Joe Van Loan, Curtis McNair, David McNeil
Later '60s:	Jimmy Foster, Raymond Reid, David McNeil

The early Verve sides were recorded in 1956 and 1957, the later ones in 1959. (There was a 1958 session, from which nothing was ever issued; the singers are unknown.) Joe Van Loan was a tenor who could hit even higher notes than Bill Kenny (although his voice wasn't as sweet); he had been with the Ravens for several years. David McNeil had been with the Larks and Dominoes, Raymond Reid with the Shadows, and Curtis McNair with the Titans. Charlie chose his talent well.

In March 1963, Charlie and Deek reunited in a $420,000 lawsuit against Stanley Morgan's "World-Famous Ink Spots," who were appearing in Las Vegas. Charlie and Deek claimed that they had received a "Federal Service Trade Mark" in 1956, which granted them exclusive rights to use the "Ink Spots" name. The problem, as stated, was that when either Fuqua or Watson would try to appear in Las Vegas, they would be told that an Ink Spots group had already performed, and for less money than they were asking. Unfortunately, neither this nor any other lawsuit ever had the effect of suppressing any of the dozens of Ink Spots groups appearing over the years.

From 1932 through 1971 (except for his service in World War II), Charlie Fuqua was a member of one Ink Spots group or another. In December 1971, following a brief illness, he died at the age of 60.

Charlie Fuqua's Ink Spots (King and Verve singles only)

KING

1297	Ebb Tide	11/11/53	K9342	12/53
	If You Should Say Goodbye	11/11/53	K9343	
1304	Changing Partners	12/11/53	K9361	01/54
	Stranger In Paradise	12/11/53	K9360	
1336	Melody Of Love	12/11/53	K9363	04/54
	Am I Too Late?	09/17/53	K9334	
1378	Planting Rice	07/11/54	K9472	07/54
	Yesterdays	07/11/54	K9470	
1425	Someone's Rocking My Dreamboat	09/17/53	K9336	01/55
	When You Come To The End Of			
	The Day	07/11/54	K9471	
1429	Melody Of Love	12/11/53	K9363	12/54
	There Is Something Missing	12/11/53	K9362	
1512	Don't Laugh At Me	08/27/55	K8585	09/55
	Keep It Movin'	08/27/55	K8587	
4670	Here In My Lonely Room	09/17/53	K9335	12/53
	Flowers, Mister Florist, Please	09/17/53	K9333	
4857	Command Me	08/27/55	K8588	11/55
	I'll Walk A Country Mile	08/27/55	K8586	
Unreleased: Doin'		07/11/54	K9469	

VERVE (singles only)

10071	Darling, Don't Cry	06/25/57	21103	07/57
	You Name It	06/25/57	21101	
10094	If I'd Only Known You Then	06/25/57	21102	—/57
	The Very Best Luck In The World	06/25/57	21100	
10198	Secret Love	08/20/59	22860	10/59
	A Little Bird Told Me	08/31/59	22880	

NOTE: No attempt has been made to trace the subsequent recordings and personnel changes of Charlie's Ink Spots group. Most recordings of "Ink Spots" groups from this point on are on budget albums, which give sketchy, if any, details as to who the recording group is. Album covers are not reliable: there is sometimes just a drawing of the group; many times there's just a nondescript cover design.

1956: Charlie Owens, Jimmy Holmes, Harold Jackson, Charlie Fuqua.

1959 (from top): David McNeil, Leon "Lucky" Antoine, Joe Skyles, Charlie Fuqua.

Ca. 1960: (top) David McNeil, Curtis McNair, Joe Van Loan; (bottom) Charlie Fuqua.

Ca. 1967: Raymond Reid, David McNeil, Jimmy Foster; (bottom) Charlie Fuqua.

Intermezzo VII:
Deek Watson

While not being on any further hit records, Deek Watson wasn't exactly quiet in the late '40s. In November 1948, he was arrested for assault "after he had run amok and wrecked an apartment on Sugar Hill in Harlem"[1] (the charges were withdrawn the next day). In February 1949, it was reported that Deek had been arrested for possessing two marijuana cigarettes.[2]

Following his career with the Brown Dots, and prior to joining Charlie's Ink Spots, Deek had done a novelty comedy act. He appeared as a disk jockey, interviewing marionettes that had been created to look like the famous black artists of the day, including Lena Horne, Billy Eckstine, Louis Armstrong, Ella Fitzgerald, Cab Calloway, Eddie "Rochester" Anderson, Louis Jordan, and (surprise, surprise) the Ink Spots. The article didn't say who provided the voices for the puppets, but between "interviews" Deek would play the records of the real artists.[3]

Deek never got to the recording studio with Charlie Fuqua's Ink Spots, having left in mid-1953. In early 1954, he recorded as a soloist for Jubilee Records ("Why Does A Drink Make You Think"/"Brown Gal"), as "Deek Watson, The Brown Dot" and then formed his own series of Ink Spots groups, which recorded for "budget" labels, such as Waldorf.

Bill Kenny was so sick of the Ink Spots hassles that in May 1955 he sold his rights in the name back to Deek Watson (who had sold them to Bill and Charlie back in 1945). Watson, of course, had an Ink Spots group at the time. Part of the deal was that Kenny would share in the earnings of

Watson's group.[4] Naturally, Charlie Fuqua and Universal Attractions sued to keep Deek from using the name:

> Fuqua alleges that during the latter part of 1947 he and Bill Kenny, lead tenor of the original Ink Spots who is now doing a single, entered into an agreement with Watson whereby the latter agreed to refrain from using the name of Ink Spots in any manner which may indicate his former association with that group. It's charged that the present useage [sic] is a violation of that written agreement.[5]

The same judge who handled the 1944 mega-suit (Isidore Wasservogel), decided in favor of Watson. He said that "neither of the principals in the case, Fuqua or Watson, established a personal proprietary right to the name Ink Spots." And, "When [Hoppy] Jones died, the original partnership terminated and the group with which the name was identified ceased to exist." He went on to say, in effect, that *none* of them (Charlie, Deek, or even Bill) should really be able to use the name by himself: "The pecuniary value of this trade name was derived solely as a result of the skills of the four original members and therefore could not be truthfully used by the others after the group disbanded. Thus, when plaintiffs [Fuqua and Universal Attractions] advertise their group as the Ink Spots, they are, in effect, perpetrating a fraud upon the public by such misrepresentation."[6] Either he really felt sorry for Deek or he was expressing legal disgust at all the wrangling that had gone on over the years.

Probably to end (they thought) any more litigation, Charlie and Deek received a "federal service trade mark" (as the *Chicago Defender* called it; Deek called it a "federal copyright") in 1956, to reserve the name "Ink Spots" for themselves. At least it would preclude them suing each other!

Deek and Charlie would team up at least once more, in 1963; not to sing, but to sue Stanley Morgan and his "World-Famous Ink Spots," who were appearing at the New Frontier Hotel in Las Vegas. This case was tried in a federal court, since it was an infringement of their federal trademark. Whatever its outcome, it has *never* permanently stopped anyone from using the Ink Spots name, from that day to this.

Deek's groups are even more difficult to document than Charlie's. Like Charlie's group, they also recorded for a variety of "budget" labels. There are only a couple of photographs of Deek's later groups. This is all that's known:

Ca. 1955   Leonard Puzey, Bernie Mackey, Sam Pierce
Ca. 1956   Lorenzo Conyers, Bernie Mackey, Johnny Reed

Puzey had been the second tenor of the Ravens and Reed had been the bass of the Orioles. This first of Deek's groups wasn't together long; Deek wanted Puzey to sing high tenor, but, being a second tenor, his voice wasn't high enough to imitate Bill Kenny's. This made him very uncomfortable and he felt out of character.[7] He ended up alternating the talking parts with Sam Pierce. After playing a few engagements in Massachusetts, they broke up. The latter group was together longer, but around 1958, they decided to continue on without Deek (as the "Fabulous Ink Spots"), and the lineup, through 1959, went something like this:

Lorenzo Conyers, Essex Scott, Bernie Mackey, Johnny Reed
Orlando Roberson, Essex Scott, Bernie Mackey, Johnny Reed
Orlando Roberson, Essex Scott, Bernie Mackey, Sam Pierce
Lorenzo Conyers, Essex Scott, Bernie Mackey, Adriel McDonald

In January 1960, the Conyers-Scott-Mackey-McDonald group was playing the Montmartre in Miami Beach, when Scott and some friends rented a fishing boat; the boat later turned up empty and no bodies were found. In the '60s, Adriel and Bernie went their own ways, each forming a succession of Ink Spots groups.

Deek's next group, formed around 1958, consisted of Ollie Crawford (who had been with the Big Three Trio in the late '40s), Gene Miller, and Henry Baxter.

Deek couldn't seem to change his act, though, and it got him into trouble on several occasions. He was just too good at rolling his eyes and jiving around, and, after a certain point, this infuriated the black community. In 1962 Ollie Crawford was interviewed by the *Chicago Daily Defender* and related how Deek had been "kicked upstairs" by their booking agent:

In 1959 Crawford took over the leadership at the request
of Joe Glaser, president of Associated Booking Corporation.

According to Ollie, "Deek's voice went hay-wire and his timing was off." They decided to give him a leave of absence with pay. He still appears with the Ink Spots when they have important TV dates. At other times he works as a single in Las Vegas.

Crawford does not pretend that he is unhappy because Watson is no longer a full-fledged member of the quartet. In fact, it is quite evident that he is overjoyed with the situation.

"For one thing," Crawford said, "Deek thinks that eyeball-rolling and Uncle Tom techniques are still fashionable. But that day is long gone. Why there were times in the past few years that I was ashamed to be on the same stage with him.

"Once in Corpus Christi, Texas, we appeared on a local television station and Deek really went into his act. To him it was showmanship, but to the people of Corpus Christi it was a disgrace."[8]

Crawford went on to say that whenever the opportunity presented itself they "slip in a 'twist' number or two." While I have repeatedly said that the Ink Spots didn't change with the times, this still boggles the mind.

Deek's days with Ink Spots groups were clearly numbered. After the expulsion from Ollie Crawford's Ink Spots (in which he was replaced by Abel DeCosta, who had been with the Blenders and the Cues), he mostly appeared as a single, although he spent some time with Joe Boatner's Ink Spots in the mid-1960s.

Deek published *The Story Of The Ink Spots* in 1967, and died in November 1969, the victim of a stroke at age 56.

Ca. 1956: (top) Lorenzo Conyers; (bottom) Johnny Reed, Deek Watson, Bernie Mackey.

Without Deek (ca. 1959): (top) Essex Scott; (bottom) Bernie Mackey, Orlando Roberson, Johnny Reed.

1953

Stalin dies; Georgi Malenkov becomes the new leader of the USSR. East Berlin workers riot. Armistice in Korea. Convicted atomic spies Julius and Ethel Rosenberg executed (recent evidence from Khrushchev's diaries indicates that they probably were guilty).

The competition: Changing Partners, Crying In The Chapel, The Doggie In The Window, Don't Let The Stars Get In Your Eyes, Dragnet, Ebb Tide, Eh Cumpari, Have You Heard, I Believe, I Love Paris, I'm Walking Behind You, Keep It A Secret, No Other Love, Oh My Papa, Pretend, P.S. I Love You, Rags To Riches, Ricochet, Side By Side, Song From "Moulin Rouge," Stranger In Paradise, That's Amore, Till I Waltz Again With You, Vaya Con Dios, Your Cheating Heart.

In March 1953, the Gale Agency was back in the legal picture again. Moe Gale sought a temporary injunction against Fuqua and Universal Attractions, to stop them from using the name "Ink Spots." Gale claimed that he had a contract with the Ink Spots that ran until July 1954, and he wanted Charlie to hold off using the name until that time. His reasoning:

The offering to the public of two "Ink Spots," the complaint alleges, will cause irreparable damage to the name, cause confusion, and hurt the earning power of the act.[1]

The New York State Supreme Court (which must have been thoroughly sick of the Ink Spots by this time) refused to grant the injunction, pending a trial:

Gale Agency, Inc. this week [3/28] was denied its motion for a temporary injunction to stop Charlie Fuqua and Universal Attractions from using the name "Ink Spots" with his quartet. New York Supreme Court Justice Ernest Hammer ruled that there was no ground to issue an injunction in advance of the trial to determine who has the right to the name.[2]

At some point in 1953, Teddy Williams left the Ink Spots and was replaced by Ernie Brown (second tenor and guitar). It's probable that he was the same Ernie Brown who had been with the Blenders a couple of years earlier. Unfortunately, little is known at this point about late members Ernie Brown, Teddy Williams, or Jimmy Kennedy; Bill Kenny seemed to treat them as pickup singers. However, this was memorable as the last personnel change the Decca Ink Spots would undergo.

While the Ink Spots had their troubles in 1953, they weren't the only ones. Christine Jorgensen, the first man to undergo a publicized sex-change operation, was booked into the Sahara Hotel in Las Vegas (in the long-standing tradition of personal appearances by those the public would consider an "oddity" or "notorious"). The chorines (the "Sa-Harem") refused to let Christine use the ladies' room, since they weren't sure if they were dealing with a man or a woman. One was quoted as saying, "How the hell do we know!"[3] Also, in that same year, Audrey Williams and Billie Jean Williams were battling it out in court for the right to use the title "Mrs. Hank Williams" (after Hank's unfortunate demise a few months earlier). They too, saw the value of personal appearances.

The end of the Decca Ink Spots came in late 1953, after Kenny and the Brown-Kennedy-McDonald-Francis group had done a live appearance with Ed Sullivan in Connecticut. Everything had gone well and Sullivan asked the group to appear at a show for returning Korean War veterans. Kenny accepted, and then privately informed the group that he couldn't afford to

pay them for the appearance—so he was going alone. The unusual thing
about this is that Kenny had always taken the group along and paid them,
even when he didn't let them perform. Figuring that this action on his part
didn't bode well for their future, they disbanded immediately. Sullivan was
so angry that he placed Kenny nearly at the bottom of the bill, headlining
the Step Brothers instead.[4] This took place late in the year, as "Bill Kenny
and the Ink Spots" played the Seville (in Montreal) in late October.

Adriel McDonald subsequently joined the Sandmen, whose lead singer,
Benjamin Peay, later achieved fame as a solo artist—after he'd changed
his name to Brook Benton. It almost goes without saying that McDonald
later formed his own Ink Spots group.

The last hurrah of the Ink Spots was when they appeared in *Down Beat*'s
17th annual poll, barely hanging on at #19.[5]

In the early '50s there was a veritable explosion of vocal groups, both
in the pop and rhythm and blues fields, many of whom were patterned after
the Ink Spots. Lots of these groups had a good deal of talent; many others
got by on vocal tricks or just plain luck. But once upon a time a vocal group
was a vocal group and needed no apologies. One of those was the Pied Pipers,
who had been with Tommy Dorsey's orchestra in the early '40s, backing
Frank Sinatra, among others. Here's what original member Chuck Lowry
had to say about 1953's crop of singers:

> Present day vocal groups scream and shout like the drunks
> that get together at the peak of a party. They feel the urge to
> sing and think they can because they manage to hit a three-part
> chord now and then. Sure, you can quote me, and I'll mention
> names because it's true to an extent of all of them—the Lancers,
> the Red Caps, the Ames Brothers, the Billy Williams Quartette,
> the Four Knights, the Four Lads, the four this or that. They
> ought to call themselves the Four Flushers. They're all awful.[6]

This is strong stuff. Amazingly, his vituperation isn't directed against
a single no-talent group. The Lancers, Ames Brothers, and Four Lads were
white pop groups that had hit records because they deserved them. The Billy
Williams Quartette was black, but with a distinct pop sound; they were
featured regulars on Sid Caesar's "Your Show Of Shows." Both the Red
Caps and Four Knights combined the best of rhythm and blues and pop in

their singing. But *why* did Lowry feel this way? What caused him to despise vocal groups in this manner? Fortunately, he gives us the answer:

> Those lousy Ink Spots started the decline. That Bill Kenny whining, with three nondescript, so-called singers moaning in the background. The successful vocal groups of other days—even those now outmoded—put the emphasis on a precise blending of voices that produced a distinctive musical sound and if a number called for swing—they could swing it.[7]

Everyone's a critic!

To say it was "the end of an era" is trite; but most trite phrases are used because they readily convey a meaning. The Ink Spots had been associated with Decca for seventeen years. While it's true that Bill Kenny hadn't let them record since Herb had departed in 1951, Decca ads continued to tout the group (while printing out-of-date photos). Only Bill Kenny solos would be forthcoming, but Decca was, on occasion, to dig into its vaults and reissue old Ink Spots sides over the years. Certainly with the host of offspring and pseudo Ink Spots groups that were to spring up over the years, there would be no lack of records for their fans to purchase.

SONGS RECORDED

03/27/53	84211	I Keep Thinking Of You (BK)
	84212	Who's To Blame (BK)
08/28/53	85122	When The Chimes Ring (At Evening) (BK)
	85123	I Believe In The Man In The Sky (BK)
	85124	Vows (BK)

NOTE: (BK) indicates the song was credited only to Bill Kenny on the label.

RECORDS RELEASED

DECCA

28677	I Keep Thinking Of You (BK)	03/27/53	84211	04/53
	Who's To Blame (BK)	03/27/53	84212	
28738	Don't Mind The Rain (BK)	01/30/52	82226	07/53
	Do You Know What It Means To Be Lonely (BK)	01/03/52	82068	
28868	When The Chimes Ring (At Evening) (BK)	08/28/53	85122	10/53
	I Believe In The Man In The Sky (BK)	08/28/53	85123	

RECORD REVIEWS

I KEEP THINKING OF YOU
> Bill Kenny chants this ditty with his usual type of phrasing and flashy style. It's a smooth, pretty rendition, and one of Kenny's best in quite a while. Good for many many spins and a disk worth watching. (78)

WHO'S TO BLAME
> Bill Kenny, of the Ink Spots, gives this weeper his distinctive treatment. (75) (*Billboard*, 4/18/53)

DO YOU KNOW WHAT IT MEANS TO BE LONELY

Bill Kenny is tender and warm with his vocal on this new ditty, while [what the reviewer thought were] the Ink Spots back him with soft humming. The second chorus is talked like most of Ink Spots' slicings. Their fans will want this one, even tho the format is now rather old-fashioned. (72)

DON'T MIND THE RAIN

The oldie receives a good rendition from Bill Kenny and the group, backed brightly by a rhythm combo. (69) (*Billboard*, 7/11/53)

I BELIEVE IN THE MAN IN THE SKY

Kenny takes a crack at a religioso-pop tune and turns in a very sincere reading. He's backed by a quiet ork and chorus. (71)

WHEN THE CHIMES RING

Same comments this side. (70) (*Billboard*, 10/11/53)

Intermezzo VIII:
Bill Kenny

Around the time that the Ink Spots dissolved, Bill Kenny became a resident of Canada (recall that his wife, Audrey, was Canadian). From then on he recorded and performed only as a solo artist. The solo career of "Mr. Ink Spot" (as he billed himself) began in earnest in November 1954, with an appearance at New York's Copacabana. He told an interviewer:

> People complained that I wasn't singing as much as I ought to. They felt cheated, somehow, because they had come to think of me as a single vocalist even though we were a group act.[1]

Kenny was as good as his word, since his performances met with enthusiastic response from nightclub patrons. *Variety* reported in early 1954:

> Bill Kenny, back on the nitery circuit after a year in which "the roof fell in"—a mess of tribulations comprising loss of voice for several months and two of family bereavements—states he's cut out previous onstage sermonizing and philosophies-amid-song "because they (spenders) don't want it in a night club." But he has a new act for a different aud[ience] consisting of "impassioned pleading for racial tolerance."

Singer, with bistro act enhanced via instrumental and vocal gimmicks, is donating daytime hours to addressing PTA, Kinsmen and similar service orgs about ethnic bias and abuses. "I'm voluble and get 'em mad, but they call me back," he asserts, adding that such harangues are his "special biz."[2]

Note that, even though it wouldn't be until November 1954 that he announced he was going solo, there is no mention of any Ink Spots group in that March 1954 article.

Down Beat gave this report of Kenny's new solo career in January 1955:

Actually, for the last five years Bill Kenny's Decca records have been made with such groups as the Ray Charles Singers, the Songspinners [sic], and Gordon Jenkins even though the Ink Spots name was used.[3]

Although Bill had the "Ink Spots Trio" in the mid-50s, this was strictly an instrumental unit:

Bill Kenny is topping here [Glasgow, Scotland] in vaude with an instrumental Ink Spots trio as backing. Group comprises Everett Barksdale on guitar, Andy Maize on piano, and Harry Prather on bass. Kenny has a 10-weeks' tour skedded, with the Edinburgh Empire slated for June 4 week.

On his return to the U.S. in the fall he has dates pencilled in for Latin Quarter, N.Y., Gatineau Club, Ottawa, and El Morocco, Montreal. He'll also probably play the Town Casino, Buffalo.[4]

When his contract with Decca ran out in mid-1955, Bill switched to RCA-Victor's Label "X," which was subsequently renamed "Vik." While there, he updated his roots:

"If I Didn't Care," 1939 tune click, has been renovated for the new disk market. Vik Records is issuing a new concept of the Bill Kenny-Ink Spots hit under the new title of "Now You Say You Care."

Song has been updated by Jack Lawrence, who wrote the original, and has been etched by Bill Kenny.

Another facet to the release is that the tune has been coupled in two styles, the original slow ballad mood and in an upbeat tempo.[5]

There was at least one other occasion during which Bill appeared with an Ink Spots group. In the early '60s, bass Joe Boatner had an Ink Spots group which consisted of Freddy Houston (high tenor), Richard Lanham (second tenor—in 1957, at age 12, he was the lead of a Rock and Roll group called the Tempo-Tones), and Billy Byrd (baritone). Boatner was friends with Deek Watson, who occasionally appeared with the group. More important, Boatner ran a competent and professional organization, which impressed Kenny. So when Joe asked Bill to join them for some appearances in Canada, Bill accepted and did several engagements with them over a period of a few months.[6]

An article about Bill Kenny ran in the *Boston Herald* in 1966, and said, in part:

> When Bill joined the first Ink Spots in 1939, they were a strictly instrumental group from Indianapolis, and just about to disband. . . . The other original members were Happy [sic] Jones on bass, Charlie Fuqua on guitar and Deek Watson, rhythm. . . . When Happy [sic] Jones died in 1944, he was replaced by his twin brother. . . . [Kenny] now has his own network television show in Canada, and this year returned to the recording field [on the Dot label].[7]

Considering that Bill joined in 1936, the Spots weren't usually an instrumental group (and never so on record), the name was "Hoppy," not "Happy," and Hoppy didn't have a twin brother (presumably this refers to *Bill's* twin brother, Herb), the obituary was fairly accurate. The hastily mentioned TV show, broadcast each Sunday on the CBC, ran for eight weeks (May 22 to July 10, 1966). It was an easy-listening format, in which Bill was backed by a group called the Accents and the Fraser MacPherson Orchestra; he hosted a different guest each week.

In 1969 Kenny almost died from a bout with pneumonia, brought on by a near-fatal fire. In July gasoline fumes entered his car and caught fire when he lit a cigar. He suffered extensive burns and spent weeks in the hospital. Seemingly cured, he started performing again, only to have a delayed shock reaction and a case of pneumonia.

The pneumonia receded, and in 1971 Bill returned to singing. Then another tragedy struck: a bout with myasthenia gravis, around the beginning of 1973. This time Bill couldn't just rest it off. In October 1973 he had an operation to remove his thymus gland; this cleared up the condition and he began singing again, to enthusiastic audiences.

Bill Kenny, the voice most associated with the Ink Spots, died in March 1978, at age 63.

Amazingly, Kenny's obituary in the otherwise prestigious *New York Times* seemed to bring it all together:

> . . . He was 55 years old [which would mean that he joined the group when he was 13].

> . . . He joined the group when he was 17 years old, in 1939 [1936], to replace Slim Greene [Jerry Daniels], who had died [poor Slim, it probably put a crimp in his subsequent recording career].

> . . .The quartet was formed in about 1933.

> In 1932 they came to New York [a year before they formed, per the above] to perform but their only regular work was as porters backstage at the old Paramount Theater in Times Square for $25 a week each. [It reaches the point where you get a warm glow seeing this evergreen trotted out again.][8]

I'd like to close with an insight into Bill's personality. We tend to think of entertainers in the abstract, but it's stories like these, that serve to humanize them:

> In the 1940s and 50s [writes Claire Levine], my parents owned a candy store on Merrick Road in Jamaica. Bill Kenny lived not far away, in a fashionable section called Addisleigh Park. He was very uncomfortable when flying, but it was necessary in order to meet various commitments. To calm him, he used

to come into the store and purchase 6 or 10 comic books to read on the plane. As soon as he landed, he gave them to the first kid he saw at the airport.[9]

Bill "Mr. Ink Spot" Kenny.

Below are the remaining Ink Spots/Bill Kenny Decca releases.

SONGS RECORDED

02/18/54	85883	What More Can I Do (BK)
	85884	Sentimental Baby (BK)
	85885	The Rose Of Roses (BK)

RECORDS RELEASED

DECCA

28982	Don't Put It Off Till Sunday (BK)	04/14/52	82678	02/54
	Just For Today (BK)	04/14/52	82677	
29070	Vows (BK)	08/28/53	85124	03/54
	The Rose Of Roses (BK)	02/18/54	85885	
29163	What More Can I Do (BK)	02/18/54	85883	07/54
	Sentimental Baby (BK)	02/18/54	85884	
29750	Memories Of You	10/03/39	66463	11/55
	It's Funny To Everyone But Me	05/17/39	65584	
29957	Ev'ry Night About This Time	06/23/42	70917	06/56
	Driftwood	02/04/41	68655	
29991	My Prayer	09/19/39	66608	07/56
	Bewildered	01/19/49	74699	
30058	The Best Things In Life Are Free	12/23/47	74396	09/56
	I Don't Stand A Ghost Of A Chance With You	08/01/51	81324	
25533	All My Life	06/15/50	L 5671	10/61
	You Were Only Fooling	09/14/48	74599	

NOTE: (BK) indicates the song was credited only to Bill Kenny on the label. Master numbers with an "L" prefix were recorded in Los Angeles.

RECORD REVIEWS

JUST FOR TODAY
Religious ballad is projected with sincere feeling and emotional warmth by Kenny. Background by organ and chorus is effective. (73)

DON'T PUT IT OFF TILL SUNDAY
Another fine inspirational waxing by the singer. Good coupling. (72) (*Billboard*, 2/6/54)

THE ROSE OF ROSES
Bill Kenny has a smart rhythm ditty here. The side has an excellent sound, stemming from Sy Oliver's distinctive arrangement for chorus and ork. This disk should get attention. (74)

VOWS
Bill Kenny gives this ballad his distinctive rendition. Good ork backing is conducted by Sy Oliver. (69) (*Billboard*, 3/27/54)

SENTIMENTAL BABY
Here's the lead singer of the Ink Spots singing lead for another group in a switch to the shuffle tempo style which groups have found so successful of late. Result is a good hunk of wax which might make noise. (75)

WHAT MORE CAN I DO
Kenny sings lead here, too, but in a different style—closer to what the Ink Spots have been selling for years. Good ballad material. (73) (*Billboard*, 7/24/54)

Ruthie Bowen and Audrey Kenny (ca. 1951).

Da Capo:
Buck Ram and the Platters

One current theory of evolution is that the dinosaurs didn't really die out; they're still with us today—as birds. It's possible to use the same logic to determine what happened to the sound of the Ink Spots. Just as the dinosaurs couldn't adapt to some changing condition, be it vegetation, climate, or a meteor in the backyard, the Ink Spots didn't adapt either. Year after year they continued singing in the same old style, seemingly not caring what the latest trends in popular music were. There came a point when they (i.e., the multiple Ink Spots of the '50s, '60s, etc.) were reduced to singing only the songs that had made the "Ink Spots" name famous.

And yet . . . there was something else.

Samuel "Buck" Ram was a musician (violin and saxophone), arranger, songwriter, and lawyer (a profession studied simply to please his parents; he never practiced). He worked for Mills Music as an arranger and toured with some swing bands (Ina Ray Hutton, Duke Ellington, Count Basie, and the Dorseys), also as an arranger.

He became the manager of the popular Three Suns, who had a tremendous 1947 hit with "Peg O' My Heart." The instrumental theme song of this trio, "Twilight Time," was written by its members (Al Nevins, Morty Nevins, and Artie Dunn); at some point Buck Ram put words to it. A talented song-writer, Buck also wrote the words to "I'll Be Home For Christmas" and "For The First Time" (the English version of "Come Prima").

Ram was heavily involved with jazz musicians. *Billboard* reviewed a December 1945 record ("Swing Street"/"Twilight In Terehari") which was credited to "Buck Ram." While not saying a word about what Ram did on the record, it mentioned all the others present: Teddy Wilson (piano), Red Norvo (vibes), Earl Bostic (alto sax), Don Byas (tenor sax), and Slam Stewart (bass).[1]

Ram was obviously in love with music, and more than that, he obviously loved the Ink Spots. (The most intriguing piece of information is one that I haven't been able to substantiate: that he had actually done some arranging for the Ink Spots in the '40s; he did write two songs that they recorded: "Ring, Telephone, Ring" and "I'll Lose A Friend Tomorrow," but that, in itself, isn't enough to tie him to the Spots.) The Platters-Ink Spots connection is partly conjecture, but the pieces fit.

In 1953 Ram opened a talent agency in Los Angeles and began managing some of the local acts, one of which was Tony Williams and the Platters. Before coming to Ram, they had obtained a recording contract with Federal Records, and had already done one session. However, their career was going nowhere. Ram saw a real potential in them (that they weren't even close to either realizing or recognizing). He worked with them more than any other of his acts and tried to polish their sound and their appearance, rehearsing them day and night.

When he thought they were ready, he switched them to Mercury Records, where he rehearsed them even more and wrote songs for them. They chose, as their first Mercury release, "Only You," a Ram-written song that they had previously recorded for Federal. The polished and re-recorded "Only You" became a monster hit. (The version that the Platters had recorded for Federal was deemed by the company to be so bad that it wasn't released until the Mercury version took off—and then only to make a few bucks from it.)

The Platters followed with a string of hits: "The Great Pretender," "(You've Got) The Magic Touch," "My Prayer," "Twilight Time" (shades of the Three Suns), and "Smoke Gets In Your Eyes." Somewhat lesser hits were "Enchanted," "My Dream," "Heaven On Earth," and "I'm Sorry." Only "My Prayer" and "Smoke Gets In Your Eyes" were *not* written by Buck Ram.

The point of all this: a group (four men and a lady), a high tenor lead, ballads, love songs. Sound like a familiar formula? Only the presence of thrush Zola Taylor was a bit different from the Ink Spots (but didn't they have hits with Ella Fitzgerald?). And it worked. In the middle of the explosion of rock and roll, the Platters were different. The music they sang harkened back to a different era, but the arrangements made it more contemporary.

They were an instant smash. Number 1 hits. Worldwide appearances. As popular in the '50s as the Ink Spots had been in the '40s. And it couldn't have been an accident. I believe that Buck Ram should be given credit for showing the world that the Ink Spots sound *could* evolve.

There's more. In the early '60s, what were the Platters recording? "To Each His Own," "If I Didn't Care," "I'll Never Smile Again," and "Java Jive," all songs done by (tah-dah) the Ink Spots. There is no doubt in my mind that the Platters were the natural successors to the Ink Spots. Other parallels: as the years went on, Tony Williams' tenor lead predominated in the group, to the point where the others, who once shared the lead, were pushed into the background. Miraculously, they all stayed together, until Williams himself left in 1960—to do a solo act, which went nowhere. And since that time, the Platters have had almost as many offshoot groups as the Ink Spots.

Just to prove that things come full circle, in 1981 I saw a performance of one of the many Ink Spots groups around, and in their repertoire were some Platters songs! Enough said.

The Platters: (top) Tony Williams, Paul Robi; (bottom) Zola Taylor, David Lynch, Herb Reed.

Coda

Despite the turbulent upheavals that the original Ink Spots unit underwent, scores of pseudo-Ink Spots have continued to sing since the early '50s. Some of the groups were started by Charlie or Deek, some by those who had sung with them, and some just seemed to spring into existence spontaneously. The name "Ink Spots" has had phenomenal staying power; unfortunately, none of the groups using that title today include any original members. Of the fourteen men who sang with the Victor/Decca group, Jerry Daniels, Charlie Fuqua, Deek Watson, Hoppy Jones, Bill Kenny, Bernie Mackey, Cliff Givens, Billy Bowen, Herb Kenny, and Adriel McDonald have all passed away. Huey Long is still alive, turning 93 in April 1998. Teddy Williams, Ernie Brown, and Jimmy Kennedy were mystery men in the early '50s, and remain so today; they've never turned up in any Ink Spots group that I've ever encountered.

Most of the current groups don't have anyone who was even remotely associated with the Decca Ink Spots. Scores of record albums have been released by these groups, and the public has supported them with incredible regularity, or at least loyalty to what they remember as the Ink Spots sound. However, it's always fascinating to compare the sound of these groups with that of the originals; it's even more fascinating to listen to some of the stories they tell of having been with the Decca group. Now that you know who's who (or, at least, who was who), see Bill Godwin's Ink Spots, or Harold Winley's, or Ray Pollard's, or any of the others and compare for yourself.

Every now and then someone shows up with his lawyers and tries to get the other groups squashed, but no one ever gets very far in permanently suppressing other "Ink Spots" groups.

In 1987 the National Academy of Recording Arts and Sciences elected "If I Didn't Care" to its Hall of Fame ("honoring records of lasting qualitative or historical significance"). Two years later, the Ink Spots were inducted into the Rock and Roll Hall of Fame in the "forefathers" category, since they were, stylistically and fundamentally, responsible for rock and roll group singing. In April 1992 the Ink Spots were inducted into the United In Group Harmony Association's Hall of Fame as an honorary pioneer rhythm and blues group. The highlight of that show, for me, was having the honor of introducing Jerry Daniels to Herb Kenny (they had never met before). Most recently, in August 1993, the Apollo Theater honored the Ink Spots by inducting them into *its* Hall of Fame. Even though the biography included "facts" such as the members of the group "meeting a few blocks from here," at least they received the well-deserved recognition of the Apollo community. Even in 1994 the Ink Spots were remembered: "If I Didn't Care" played over the opening credits of the movie *The Shawshank Redemption*.

If the Mills Brothers were primarily responsible for opening the airwaves to black artists in the early '30s, then the Ink Spots were the first black group to release records which consistently sold to white as well as black audiences. Certainly the Ink Spots broke down many of the racial barriers which had been zealously guarded in the music industry. Although it is true that the Ink Spots' style had become clichéd by the late '40s, their continuing success served as an inspiration to hundreds of ensuing black groups—from the Ravens and Orioles to the Platters and certainly to some sweet soul groups, such as the Stylistics. What all these vocal groups have in common is that they are part of a tradition of singing bluesy, romantic ballads in harmony. In fifty years, the appeal of this style doesn't seem to have diminished one bit.

April 1992: Herb Kenny and Jerry Daniels meet at last. (Courtesy of Mike Caldarulo.)

"We're in trouble, Frank; they can't make it. They've been desorbed."

Still packing them in after fifty years. This 1989 cartoon was drawn by George Hardy to illustrate the definition of the word "desorb" (a verb meaning to remove by reversing absorption). While it has nothing in particular to do with the Ink Spots, it relies on people knowing who the Ink Spots are. (Reprinted with permission from Lost Words Of The English Language *by Robert Schachner and John Whited. Copyright 1989 Adams Media Corporation.)*

The Recordings:
In Alphabetical Order

This list includes only the first release of a song on Victor or Decca. Also included are the two sides issued on Brunswick (United Kingdom) that were never released in the United States and two sides on 20th Century Fox that were never issued on Decca (even though they weren't commercially released by the movie company). Although there were many unreleased sides, most of them were first tries at a song that was re-recorded and subsequently released. Only those unreleased titles which were *never* re-recorded are found here (*all* masters are accounted for in the text, however). (BK) = released as by Bill Kenny; (EF) = Ella Fitzgerald and the Ink Spots; (U) = unreleased. Master numbers with an "L" prefix were recorded in Los Angeles. Dashes are used for unreleased masters to indicate no record number and release date. * = date approximate.

Label/Number	Title	Date Recorded	Master Number	Date Released
Decca 2707	Address Unknown			
		08/17/39	66120	10/39*
Decca 1154	Alabama Barbecue			
		02/05/37	61581	03/37*
Decca 24496	Aladdin's Lamp			
		08/18/47	74067	09/48

Decca 27996	All My Life			
		06/15/50	L 5671	03/52
Decca 24140	Always			
		02/27/47	73807	09/47
Decca 24517	Am I Asking Too Much			
		10/19/48	74608	11/48
Decca 27494	And Then I Prayed			
		02/15/51	80552	04/51
Decca 23900	Ask Anyone Who Knows			
		02/27/47	73806	06/47
Decca 24585	As You Desire Me			
		01/19/49	74698	03/49
Decca 14588	At The End Of The Day (BK)			
		08/01/51	81326	09/51
Decca 14538	Ave Maria (BK)			
		10/27/50	80101	12/50
Decca 24327	Best Things In Life Are Free, The			
		12/23/47	74396	02/48
Decca 24566	Bewildered			
		01/19/49	74699	02/49
Decca 2841	Bless You (For Being An Angel)			
		10/11/39	66753	12/39*
Decca 2044	Brown Gal			
		08/31/38	64486	10/38*
Decca 28289	Bundle From Heaven, A (BK)			
		01/30/52	82227	07/52
Decca 23900	Can You Look Me In The Eyes			
		02/27/47	73803	06/47
Decca 27464	Castles In The Sand			
		10/23/50	80064	03/51
Decca 883	Christopher Columbus			
		06/18/36	61191	08/36*
Decca 3077	Coquette			
		08/17/39	66121	04/40
Decca 18587	Cow–Cow Boogie (EF)			
		11/03/43	71482	02/44
———	Did You Tell Me A Lie (U)			
		01/03/52	82069	———
Decca 3432	Do I Worry?			
		08/08/40	67970	11/40
Decca 27493	Do Something For Me			
		02/15/51	80554	04/51

Decca 24111	Do You Feel That Way, Too?		
	03/05/47	73814	08/47
Decca 28738	Do You Know What It Means To Be Lonely (BK)		
	01/03/52	82068	07/53
Decca 18583	Don't Believe Everything You Dream		
	11/17/43	71514	01/44
———	Don't Be Sorry (U)		
	12/23/47	74397	———
Brunswick 04183	Don't Ever Break A Promise		
	08/20/40	67991	—/40
Decca 18503	Don't Get Around Much Anymore		
	07/28/42	71237	10/42
Decca 4303	Don't Leave Now		
	08/21/41	69671	04/42
Decca 1731	Don't Let Old Age Creep Upon You		
	02/05/37	61582	03/38*
Victor 24876	Don't 'Low No Swingin' In Here		
	01/04/35	BS-87271	03/35
Decca 28738	Don't Mind The Rain (BK)		
	01/30/52	82226	07/53
Decca 28982	Don't Put It Off Till Sunday (BK)		
	04/14/52	82678	02/54
Decca 18383	Don't Tell A Lie About Me, Dear		
	05/19/42	70762	06/42
Decca 27259	Dream Awhile		
	09/27/50	76909	10/50
Decca 3872	Driftwood		
	02/04/41	68655	07/41
Decca 24741	Echoes		
	06/27/49	75029	09/49
Decca 23695	Either It's Love Or It Isn't		
	09/10/46	73677	10/46
Decca 18817	Everyone Is Saying Hello Again		
	02/21/46	73390	04/46
Decca 18461	Ev'ry Night About This Time		
	06/23/42	70917	08/42
Decca 4303	Foo-gee		
	10/06/41	69786	04/42
Decca 27493	Fool Grows Wise, A		
	01/22/51	80441	04/51
Decca 28462	Forgetting You (BK)		
	09/02/52	83338	11/52

Decca 27391	Friend Of Johnny's, A			
		10/23/50	80066	01/51
Decca 14562	Gentle Carpenter Of Bethlehem, The (BK)			
		03/20/51	80724	05/51
Decca 2790	Give Her My Love			
		09/19/39	66609	11/39*
Decca 18817	Gypsy, The			
		02/19/46	73387	04/46
Decca 28219	Hand Of God, The (BK)			
		04/14/52	82679	06/52
Decca 3987	Hey, Doc			
		07/25/41	69567	09/41
Decca 14562	His Eye Is On The Sparrow (BK)			
		03/20/51	80723	05/51
Decca 24192	Home Is Where The Heart Is			
		08/18/47	74066	10/47
Decca 27996	Honest And Truly			
		10/12/51	81683	03/52
Decca 28868	I Believe In The Man In The Sky (BK)			
		08/28/53	85123	10/53
Decca 18542	I Can't Stand Losing You			
		12/23/40	68535	03/43
Decca 3346	I Could Make You Care			
		08/08/40	67969	09/40
Decca 28462	I Counted On You (BK)			
		01/30/52	82225	11/52
Decca 18864	I Cover The Waterfront			
		03/18/46	73453	04/46
Decca 18711	I'd Climb The Highest Mountain			
		12/30/40	68540	09/45
Decca 27742	I Don't Stand A Ghost Of A Chance With You			
		08/01/51	81324	09/51
Decca 2841	I Don't Want Sympathy, I Want Love			
		08/17/39	66119	12/39*
Decca 3987	I Don't Want To Set The World On Fire			
		08/21/41	69660	09/41
Decca 27391	If			
		10/23/50	80065	01/51
Decca 18528	If I Cared A Little Bit Less			
		07/28/42	71236	11/42
Decca 2286	If I Didn't Care			
		01/12/39	64891	02/39

Decca 27946	If I Forget You (BK)			
		01/03/52	82065	01/52
Decca 24672	If You Had To Hurt Someone			
		11/24/47	74159	07/49
Decca 23695	I Get The Blues When It Rains			
		07/08/46	L 4225	10/46
Decca 27326	I Hear A Choir (BK)			
		10/27/50	80103	12/50
Decca 18657	I Hope To Die If I Told A Lie			
		08/29/44	72368	03/45
Decca 28677	I Keep Thinking Of You (BK)			
		03/27/53	84211	04/53
Decca 18579	I'll Get By			
		12/22/43	71610	04/44
Decca 24261	I'll Lose A Friend Tomorrow			
		10/02/45	73058	11/47
Decca 24286	I'll Make Up For Everything			
		11/21/47	74151	01/48
Decca 18542	I'll Never Make The Same Mistake Again			
		07/28/42	71234	03/43
Decca 3346	I'll Never Smile Again			
		08/08/40	67968	09/40
Decca 23399	I'm Beginning To See The Light (EF)			
		02/26/45	72746	03/45
Decca 3077	I'm Getting Sentimental Over You			
		10/11/39	66752	04/40
Decca 18755	I'm Gonna Turn Off The Teardrops			
		10/02/45	73057	01/46
Decca 28078	I'm Heading Back To Paradise (BK)			
		01/03/52	82067	04/52
Decca 27742	I'm Lucky I Have You			
		08/01/51	81325	09/51
Decca 23356	I'm Making Believe (EF)			
		08/30/44	72371	10/44
Decca 18461	I'm Not The Same Old Me			
		10/06/41	69788	08/42
Decca 3468	I'm Only Human			
		06/24/40	67899	11/40
Decca 3806	I'm Still Without A Sweetheart			
		12/23/40	68537	05/41
Decca 2966	I'm Through			
		10/06/39	66738	01/40

Decca 28078	I Must Say Goodbye		
	01/30/52	82228	04/52
Decca 23615	I Never Had A Dream Come True		
	03/18/46	73449	08/46
Decca 24111	Information Please		
	02/27/47	73804	08/47
———	In The Doorway (U)		
	08/21/40	67999	———
Decca 23356	Into Each Life Some Rain Must Fall (EF)		
	08/30/44	72370	10/44
Decca 14588	I See God (BK)		
	08/01/51	81327	09/51
Decca 4112	Is It A Sin?		
	11/17/41	69950	01/42
Decca 27419	I Still Feel The Same About You (EF)		
	12/20/50	80292	02/51
Decca 27326	It Is No Secret (BK)		
	10/27/50	80104	12/50
Decca 4194	It Isn't A Dream Anymore		
	08/12/41	69633	03/42
Decca 24585	It Only Happens Once		
	02/07/49	74747	03/49
Decca 4112	It's A Sin To Tell A Lie		
	11/17/41	69949	01/42
Decca 24286	It's All Over But The Crying		
	11/21/47	74150	01/48
Decca 2507	It's Funny To Everyone But Me		
	05/17/39	65584	06/39*
20th Cent. Fox 57	I've Got A Bone To Pick With You		
	??/??/??	TCF-57	—/41
Decca 23851	I Want To Thank Your Folks		
	02/27/47	73802	04/47
Decca 27102	I Was Dancing With Someone		
	06/15/50	L 5669	07/50
Decca 23851	I Wasn't Made For Love		
	03/18/46	73454	04/47
Brunswick 03673	I Wish I Could Say The Same		
	12/23/40	68539	—/40
Decca 1870	I Wish You The Best Of Everything		
	05/19/38	63813	05/38
Decca 24327	I Woke Up With A Teardrop In My Eye		
	11/24/47	74157	02/48

Decca 3432	Java Jive		
	07/16/40	67931	11/40
Decca 18466	Just As Though You Were Here		
	07/28/42	71235	08/42
Decca 2507	Just For A Thrill		
	01/12/39	64892	06/39*
Decca 24173	Just For Me		
	10/03/45	73063	09/47
Decca 24461	Just For Now		
	12/23/47	74394	07/48
Decca 28982	Just For Today (BK)		
	04/14/52	82677	02/54
Decca 24173	Just Plain Love		
	07/16/47	L 4469	09/47
Decca 1036	Keep Away From My Door Step		
	06/18/36	61190	12/36*
Decca 3958	Keep Cool, Fool		
	07/25/41	69565	08/41
———	Keep On The Sunny Side (U)		
	10/03/45	73062	———
Decca 14593	Keep On The Sunny Side Of Life (BK)		
	09/04/51	81482	10/51
Decca 24611	Kiss And A Rose, A		
	02/07/49	74748	04/49
Decca 2286	Knock Kneed Sal		
	01/12/39	64893	02/39
———	Knock Me A Kiss (U)		
	06/23/42	70918	———
Decca 24611	Knock On The Door, A		
	12/23/47	74395	04/49
Decca 24741	Land Of Love		
	06/27/49	75026	09/49
Decca 1251	Let's Call The Whole Thing Off		
	04/09/37	62121	05/37*
Decca 27419	Little Small Town Girl (EF)		
	12/20/50	80291	02/51
Decca 14538	Lord's Prayer, The (BK)		
	10/27/50	80102	12/50
Decca 24887	Lost In A Dream		
	01/16/50	75717	02/50
Decca 18583	Lovely Way To Spend An Evening, A		
	12/22/43	71609	01/44

Decca 3258	Maybe			
		06/11/40	67863	07/40
Decca 18657	Maybe It's All For The Best			
		08/29/44	72369	03/45
Decca 2966	Memories Of You			
		10/03/39	66463	01/40
Decca 18528	Mine All Mine, My My			
		10/06/41	69787	11/42
Decca 28412	Moonlight Mystery (BK)			
		09/02/52	83337	10/52
Decca 27632	More Of The Same Sweet You			
		01/17/51	80394	07/51
Decca 24496	My Baby Didn't Even Say Goodbye			
		11/07/46	73741	09/48
Decca 27844	My First And My Last Love (BK)			
		10/12/51	81681	11/51*
Decca 3379	My Greatest Mistake			
		08/20/40	67990	10/40
Decca 2790	My Prayer			
		09/19/39	66608	11/39*
Decca 24933	My Reward			
		01/16/50	75718	03/50
Decca 24566	No Orchids For My Lady			
		01/19/49	74697	02/49
Decca 4045	Nothin'			
		08/12/41	69634	11/41
Decca 1789	Oh! Red			
		03/25/38	63494	04/38*
Decca 883	Old Joe's Hitting The Jug			
		06/18/36	61189	08/36*
Decca 27844	Once (BK)			
		10/12/51	81682	11/51*
Decca 27256	Our Lady Of Fatima (BK)			
		09/27/50	76907	10/50
Decca 27946	Please Mr. Sun (BK)			
		01/03/52	82066	01/52
Decca 3626	Please Take A Letter, Miss Brown			
		01/23/41	TNY-911	02/41
Decca 2044	Pork Chops And Gravy			
		08/31/38	64485	10/38*
Decca 14547	Precious Memories (BK)			
		01/17/51	80397	03/51

Decca 18864	Prisoner Of Love			
		03/18/46	73448	04/46
Decca 3468	Puttin' And Takin'			
		07/16/40	67930	11/40
Decca 24517	Recess In Heaven			
		10/19/48	74609	11/48
Decca 27214	Right About Now			
		06/15/50	L 5672	09/50
Decca 3626	Ring, Telephone, Ring			
		12/23/40	68533	02/41
Decca 29070	Rose Of Roses, The (BK)			
		02/18/54	85885	03/54
Decca 24507	Say Something Sweet To Your Sweetheart			
		09/14/48	74598	10/48
Decca 29163	Sentimental Baby (BK)			
		02/18/54	85884	07/54
Decca 4194	Shout, Brother, Shout			
		10/13/41	69808	03/42
Decca 24192	Sincerely Yours			
		08/18/47	74068	10/47
Decca 1251	Slap That Bass			
		04/09/37	62123	05/37*
Decca 28219	Soldier's Rosary, A (BK)			
		04/14/52	82676	06/52
Decca 27494	Somebody Bigger Than You And I			
		02/15/51	80553	04/51
Decca 18579	Someday I'll Meet You Again			
		01/06/44	71620	04/44
Decca 4045	Someone's Rocking My Dream Boat			
		10/13/41	69807	11/41
Decca 27102	Sometime			
		06/15/50	L 5670	07/50
Decca 28289	Sorry You Said Goodbye (BK)			
		02/15/51	80551	07/52
Decca 3806	So Sorry			
		12/23/40	68532	05/41
Decca 1036	Stomping At The Savoy			
		06/18/36	61188	12/36*
Decca 3288	Stop Pretending			
		06/24/40	67898	08/40
Decca 27256	Stranger In The City (BK)			
		09/27/50	76906	10/50

Decca 18503	Street Of Dreams			
		07/28/42	71233	10/42
Decca 18755	Sweetest Dream, The			
		10/03/45	73061	01/46
Victor 24876	Swing, Gate, Swing			
		01/04/35	BS-87272	03/35
Decca 1236	Swing High, Swing Low			
		04/09/37	62122	04/37*
Victor 24851	Swinging On The Strings			
		01/04/35	BS-87269	01/35
Decca 817	Tain't Nobody's Biz-ness If I Do			
		05/12/36	61105	06/36*
Decca 27464	Tell Me You Love Me			
		01/22/51	80442	03/51
Decca 1789	That Cat Is High			
		03/25/38	63495	04/38*
Decca 23399	That's The Way It Is (EF)			
		02/26/45	72747	03/45
Decca 3720	That's When Your Heartaches Begin			
		12/23/40	68536	05/41
Decca 23809	That's Where I Came In			
		11/07/46	73738	01/47
Decca 14593	These Things Shall Pass (BK)			
		09/04/51	81481	10/51
Decca 18466	This Is Worth Fighting For			
		07/28/42	71238	08/42
Decca 18711	Thoughtless			
		10/06/39	66737	09/45
Decca 27259	Time Out For Tears			
		09/27/50	76908	10/50
Decca 23615	To Each His Own			
		07/08/46	L 4226	08/46
Decca 24672	To Remind Me Of You			
		12/29/47	74454	07/49
Decca 28164	Under The Honeysuckle Vine (BK)			
		04/07/52	82650	05/52
Decca 3958	Until The Real Thing Comes Along			
		07/25/41	69566	08/41
Decca 14547	Vision Of Bernadette , The (BK)			
		01/17/51	80396	03/51
Decca 29070	Vows (BK)			
		08/28/53	85124	03/54

———	Wanting You (U)			
		11/24/47	74158	———
Decca 27214	Way It Used To Be, The			
		06/15/50	L 5673	09/50
Decca 3379	We Three (My Echo, My Shadow, And Me)			
		07/16/40	67928	10/40
Decca 3656	We'll Meet Again			
		02/04/41	68656	03/41
Decca 3195	What Can I Do			
		10/06/39	66739	06/40
Decca 27632	What Can You Do			
		10/23/50	80063	07/51
Decca 3720	What Good Would It Do?			
		12/30/40	68541	05/41
Decca 29163	What More Can I Do (BK)			
		02/18/54	85883	07/54
Decca 28868	When The Chimes Ring (At Evening) (BK)			
		08/28/53	85122	10/53
Decca 1870	When The Sun Goes Down			
		05/19/38	63814	05/38*
Decca 3195	When The Swallows Come Back To Capistrano			
		05/13/40	67718	06/40
Decca 24261	When You Come To The End Of The Day			
		11/07/46	73739	11/47
Decca 24461	Where Flamingoes Fly			
		12/22/47	74385	07/48
20th Cent. Fox 56	Where You Are			
		??/??/??	TCF-56	—/41
Decca 3258	Whispering Grass			
		06/11/40	67862	07/40
Decca 24140	White Christmas			
		02/27/47	73805	09/47
Decca 1236	Whoa Babe			
		04/09/37	62120	04/37*
Decca 24693	Who Do You Know In Heaven			
		06/27/49	75027	08/49
Decca 28677	Who's To Blame (BK)			
		03/27/53	84212	04/53
Decca 18383	Who Wouldn't Love You?			
		05/19/42	70763	06/42
Decca 3872	Why Didn't You Tell Me?			
		12/23/40	68538	07/41

Decca 24887	With My Eyes Wide Open, I'm Dreaming		
	01/16/50	75716	02/50
Decca 1154	With Plenty Of Money And You		
	02/05/37	61583	03/37*
Decca 1731	Yes–suh!		
	02/05/37	61584	03/38*
Decca 28412	You Are Happiness (BK)		
	04/07/52	82648	10/52
Decca 2707	You Bring Me Down		
	08/17/39	66118	10/39*
Decca 23809	You Can't See The Sun When You're Crying		
	11/07/46	73740	01/47
Decca 24933	You Left Me Everything But You		
	01/16/50	75715	03/50
Decca 28164	You May Be The Sweetheart Of Somebody Else		
	04/07/52	82649	05/52
Decca 24693	You're Breaking My Heart		
	06/27/49	75028	08/49
Decca 3288	You're Breaking My Heart All Over Again		
	06/24/40	67900	08/40
Decca 3656	You're Looking For Romance		
	12/23/40	68534	03/41
Victor 24851	Your Feet's Too Big		
	01/04/35	BS-87270	01/35
Decca 817	Your Feet's Too Big		
	05/12/36	61104	06/36*
Decca 24507	You Were Only Fooling		
	09/14/48	74599	10/48

The Recordings: Decca Albums (through 1959 only)

A477—The Ink Spots (8/46) (reissued as DL5056 10/50)

If I Didn't Care	Java Jive
Whispering Grass	I'll Never Smile Again
Maybe	Do I Worry?
We Three	Until The Real Thing Comes Along

A594—The Ink Spots, Volume 2 (9/47) (reissued as DL5071 10/50)

We'll Meet Again	Coquette
Just For A Thrill	My Greatest Mistake
I'll Get By	I'd Climb The Highest Mountain
I'm Getting Sentimental Over You	When The Swallows Come Back To Capistrano

A667—The Ink Spots Souvenir Album, Volume 3 (7/48)

I Wasn't Made For Love	Information, Please
Either It's Love Or It Isn't	Sincerely Yours
Home Is Where The Heart Is	Do You Feel That Way, Too?
I Get The Blues When It Rains	I Want To Thank Your Folks

A657—Ella Fitzgerald And The Ink Spots (8/48)

Cow-Cow Boogie	I'm Making Believe
I'm Beginning To See The Light	Into Each Life Some Rain Must Fall
I'm Gonna Turn Off The Teardrops	That's The Way It Is

DL5333—Pecious Memories (5/51) (also A854)

Stranger In The City	Our Lady Of Fatima
Ave Maria	The Lord's Prayer
I Hear A Choir	It Is No Secret
The Vision Of Bernadette	Precious Memories

NOTE: The 12-inch LP DL8683 also included "The Hand Of God" and "Somebody Bigger Than You And I"

DL5541—Street Of Dreams (8/54)

Address Unknown	Please Take A Letter Miss Brown
Thoughtless	Someone's Rocking My Dream Boat
I Cover The Waterfront	Don't Get Around Much Anymore
Street Of Dreams	I Don't Want To Set The World On Fire

DL8154—The Best Of The Ink Spots (8/55)

If I Didn't Care	Just For A Thrill
Whispering Grass	I'm Getting Sentimental Over You
Maybe	We Three
I'll Never Smile Again	Java Jive
Do I Worry?	We'll Meet Again
Coquette	Until The Real Thing Comes Along

DL8232—Time Out For Tears (8/56)

Prisoner Of Love	I Get The Blues When It Rains
No Orchids For My Lady	Bewildered
Time Out For Tears	Forgetting You
Memories Of You	It's Funny To Everyone But Me
Always	Just As Though You Were Here
I Don't Stand A Ghost Of A Chance With You	You're Breaking My Heart All Over Again

VL3606—Sincerely Yours (6/58) (on Vocalion, a Decca subsidiary)

All My Life	The Best Things In Life Are Free
As You Desire Me	Dream Awhile
Honest And Truly	I Hope To Die If I Told A Lie
If	I Want To Thank Your Folks
Please Mr. Sun	Sincerely Yours
With My Eyes Wide Open I'm Dreaming	You Were Only Fooling

DL8768—Torch Time (8/58)

My Prayer

So Sorry

Driftwood

That's Where I Came In

Ev'ry Night About This Time

When The Swallows Come
Back To Capistrano

Puttin' And Takin'

Ring, Telephone, Ring

It's A Sin To Tell A Lie

To Each His Own

A Lovely Way To Spend An Evening

When You Come To The End Of The
Day

The Recordings: Decca Extended-Play Records (EPs) (issued in the 1950s)

ED 2008	The Gypsy/To Each His Own// Bless You/With My Eyes Wide Open I'm Dreaming	05/53
ED 2040	Into Each Life Some Rain Must Fall/ I'm Beginning To See The Light// Cow-Cow Boogie/I'm Making Believe	07/53
ED 2047	Don't Get Around Much Anymore/My Prayer// It's Funny To Everyone But Me/It's A Sin To Tell A Lie	07/53
ED 2048	We'll Meet Again/My Greatest Mistake// Prisoner Of Love/Memories Of You	07/53
91099	If I Didn't Care/Whispering Grass// Do I Worry?/Java Jive	08/53
91100	We Three (My Echo, My Shadow And Me)/Maybe// I'll Never Smile Again/Until The Real Thing Comes Along	08/53
91115	We'll Meet Again/My Greatest Mistake// I'll Get By/Just For A Thrill	08/53
91116	I'd Climb The Highest Mountain/ I'm Gettin' Sentimental Over You// Coquette/When The Swallows Come Back To Capistrano	08/53
91309	Street Of Dreams/Please Take A Letter Miss Brown// Address Unknown/Don't Get Around Much Anymore	08/54
91310	Someone's Rocking My Dream Boat/ I Don't Want To Set The World On Fire// I Cover The Waterfront/Thoughtless	08/54

91695	Time Out For Tears/Memories Of You//	08/56
	I Don't Stand A Ghost Of A Chance With You/	
	Prisoner Of Love	
91696	Forgetting You/I Get The Blues When It Rains//	08/56
	Just As Though You Were Here/Always	

Notes

Introduction (page xiii)

1. Herb Kenny, as quoted in the *Howard County Sun*, July 25, 1990.
2. Decca Records, liner notes for release number 1-706 (part of Decca's Curtain Call series, 1952).
3. Decca Records liner notes for 1-706.

Prelude: The 1920s to 1931 (page 1)

1. Claire Keefner, "Remembering The Big Time" in the *Alaska Ruralite*, January 1987, 4. The article is based on an interview with Mifflin "Miff" Campbell, at the time an 80-year-old Alaska resident. He died in April 1995.
2. Interview with Jerry Daniels, 6/8/92.
3. Deek Watson (with Lee Stephenson), *The Story of the Ink Spots* (Vantage Press, New York, 1967), 13.
4. Interview with Jerry Daniels, 6/8/92.
5. Interview with Bernie Mackey, 7/18/76.

1932 (page 7)

1. Interview with Jerry Daniels, 9/8/75.
2. Ibid.
3. Ibid.

1933 (page 11)

1. Interview with Jerry Daniels, 10/24/91.

1934 (page 15)

1. Jack Schiffman, *Uptown, The Story of Harlem's Apollo Theatre* (Cowles, New York, 1971), 153.
2. Schiffman, 159.
3. Earl Wilson column, *New York Post*, April 28, 1941.
4. *Variety*, September 18, 1934, 49.
5. *Variety*, October 2, 1934, 70.
6. Deek Watson, 25
7. Watson, 25.
8. Interview with Jerry Daniels, 10/31/91.
9. Watson, 26.
10. Interview with Daniels, 10/31/91.

1935 (page 23)

1. *Baltimore Afro-American*, February 23, 1935.
2. Interview with Jerry Daniels, 9/8/75.
3. *Baltimore Afro-American*, March 16, 1935.
4. *Baltimore Afro-American*, April 13, 1935.
5. *Baltimore Afro-American*, May 11, 1935.

1936 (page 29)

1. Interview with Jerry Daniels, 9/8/75.
2. Interview with Herb Kenny, 12/29/91.
3. Deek Watson, 31.

Intermezzo I: Jerry Daniels (page 35)

1. Interview with Jerry Daniels, 9/8/75.

1937 (page 39)

1. *Variety*, January 27, 1937, 47.
2. *Variety*, May 18, 1938, 41.
3. *Variety*, June 23, 1937, 53.
4. *Variety*, January 27, 1937, 43.
5. *Variety*, March 10, 1937, 45.
6. *Variety*, August 11, 1937, 47.
7. *Variety*, August 11, 1937, 47.
8. *Variety*, May 12, 1937, 34.

1938 (page 45)

1. *New York Amsterdam News*, January 7, 1939, 16.

1939 (page 49)

1. This song was never recorded by the Ink Spots, but it appears on a 1980 album that presented two full Ink Spots radio shows. "The Old Spinning Wheel" was from an August 9, 1935, WJZ show. The album ("The Ink Spots 'On The Air,'" Totem 1020) also contains their WFIL broadcast of July 12, 1939, as well as some tunes broadcast on the Kraft Music Hall show of February 27, 1941 (with host Bing Crosby), and one contribution to Armed Forces Radio Service (AFRS): a Jubilee program from 1944. Other songs that they sang on the 1935 show were "Did You Ever See A Dream Walking?" "Babs," and "Baby Brown."
2. *Chicago Defender*, June 30, 1945, 20.

1940 (page 59)

1. *Down Beat*, April 25, 1940.
2. *Billboard*, January 13, 1940, 9.
3. *Chicago Defender*, April 13, 1940, 10.
4. *Billboard*, January 20, 1940, 74.
5. *Cleveland Call And Post*, January 11, 1940, 3.
6. *Chicago Defender*, October 19, 1940, 19.
7. *Down Beat*, December 1, 1940.
8. Jack Schiffman, 140.
9. *Variety*, February 7, 1940.

10. *Billboard*, special "Talent and Tunes on Music Machines" supplement, September 28, 1940, 12.

11. *Billboard*, November 23, 1940, 13.

1941 (page 75)

1. *Metronome*, April 1941.

2. *Chicago Defender*, May 10, 1941, 10.

3. Earl Wilson column, *The New York Post*, April 28, 1941.

4. *Down Beat*, October 15, 1940.

5. Interview with Bill Doggett, 1/15/92.

6. *Billboard*, January 17, 1942, 21.

1942 (page 89)

1. *Billboard*, February 21, 1942.

2. "The Ink Spots 'On The Air,'" (Totem 1020, 1980). See note 1 under heading "1939." It contains this one, undated cut labeled "test pressing."

3. Interview with Bill Doggett, 1/15/92.

4. Interview with Doggett, 1/15/92.

5. *Billboard*, December 12, 1942.

Shellac (page 99)

1. *Billboard*, January 10, 1942.

2. *Billboard*, September 5, 1942, 19.

3. *Billboard*, September 26, 1942, 59.

4. *Billboard*, November 14, 1942, 20.

5. *Billboard*, November 14, 1942.

6. *Billboard*, May 1, 1943, 62.

7. *Billboard*, June 5, 1943, 62.

8. *Billboard*, February 26, 1944, 16.

9. *Billboard*, September 23, 1944, 72.

10. *Billboard*, October 28, 1944.

11. *Billboard*, July 6, 1946, 21.

1943 (page 107)

1. Deek Watson, 54.
2. *Down Beat*, August 15, 1943.
3. *Billboard*, August 7, 1943.
4. Watson, 47.
5. Watson, 59.
6. *Down Beat*, February 1, 1944.
7. *Billboard*, October 14, 1942.
8. *Billboard*, November 13, 1943, 16.

1944 (page 117)

1. Interview with Bernie Mackey, 7/18/76.
2. *Billboard*, March 4, 1944, 4.
3. Ad appearing in the *Chicago Defender*, April 1, 1944, 4.
4. *Billboard*, June 3, 1944, 12.
5. Deek Watson, 60.
6. *Billboard*, July 22, 1944, 15.
7. *Billboard*, July 15, 1944.
8. Interview with Mackey, 7/18/76.
9. Interview with Mackey, 7/18/76.
10. Interview with Billy Bowen, 10/6/76.
11. Interview with Bill Doggett, 1/15/92.
12. Interview with Ray Tunia, 7/11/76.
13. *Billboard*, October 28, 1944.
14. *Down Beat*, November 15, 1944. (They called him Cliff "Gibbons," and claimed he was with the Southern "Suns," but at least the date is confirmed.)
15. *Billboard*, October 14, 1944, 12.
16. *Billboard*, December 23, 1944.
17. *Chicago Defender*, November 25, 1944, 7.
18. *Variety*, December 13, 1944.
19. *Billboard*, November 11, 1944.
20. *Billboard*, November 25, 1944.
21. Interview with Mackey, 7/18/76.

Intermezzo II: Hoppy Jones (page 133)

1. Earl Wilson column, *New York Post*, April 28, 1941.
2. *Down Beat*, January 12, 1955, 2.

1945 (page 135)

1. *Variety*, January 10, 1945.
2. *Metronome*, February 1945.
3. Interview with Herb Kenny, 12/29/91.
4. *Billboard*, February 3, 1945, 13.
5. Interview with Kenny, 12/29/91.
6. *Billboard*, May 19, 1945, 21.
7. *Billboard*, May 26, 1945, 18.
8. *Baltimore Afro-American*, December 13, 1947, 6.
9. *Billboard*, April 7, 1945.
10. *Billboard*, July 7, 1945.
11. Interview with Huey Long, 7/1/92.
12. Ibid.
13. Ibid.
14. Interview with Bernie Mackey, 7/18/76.
15. Interview with Kenny, 8/22/76.
16. *Chicago Defender*, November 20, 1948.
17. Interview with Kenny, 8/22/76.
18. Interview with Kenny, 1/25/92.
19. *Variety*, August 15, 1945, 39.
20. *Billboard*, October 20, 1945.

Intermezzo III: The Brown Dots (page 147)

1. *Variety*, January 10, 1945.
2. Interview with Jimmie Nabbie, 7/31/74.
3. *Chicago Defender*, February 10, 1945, 9.
4. Marv Goldberg and Mike Redmond, "The Brown Dots And The Four Tunes," *Yesterday's Memories*, No. 1, March 1975, 14.
5. *Variety*, March 7, 1945, 49.
6. *Baltimore Afro-American*, June 29, 1946.
7. *Michigan Chronicle*, October 5, 1946, 16.
8. Interview with Jimmie Nabbie, 7/31/74.
9. *New York Amsterdam News*, January 1, 1949, 19.

1946 (page 157)

1. *Chicago Defender*, April 20, 1946, 26.
2. *New York Amsterdam News*, December 28, 1946, 5.
3. Interview with Ray Tunia, 7/11/76.
4. *Billboard*, January 4, 1947, 3.

1947 (page 169)

1. *The Billboard*, May 24, 1947.
2. *The Billboard*, September 6, 1947 (cover photo and a small accompanying article).
3. *Down Beat*, September 24, 1947.
4. *Billboard*, September 20, 1947, 29.
5. Unknown publication, October 18, 1947.
6. *Billboard*, October 18, 1947, 41.
7. *Baltimore Afro-American*, December 13, 1947, 6.
8. Interview with Herb Kenny, 12/22/91.
9. *Billboard*, December 13, 1947.
10. *Variety*, October 4, 1947.
11. *Billboard*, January 3, 1948.

1948 (page 181)

1. *Billboard*, January 24, 1948, 19.
2. *Chicago Defender*, February 28, 1948, 28.
3. *Billboard*, April 3, 1948, 16.
4. *Cleveland Call And Post*, September 18, 1948, 9B.
5. *Billboard*, October 2, 1948, 21.
6. *Billboard*, December 25, 1948, 21.
7. *Michigan Chronicle*, January 1, 1949.
8. *Billboard*, January 8, 1949, 36.

1949 (page 189)

1. *Cleveland Call And Post*, July 9, 1949, 8B.
2. *Cleveland Call And Post*, July 23, 1949, 8B.
3. *Cleveland Call And Post*, July 23, 1949, 8B.
4. *Cleveland Call And Post*, October 8, 1949, 9B.
5. *Cleveland Call And Post*, November 19, 1949, 9B.
6. *Billboard*, October 22, 1949.
7. *Baltimore Afro-American*, September 24, 1949, 8.

1950 (page 199)

1. Interview with Herb Kenny, 8/22/76.
2. Interview with Kenny, 1/25/92.
3. *Billboard*, August 1950.
4. *New York Amsterdam News*, March 9, 1946, 2.
5. *Cleveland Call And Post*, April 16, 1949, 9B.
6. Interview with Kenny, 12/29/91.
7. *Baltimore Afro-American*, May 27, 1950, 8.
8. Ad appearing in the *Chicago Defender*, April 15, 1950.
9. *Chicago Defender*, June 3, 1950, 31.
10. *Billboard*, June 17, 1950, 15.
11. *Billboard*, June 24, 1950, 37.
12. *Billboard*, October 7, 1950.
13. *Billboard*, September 2, 1950, 12.
14. *Billboard*, November 4, 1950, 16.
15. *Billboard*, November 4, 1950, 20.
16. *Billboard*, November 18, 1950, 11.
17. *Billboard*, December 16, 1950, 11.

1951 (page 211)

1. *Billboard*, April 14, 1951.
2. *Billboard*, April 28, 1951, 14.
3. Interview with Adriel McDonald, 9/27/76.
4. Interview with Billy Bowen, 10/6/76.
5. *Chicago Defender*, June 2, 1951, 51
6. *Billboard*, June 30, 1951, 11.

7. *Billboard*, February 27, 1954, 1.
8. *Billboard*, September 1, 1951, 14.
9. *Billboard*, February 26, 1954, 16.

Intermezzo IV: Herb Kenny (page 223)

1. Interview with Herb Kenny, 8/22/76.

1952 (page 227)

1. Interview with Adriel McDonald, 9/27/76.
2. *Billboard*, March 15, 1952, 3.
3. *Billboard*, June 7, 1952, 1.
4. *Chicago Defender*, July 12, 1952, 17.
5. *Baltimore Afro-American*, August 23, 1952, 14.
6. *Billboard*, August 15, 1952.
7. *Baltimore Afro-American*, August 23, 1952, 14.
8. *Billboard*, July 19, 1952, 20.

Intermezzo V: Billy Bowen (page 237)

1. Interview with Billy Bowen, 10/6/76.

Intermezzo VI: Charlie Fuqua's Ink Spots (page 239)

1. *Baltimore Afro-American*, October 4, 1952, 7.
2. *Chicago Defender*, November 1, 1952, 20.

Intermezzo VII: Deek Watson (page 247)

1. *Baltimore Afro-American*, December 4, 1948, 3.
2. *Baltimore Afro-American*, February 19, 1949, 7
3. *Baltimore Afro-American*, May 3, 1952, 7.
4. *Variety*, June 8, 1955.
5. *Variety*, July 27, 1955.

6. *Variety*, November 16, 1955.
7. Interview with Leonard Puzey, 2/7/92.
8. *Chicago Daily Defender*, September 10, 1962, 17.

1953 (page 253)

1. *Billboard*, March 28, 1953, 17.
2. *Billboard*, April 4, 1953, 17.
3. *Billboard*, November 21, 1953, 1.
4. Interview with Adriel McDonald, 9/27/76.
5. *Down Beat*, December 30, 1953, 6.
6. *Down Beat*, December 30, 1953, 3.
7. *Ibid.*

Intermezzo VIII: Bill Kenny (page 259)

1. Win Fanning (unknown publication), November 1954.
2. *Variety*, March 24, 1954.
3. *Down Beat*, January 12, 1955.
4. *Variety*, May 30, 1956.
5. *Variety*, August 8, 1956.
6. Interview with Richard Lanham, 2/15/92.
7. Allan Eaton in the *Boston Herald*, November 27, 1966, 19.
8. *New York Times*, March 25, 1978.
9. Letter from Claire Levine, dated December 29, 1995.

Da Capo: Buck Ram and the Platters (page 267)
1. *Billboard*, December 22, 1945, 31.

Bibliography

Baltimore Afro-American (various issues)
Billboard (various issues)
Bim Bam Boom (issue 6, July 1972—the Platters)
Boston Herald (11/27/66)
Chicago Defender (various issues)
Cleveland Call And Post (various issues)
Down Beat (various issues)
Golden Valley (Alaska) Ruralite (January 1987)
It Will Stand (issue 17/18, December 1980—the Platters)
Kliment, Bud. *Ella Fitzgerald: First Lady Of American Song.* Chelsea House, 1988
Mays, Willie (with Lou Sahadi). *Say Hey: The Autobiography of Willie Mays*, Pocket Books, New York, 1989
Metronome (various issues)
Michigan Chronicle (10/5/46 and 1/1/49)
New York Amsterdam News (1/1/49)
New York Post (4/28/41)
New York Times (3/25/78)
Rock and Roll Hall of Fame Induction Booklet (1989)
Schiffman, Jack. *Uptown, The Story of Harlem's Apollo Theater*, Cowles, New York, 1971
Shaw, Arnold. *Honkers And Shouters.* Collier, New York, 1978

Variety (various issues)

Watson, Deek (with Lee Stephenson). *The Story of the Ink Spots*, Vantage Press, New York, 1967

Yesterday's Memories (issues 1 [Brown Dots, March 1975] and 9 [Ink Spots, March 1977])

Index

About the Author

Marv Goldberg is a music historian in the field of rhythm and blues and rock and roll. Ever since first hearing Alan Freed in mid-1955, at the tender age of 11, he's been lost in the sounds of black vocal group music.

Having interviewed more than 150 singers, Marv has written for most of the genre publications: *Bim Bam Boom, Record Exchanger, Record Collector's Monthly, Goldmine, Big Town Review,* and the much-missed *Whiskey, Women, And....* From 1975 to 1977, he was owner/editor of *Yesterday's Memories* (with partners Mike Redmond and Marcia Vance). He currently writes a monthly column for *Discoveries* magazine, in which he's profiled the Clovers, 5 Keys, Ravens, Orioles, Penguins, Dominoes, Teenagers, and a host of less-famous groups. Another facet of his writing is the liner notes that he's done for about two dozen record albums.

A frequent guest on area oldies radio shows, he also hosts a weekly show of his own. He prides himself on not only liking rhythm and blues, but actually *listening* to the lyrics. This is his first book.

A systems analyst by day, Marv currently lives, with his wife and stuffed aardvark, in Long Island, New York.